THE THRIFTY DECORATOR

The Thrifty
DECORATOR

Jocasta Innes

Illustrations by Lynne Robinson and Richard Lowther
Special Photography by Nadia Mackenzie

CONRAN OCTOPUS

To Jason and Kate

First published 1993 by
Conran Octopus Limited, 37 Shelton Street,
London WC2H 9HN

Art Editor *Paul Welti*
Illustrator *Lynne Robinson*
Project Editor *Louise Simpson*
Special Photography *Nadia Mackenzie*
Picture Researcher *Abigail Ahern*
Copy Editor *Jennifer Alexander*
Editorial Consultant *Alison Bolus*
Editorial Assistant *Jane Chapman*
Production Controller *Jill Macey*

A CIP catalogue record for this book is available from the British Library
ISBN 1 85029 560 3 (hardback)
ISBN 1 85029 613 8 (paperback)

Typeset by Servis Filmsetting Limited
Printed and bound by Arnoldo Mondadori Editore,
Verona, Italy

Contents

FOREWORD

The DIY Revolution

The aim of this book is to graft my lengthy experience on to your limitless enthusiasm and energy, thereby enabling you to create from whatever environment you have landed in – bed-sit, semi, dilapidated terrace house or crumbling cottage – a context that fits your needs, expresses your tastes and interests, and is a comfort, reward and pleasure to return to. Times have changed since I published my first collected thoughts on this subject in the early seventies, entitled *The Pauper's Homemaking Book*. There has been a huge expansion of DIY activity, with a consequent explosion in tools, materials and services geared to the keen but needy and inexperienced home owner. My own *Paint Magic* helped widen people's notions of what they could achieve with paint – still the cheapest means to a speedy transformation job.

Bold and imaginative initiatives in the retailing world – Habitat, Homebase, Ikea, to name just a few – have increased the scope and choice available in the marketplace, at competitive prices. Magazines on home improvements or 'house mags', as I tend to call them, have increased awareness of what can be done with what you have, preaching the 'art of the possible' at every level and in every imaginable style. Set against this bustling panorama, my own seventies' book appears limited, a bit 'hippy', very much a product of its time and my own circumstances, *but* good in parts (and you should know this because some of the original text reappears here). I can scarcely improve, I am thankful to say, on my own enthusiastic, detailed and knowledgeable descriptions of how to re-cane a chair, cut and stitch a loose cover and run up curtains to the highest standards (lined and interlined, all layers herringbone stitched together to 'hang as one').

All the original costs and prices quoted of course seem laughably out of date. Was it ever possible to get a chair 'close covered' for such a small sum? Now it is more likely to cost twelve times that amount. So much for attempts to bring down inflation. Still, the message for the DIY buff holds good: daring to tackle the job yourself represents a real saving, only now the saving is hundreds rather than tens of pounds.

I must confess to a self-congratulatory throb over a few of my earlier inspirations; I was a prescient pauper. At least three of the ideas I thought good news for seventies' paupers are now top trendy offerings at all the antique fairs: silhouettes, fabric-covered boxes, decoratively punched tins. On the other hand I kick myself for not anticipating the boom in old enamelled kitchenware, colanders, roasting pans, racks for utensils and pan lids. Nor did I foresee the craze for baskets: any tatty old shopping basket with its handle reinforced with wire has a cheeky asking price, and larger receptacles – laundry baskets, wastepaper baskets, wicker trunks – can go for ridiculous prices.

What has not changed, but intensified if anything, is a shortage of spare cash and the powerful longing to create, and I quote myself, 'with the cheapest of materials and tools, that necessary, comforting ambience we call "home" '. Home is a potent word at any time, a guaranteed tear jerker, a muddle of childhood nostalgia, pride in setting up on one's own, a natural hankering for a safe place, a familiar haven when the world out there takes on an increasingly disturbing, not to say threatening, aspect. I sense that the new generation of hard-up homemakers responds even more acutely to the pressures that motivated my original book; the odds are stacked higher, in some respects, against them. The brilliant bargains and lucky strikes take more finding now that TV programmes like the *Antiques Roadshow* have made everyone smart about the contents of their attics. But with flair and perseverance you can still locate a good buy, and repair, restore and splendidly reveal its potential more easily now than in the days when 'shellac' meant nothing to your average paint retailer, and asking for 'transparent oil glaze' earned you that 'we've got a right one here' look.

Just as the foodie thing has revolutionized the contents of the supermarket shelves, so the DIY thing is stretching the boundaries of what DIY stores, builders' merchants, or small high street outlets will stock. My small, local, bustling, but relatively downmarket DIY store where I drop in for basic necessities has expanded its stock from bumpy woodchip paper, repro ceiling roses and one limited range of paints, to include such items as a centrifugal paint mixer, transparent oil glazes, borders by the yard and just recently, blow-me-down, a whole stencilling one-stop stand, offering stencils, brushes, paints, booklets. The style may be naff but the message clear: people are getting more adventurous, DIY is going sophisticated, and the manufacturers and retailers are at last taking notice.

JOCASTA INNES

CHAPTER 1

THE THRIFTY FORMULA

Getting it Together

There it is, your own place, home, a blessed notion which probably means empty rooms, blank walls showing every crack and damp stain and bare boards. There is so much you need, so much to be done, and your bank balance is a black hole. Where to begin?

Prioritizing is an unlovely word but the principle is sound: first things first. In the above-mentioned extreme case you would start by sorting out the electrics. Survival comes first. Assuming you have the bare necessities – cooker and mattress – hit the kitchen next. Eating in saves money and that's what you need most, so a table to eat off and prepare food on if need be, somewhere to sit, and depending on what you have inherited, some storage space, are all essentials. You may have inherited the semblance of a fitted kitchen, in oak-grained melamine, of painful ugliness; put up with this for now.

A solid table is a forward-looking buy. Scrubbed deal kitchen tables with drawers for cutlery used to be ubiquitous, and not overpriced. Oak gateleg tables, darkly varnished with twisty legs, are cheaper and less sought after. They look excellent stripped and limed, and the fold-down flaps save space.

A couple of weeks' occupancy of a kitchen will reveal its shortcomings: usually a lack of storage and worktops. I subscribe to the open-faced approach to storage – I like to see the things I use all the time such as pots and pans, jars, knives, spoons – and kitchen clobber is quite handsome to contemplate. Pots and pans can be hung from hooks screwed into a large wall-mounted board, or from butchers' hooks slung over one of those ceiling mounted clothes' dryers which often turn up in boot sales. Or you might happen upon an old

A traditional clothes' dryer suspended from the ceiling makes a nifty and space-saving way of storing pans, utensils and other paraphernaila of kitchen life

Oak gateleg tables are still reasonably inexpensive and widely available from junk shops and car-boot sales. With flaps extended they are perfect for family meals or entertaining; folded down, they fit snugly into the smallest of spaces

A glorious array of junk spilling out from a well-stocked shop. Some of it may be decidedly dodgy, but there are usually a few gems to be uncovered. Don't be put off by superficial appearances – look for well-made, sturdy objects that can be renovated, revamped or, if desperate, disguised

pyramid shaped metal pot-stand in a thrift shop. For extra storage, nothing beats shelves. Old floorboards from a skip or salvage company can make good solid shelving, scrubbed, stained or painted. The shelves in the brown study on pages 178–179 came in a kit from B&Q. The wood is nothing much in its original form, but painted either black or a strong colour, brackets and all, it looks quite classy and cost peanuts.

If hideaway storage is your priority, then the fashion for unfitted kitchens is weighted in your favour. You can forget the streamlined frontage of matching units featured in the glossies (not as space-saving as they purport to be unless custom-made and fiendishly expensive) and go for free-standing pieces. It's not difficult to find a simple cupboard with two doors and several drawers. Make a set of wall-mounted shelves to fit above this (see Shelving page 134), paint both parts to match and you have an *ad hoc* dresser. A slab of washstand marble or slate cut to fit on top (visit a monumental masons for this) and you have a handsome worktop to boot. Think laterally, carry relevant measurements and a small steel tape measure, and keep your eyes open. It is amazing what people throw out. Old shop fittings often end up on skips; anything which looks shabby, or a bit 'broken' (but *you* can mend it) can end up on the street on its way to the rubbish dump. Trawl the likely venues too such as architectural salvage sheds, markets, boot sales, second-hand furniture stores – the kind that display lots of junk outside on the pavement. I am told, if you are not too fastidious, that some municipal tips do a sideline in salvage items if you know where and when to drop by.

Furnishing in this harum-scarum fashion means you end up, like as not, with a stylistic hodge-podge, but no matter if it works for you. A strong colour on the walls, maybe a chequered painted floor, will help bind it all together. Paint the really ugly stuff in with the walls to lose it. Go for appealing bits and pieces to dress it up: baskets, colourful bits of china, enamelled kitchenware – colanders, roasting dishes, pots and pans – stoneware jars for your wooden spoons. This way kitchens soon fill up and look homely.

After bedding, curtains and/or blinds seem to me the essential soft furnishings. If you have a period house with original wooden shutters this need may not arise. You may not *know* you have shutters, if previous owners painted them in with the window surround in which case they may be stuck down with paint. If so, these are always worth excavating, using a hot-air gun and shavehook to peel off old paint. Missing flaps can be re-made, hinges and fastenings replaced. Shutters look good, exclude draughts and repel intruders, whilst curtains civilize a room, adding colour and softness, and of course privacy. Second-hand curtains come cheaper than antique or nearly-new, or you could make your own from bargain fabrics (see Windows, page 86, for ideas and instructions).

My favourite way of storing spoons and spatulas – a lovely stoneware jug, and all the better for the odd chip or crack

Furniture, in the sense of sofas and easy chairs, can usually be postponed until you get your ideas straight and work out what you can afford. If this seems grim, make floor cushions like the ones described on page 171 as a stop-gap. Wicker sofas and chairs strike me as a good investment – they're sturdy, relatively inexpensive (especially if you cover the cushions yourself) and have a timeless quality that suits most rooms. Waiting for the Sales could reduce the price further. Directors' chairs, with cream canvas seats, provide extra seating for a modest outlay. They fold away when they're not needed and can double up as garden or dining chairs.

Floors are less of a problem today, when minimalism has made bare boards chic. Sub-standard floors, even concrete ones, can be transformed with various paint techniques. For warmth and comfort look at rush mats, or buy old rugs going cheap because they need work doing on them. The really dilapidated ones can be cut down to make floor cushions or used to close-cover small chairs.

The minute a place begins to look half civilized is the minute you notice the lack of occasional tables, bookshelves, pictures to break up empty wall space, lamps and cushions. Lateral thinking is what's needed here and finding a solution to your needs can be fun and creative. Large sturdy cardboard boxes papered in a wild print, or draped with a cloth, can be makeshift tables till you find something more solid in a saleroom or junkshop. Bookshelves are easily erected (see page 134). Cheap old lamps turn up all over the place, usually in need of re-wiring, a new flex and a neat shade, which you could stencil for fun. One of the houses we worked on for this book had a wonderfully nostalgic spread of old family photos – wedding and christening shots going back to the early days of the century – in original frames. I thought they looked great, and provided hours of fascinating speculation. Consider framing scraps of interesting or beautiful old fabric, lace, embroideries, old prints and collect old frames whenever you see them to refurbish – even photocopies look impressive, properly mounted, in decorative frames.

Tools and Equipment

There are some basic tools and equipment any DIY operator needs, I think, to make projects run more swiftly and smoothly. I'm not talking about the sort of beautifully fitted-out corner of the garage that the superior DIY manuals show, with workbench, suites of power tools, shelves for bits and bobs and dinky racks for drill bits, screwdrivers, etc. More likely, your equipment is stuffed into a box under the stairs, or scattered alongside your current projects. Garages, if you are lucky enough to have one, are usually cold, dark places to work in, so tools and paints tend to be moved indoors anyway. It will make life easier for you to obtain a sturdy plastic toolbox. Buy one with hinged trays for smaller items, plus a roomy compartment for hammers, screwdrivers, spanners, pliers, drill bits and keep this in its own designated spot. This saves hours tracking down the scattered clobber needed for a job on hand.

A trusty toolkit, stocked with really essential items, is worth its weight in gold once you have learnt to master its contents

Power tools are bulky items (at least the seriously powerful ones are) but by far the best buy *if* you anticipate doing a lot of work yourself. Experience has taught me, and tradesmen agree, that heavy-duty power tools from a professional range are the best buy. They cost more, initially, but with time they pay for themselves in extra speed, efficiency and reliability. Now that cordless models are replacing plugged tools in the well-sorted workshop, you may find the older models – with flex and plugs – on offer cheaply in *Loot* and *Exchange & Mart*, or at boot sales and markets. Where possible try out power tools before parting with your cash. A powerful drill, with assorted masonry and wood bits, is the one indispensable; power screwdrivers are a time and muscle saver, but one can manage without. A hot-air gun, electrically powered, is another helpful gadget if you have a great deal of old paint to strip off woodwork, doors, stairs and so forth, but the old-style blowtorch paint stripper, worked off a gas canister, is cheaper (though there is more risk of scorching the wood beneath).

Hot-air gun for stripping paint

Good friends and trusting relatives may be prepared to lend out decent power tools, but be sure to return them with all their bits, especially the chuck key. Friendships can be soured by a chuck key mislaid.

A TRUSTY TOOLKIT

The following is a skeleton range of gadgets and equipment to add to when necessary items become affordable.

Collapsible aluminium stepladders

Light and stable, these are not expensive and fold down to about the size of an ironing board. One pair is essential, especially for decorating purposes. Two pairs of the same height with a rigid plank running between can make an *ad hoc* trestle when working on ceilings and stairways, if you're careful. Always make sure the platform is firmly snapped in place. A butcher's hook slung over the top rail can hold a paint kettle or a can while you work. A tough apron with pockets in which you can stuff brushes, screwdrivers, screws, etc. saves running up and down steps all the time.

Left Light collapsible aluminium ladder; **above** power drill with extension lead; **below** chuck key and drill bits

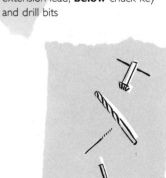

Power drill with extension lead

This is the one indispensable power tool for boring holes in brickwork, plaster, studwork and joinery. Buy packs of drill bits – carbide-tipped for masonry, separate wood bits for joinery – and make sure you have a chuck key and know how it works. Check too that the flex, both on the drill and the extension, is in good nick and not frayed or badly wired at any point along the line. Disconnect when not in use. When drilling wood, or woody materials, take the drill out now and then to clear debris from the hole. If the going gets tough, carbide bits can be lubricated with a smear of washing-up liquid. See that the screw size tallies with the bit size, and use rawlplugs to give more purchase when screwing into masonry. When screwing into party walls (internal walls) try to locate studwork (the timber uprights supporting plasterboard or laths and plaster) and bed your screws into these, using 6.5-cm (2½-in.) screws. This will ensure you get a good grip if you are putting up something heavy like a wall cupboard or bookshelves. Two-speed drills can also be fitted with a screwdriver head, for both standard and Phillips 'pozzi' screws.

Above from left to right Claw hammer, pin or tack hammer, club hammer and cold chisels (one with hand shield)

Hammers

Make sure you have a good, solid claw hammer, and a lighter tack hammer. These often turn up on market stalls. I like the balance of wooden handles, but be sure the hammer head is not loose. For really heavy demolition work you need a bolster and a bull-nosed chisel. The claw side of the claw hammer yanks out nails, but for lifting upholstery tacks get a pronged instrument called a tack lifter which is less bruising to superior wood.

Screwdrivers

Two of these are adequate but three are better, in big, medium and small sizes. Get the best quality you can afford, hardened steel, keen edged, with sizeable handles to grip well. You also need a Phillips screwdriver for screws with the star-shaped heads. The old-style ratched-operated manual screwdriver is a step nearer the power-driven sort and useful if you have lots of work to get through.

Right Tack lifter – ideal for lifting upholstery tacks out of furniture; **far right** a good toolkit should include various-sized screwdrivers and Phillips screwdrivers

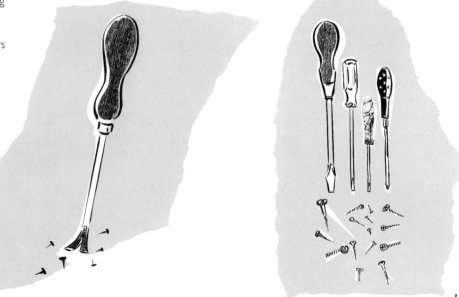

Saws

These days, if you plan your work beforehand, measuring up on paper, you can get most timber cut to size in timber yards and DIY sheds – a great energy saver. However, it is as well to keep a small panel saw for trimming and adjusting or cutting mouldings to fit. Power-operated jig-saws are a must for curvy edges and ornamental cut-outs; for reducing scrap timber to firewood you can't beat a chain-saw, but master the safety aspects first.

Left Standard saw and electric jig-saw

Planes, sanders, abrasive papers, wire wool

Most new timber comes planed and clean textured, but a plane is essential for jobs like re-surfacing old floorboards. People make furniture out of floorboards, nail holes notwithstanding, because they are well seasoned and less likely to warp or shrink. But planes are temperamental, and keeping the blades sharp and setting them properly takes skill. I am told that a small sander that fits into the palm of one's hand is a boon for smoothing down joinery and furniture, but I haven't yet encountered one. It may sound retrograde but I find the various types of abrasive papers – silicone, carbide, wet-and-dry – suit most situations where I need to round off splintered edges, smooth end grain, or refine and tidy up paintwork. I wrap the papers round a block for sanding larger stretches, but tear them into smaller pieces for smaller areas, using my fingers to sense the smoothness as I go. I'm not too fussy about the grade of paper either, but tend to rub with the grain, progressing from coarse to fine grit abrasive papers. Wet-and-dry paper, dipped in water, is efficient for cutting through glossy finishes to provide a 'key' for paint. Wire wool has a gentler action than abrasive paper (at least in the finer grades). Coarse wire wool is excellent for use with chemical paint stripper, and scrapers; a handful will reach the bits the scraper misses, and generally tidy up the surface. Fine wire wool has a polishing effect on many paints, as well as fine woods. Buy wire wool in big rolls; it is endlessly serviceable, and costs much less than packs of small pads.

Stanley and craft knives
These are invaluable for cutting anything from sisal matting (use the hook blade) to picture mounts. Keep spare blades and change them frequently. The craft knife or scalpel is for finer work, like découpage (see page 174).

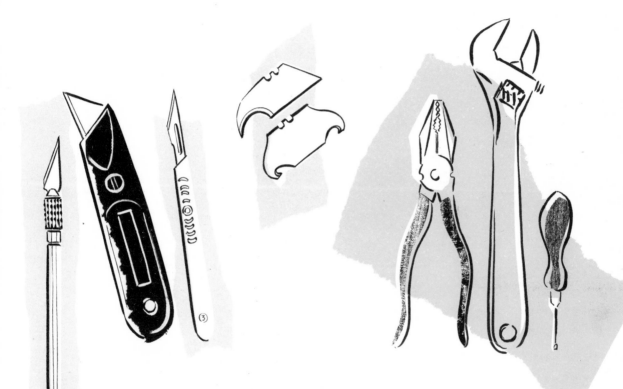

Above from left to right Craft knife, Stanley knife, scalpel, blades for Stanley knife, pliers, adjustable spanner, bradawl

Pliers/bradawl/spanner
Pliers are needed for yanking out obstinate nails (less bruising to wood or paint than the claw hammer), a bradawl for locating and starting screw holes and other punching operations, and an adjustable spanner for minor plumbing repairs, bicycle maintenance, etc. Again, look for quality, solid handles with a keen grip. When buying smaller items new, rather than second-hand, it pays to locate a trade supplier (see Suppliers page 202).

Brushes and rollers
Three standard decorating brushes are the minimum: a wide one, 10–12.5 cm (4–5 in.), but check for convenient handling as a loaded brush is heavy for small hands; a medium one, 3 cm ($1\frac{1}{4}$ in.), and a little whippy one for cutting in details, 12 mm ($\frac{1}{2}$ in.). The big one is for walls, medium for woodwork and

furniture, the little one for 'cutting out', round window panes, door panels and the like. Use rollers for fast basecoating on walls and ceilings; the fluffy ones are best for emulsions and acrylic primer. These deteriorate rather quickly in use, even with careful washing, but they are cheap to replace and save hours of labour. Long-handled versions are available for reaching inaccessible areas. Rollers do leave a faint 'orange peel' texture, but this responds well to further treatment, such as colourwashing.

Fillers

The standard makes of exterior and interior grade fillers are all good, and DIY work consumes them rapidly, so invest in a jumbo box or bag and buy from a builders' merchants. Use fillers for 'making good' cracks, holes in walls and interior or exterior woodwork. Special exterior filler is also available and claims to allow for shrinking and expansion of window frames. Alternatively, old-fashioned linseed oil putty is still used by some tradesmen for exterior filling for the same reason, but needs both extra time to harden off and extra priming. Use plastic wood in a matching shade for filling wood that will remain unpainted. Always 'seal' interior filler with an extra dab or two of the wall base paint.

Adhesives

Superglues have their uses, but in general I incline towards the newer glues, such as PVA (polyvinyl acetate – the builder's friend) and the old glues, such as glue size made from rabbit skin or other animal parts. Wallpaper paste is clean and clear for some paper sticking operations, but don't make up more than you need at one time. Epoxy resin adhesives, like Araldite, are still the most efficient and durable glues for repairing broken pots and cup handles. But don't use them on anything valuable – the current wisdom is that all restoration must be reversible, and these are not. Fast-acting Rapid Araldite is a boon, if you keep calm and your hands don't shake.

Staple gun

The 'stylist's' friend, this is essential for fabric-covered walls and for improvised draperies. Get the muscular size if possible.

Sewing machine

Last, but by no means least, comes the one mechanical aid no one attempting soft furnishings can dispense with. I have owned a succession of makes and models, of different periods and capabilities. For ordinary stitching on a small scale, a hand-turned or treadle model is fine and dirt cheap. But for machine quilting, sewing together swathes of fabric (as for loose covers) an electrically-operated and swing-needle model is a great help. But again, unless you have creative uses in mind, like appliqué, embroidery, or want to sew stretch fabrics, I don't believe the newest models justify the extra cash. Simple basic stitching is all you need for most sewing projects in this book, and old models can cope with this: they may even cope better. I have never yet come across a twentieth-century machine that produces the tiny, exquisitely even, plain stitching one finds on the turn-of-the-century cotton nighties, and other clothing.

Upholstery

Specialized equipment is mentioned in its own section (see page 140) but even if you don't plan to re-cover chairs, it can be useful to have the following: 12-mm ($\frac{1}{2}$-in.) bayonet tacks and gimp pins for replacing braid or fringing; a double-pointed strong needle, 10–15 cm (4–6 in.) for stitching through cushions, mattresses; strong linen thread and a cake of beeswax to run over the thread (beeswax makes linen thread stronger and smoother to work with). I have re-stitched old leather cases and bags with such equipment. You also need a good, stout thimble to prevent lacerated fingers, and pliers to yank threads when needed.

This list covers most of the projects and techniques you will meet in this book. Specialist, one-off materials and tools will be listed under their appropriate sections. Everything should be fairly easy to find, even in a small town, but if you find yourself stumped for something – how often one hears the excuse 'There just isn't any call for it' – go to your phone directory. A little intelligent ringing round and questioning will nearly always produce results.

Finally, for almost any homemaking enterprise, you will need stacks of jam jars, old tins, rags, boxes and so forth. You may long to chuck them all away, as they accumulate in drawers and cupboards, but you will regret it if you do. The alternative is to have every available saucer covered with drying oil paint, milk jugs full of stripper, tools lying about in drawers, tea towels impregnated with linseed oil. This is not only wasteful and squalid but potentially dangerous. Professional craftsmen, I now realize, are methodical and tidy because in the end it saves them time, effort and money. Five minutes spent cleaning brushes shows respect and in the long run saves money. I am basically a disorganized and untidy person, but I've bludgeoned myself into cleaning up and putting things away out of sheer necessity.

Places to Plunder

SKIPS

Everyone who has done any building work knows what a skip is, but in case
you haven't yet got as far as knocking down walls or digging out cellars, a skip
is a large metal container hired from contractors, and filled with building debris
of every sort for eventual removal by a skip lorry. It is illegal to put things into
someone else's skip, but not to take them out. I filled 28 skips with rubble,
plaster, rotten planking and other rubbish when I started work on my pauper's
palazzo in the East End of London, but this is unusual. In any case, the house
had been dossed in for eight years previously, and its main arteries had
become seriously blocked with decrepit gas cookers, TV sets, mattresses,
heaps of rags, polystyrene, bottle tops and much more.

Despite this mammoth clear-out, I hung on like a Pitbull to anything
recyclable. Not everyone who hires a skip is so wised-up in these matters; it is
extraordinary what treasures can be discovered if you make it your business to
check out the contents of skips parked somewhere along your daily route. I
have never found anything to match the eighteenth-century chair with one leg
missing that an antiquarian-minded neighbour unearthed and bore off
triumphantly to the nearest restorer's workshop, for a new leg to be fashioned.
But I supplied my denuded house with panelled doors, a set of shutters,
endless planks, a couple of Habitat Bauhaus chairs (with tattered caned seats,
replaced from the company's stock room), a cast-iron fireplace surround and
other goodies. Friends of mine, living in more propitious areas, claim to have
done better, fitting out their homes from cellar to attic with finds from skips.
What makes skips such a rich vein for exploration is the simple truth that one
person's junk is another person's glorious and long-sought treasure. I can never
pass a skip without a twinge of curiosity as to its contents. Not so long ago I
managed to persuade two sturdy neighbours to help me heft a large, deeply
contoured and massively heavy butcher's block from the skip-heap into the
boot of my car. It has been growing moss in my yard ever since, awaiting a
frame, drastic planing, and a bit of surgery at one end where the steel lining
has been uncovered. But every time I catch sight of an upmarket, prettified
butcher block table in one of the designer kitchen shops, with a vast price tag,
I pat myself on the back for my decisive, shall we say, intervention!

Nobody I know has ever been told off for winkling stuff out of skips, but
commonsense suggests that while a skip's contents are almost, by definition,
unwanted rubbish, the contractor or householder might not take kindly to a raid
that scatters debris over the road and leaves the contents precariously
balanced. (Councils also maintain that the contents of a skip still belong to the
person who placed them there until the skip has been removed, so be warned.)
You will usually find scaffolding planks wedging the rubbish together and these
should not be disturbed. If a doubt remains, and your dignity is precious to

Skip-trawling becomes a way of life when you are in thrifty mode. Look out for old bed-heads, chairs without their seats, steel or glazed sinks – a host of treasures that the uninitiated or seriously wealthy have passed over

you, try and waylay one of the builders on site and check it out with them. Obviously, don't rant on and on about some wonderful piece you have detected among the dross; just mention that you could use some of the stuff thrown out in the skip and would they mind if you helped yourself, carefully of course. A small gratuity can be offered if the mood seems obstructive, but in general I have found builders friendly and grateful for a diversion, and genially disposed towards the scavenging classes.

It only remains for me to suggest what could be useful in the average skip, and what you might overlook in your early scavenging career. We can take it as read that panelled doors, actual furniture (even a medicine cupboard), and the sort of bric-a-brac that made the fortune of architectural salvage companies, will not have escaped your notice. But you may have overlooked simple planks: well-seasoned floorboards, somewhat roughly uprooted and liable to be peppered with nail holes, stained with villainous floor paints or lino adhesive, and not measuring up by a long chalk to the immaculate planks your DIY manual illustrates. Appearances to the contrary, these are excellent for DIY. Professionals may object that it takes too long to plane them off or fill them, but a keen amateur will enjoy making something out of a windfall. And the fact is, old planks make up into much more appealing furniture than flimsy new deal or that sullen, heavy, substance, MDF. I know someone – very thriftily inclined – who spends his spare time fashioning cupboards, dressers and hanging shelves out of recycled floorboards, and this is one area where fortuitous wear and tear, or what we love to call 'heavy distressing', pays off. The planks are thick enough to give weight to a piece, the holes can be left (or filled if you want perfection, with plastic wood or putty) and any residual creosote or varnish-stain can simply be painted over for an instantly fetching and very fashionable 'worn' look.

Car boot sales are the cornucopias of the nineties. If you have the time and the energy to visit them regularly, you can pick up some amazing bargains

CAR BOOT SALES

The idea behind car boot sales is irresistible, or was in the early days before dealers moved in on the scene and it became difficult to tell them apart from antique fairs and junk markets. The essence of a genuine boot sale, as I understand it, is that it is an amateur, neighbourhood event – like garage sales in the USA – providing a locally publicized venue where people can bring all the junk that accumulates in a home over the years, offer it for sale at clean-sweep prices, and go home with the double satisfaction of having cleared the decks, metaphorically speaking, and earned a little cash thereby.

Boot sales of this type are still to be found, in country districts; if you see handwritten posters and the locale is somewhere like a school playing field, there is a good chance of a genuine boot sale. The point is that these turn up the real bargains because ordinary folk are rarely smart about pricing in their eagerness to get rid of old eiderdowns, lidless saucepans, piles of old records, deck chairs with torn canvas, incomplete tea sets, stud boxes and much else. Bargain hounds rarely come away empty handed from these events, and a good time is had by all.

Local papers provide details of forthcoming car boot sales, and it is up to your flair or intuition to discriminate between the real thing and the more knowing alternative, largely run by dealers. These too are worth a visit (dealers have been known to nod off), but they rarely offer such rich pickings as down-filled pillows, old kitchen knives of the non-stainless variety which sharpen up a treat, or lamps in need of re-wiring. With boot sales, it does pay to arrive early; once the stuff is sold, people leave, unlike market stalls where usually there is more stock to begin with and reserves under the table to replenish the emptying stalls.

Should you be in the position of wanting to sell rather than buy, boot sales are a good bet, since the fee for a space is nominal. If your car is too small to pack in a trestle table and the goods for sale, a plastic groundsheet will suffice. Again, arrive early to secure a good position and bring plenty of tie-on price tags or gummed stickers. If you haven't a clue what to ask, a quick recce round neighbouring stalls may yield pointers. You don't need to go to business school to work out that low prices tend to ensure a quick sale; on the other hand, if there is something in your boot that you feel may be worth a bit more, say, a hallmarked silver spoon, keep it back till you have got the feel of pricing. You might be lucky and find someone a bit more knowledgeable, who will suggest a sensible price but won't take you for a ride.

CHARITY AND THRIFT SHOPS

If you were lucky enough to live close to one of these in their heyday, a decade or more ago, you really could have imported a touch of luxury into your life very cheaply. All you had to do was assiduously and regularly comb the wares, set out with pell-mell innocence, in strange, underlit premises, staffed by dreamy OAPs, and reeking of sweaty feet. It would be cruel to enumerate the wonders I pounced on at Oxfam shops in this glowing shambolic springtime of donations to good causes. But truth to history demands that I record that you could then 'pick up' exquisite, handworked linen tablecloths, crocodile writing cases, even a somewhat beat-up 'lowboy', or linen press on bun feet, for derisory sums. Rich pickings such as these were all possible if, like me, you were able to look in almost daily with your pram on the way back from shopping in the nearest High Street, not yet a 'mall' or 'centre'.

Today most of these charitably orientated little shops dotted about our towns are sadly altered. The stuff that comes in is not what it was. The sweaty feet smell lingers, but instead of Harris tweed coats, riding boots, heavy duty aluminium saucepans designed for Agas, stoneware casseroles without lids, the goods on display veer towards tacky imported basketware, greasy paperbacks and the most lifeless form of ethnic craftwork. However, this decline is not invariable, or unilateral. It has been my recent experience that provincial charity shops are more fruitful than metropolitan ones, and that the more genteel towns – Hastings, Shaftesbury to name two – are likely to offer more besides the ethnic tat and tea towels rigid with dressing, which emerge Kleenex-like from the first wash. Look for old feather-filled pillows, cushions and eiderdowns, odds and ends of china and glass, faded chintz curtains.

Most of these shops provide an unofficial library service today. Not a lending library strictly speaking, but the most wonderful conglomeration of second-hand books, from paperback thrillers to cloth-bound classics, at such minuscule prices that you can extend your collection by the yard for less than the cost of a new hardback. The dear ladies who run these establishments are wised up, however, to the value of fine bindings or rarities, like first editions, because smart representatives from HQ call in from time to time to advise on such things. I have a weakness for these little shops and the devoted teams who run them, and the thought that a small spending spree in such a place ultimately benefits a good cause mitigates consumerist guilt. If you find yourself at weekends, or on holiday, or for any other reason, in a small provincial town, it is usually worth paying a quick visit to the local charity shops. Better still, of course, is to regularly check out one in your neighbourhood; but if you live in a bustling urban area, the competition will be that much keener. Dealers today tend to take in a few charity shops on their rounds.

MARKETS

Regular weekly markets are still held today, as they have been done for centuries, in almost every small town throughout the country. A quick word with a knowledgeable local publican, craft shop proprietor or antique dealer will supply details of days and times. On the whole these markets are given over to fresh local produce, but quite often there will be a stall or two selling junk – yesterday's junk being today's 'collectable'. Take the case of old enamelled kitchenware, usually cream and green, or spattered grey, or dingy white. This used to be thrown out gleefully in favour of bright new plastic or non-stick coated steel. Today these invariably battered relics of the innocent days of wooden wirelesses and black-and-white TV sets are fondly collected by,

Left A simple and stylish bentwood chair and a country dresser – some of the bargains that may be found in provincial markets or second-hand furniture shops

A large pine table with cutlery drawers may still be cheaper secondhand than new

I suppose, the same crowd that go for cute old wireless sets, Teasmaids, complete with 'wake-up' music and a little chromed teapot, and darling old alarm clocks that do a little dance on the bedside table while you grope about blearily trying to suppress the nerve-shattering racket. All these items may feature on a fast-forward country market junk stall, the gleanings of which are still way down the price ladder as a rule, and well worth the search.

Then there are the proper antique/junk markets which can be very swanky, held under cover all the year round, or not under cover but in minor roads or spare lots. The latter tend to mushroom with stalls overnight, and by dawn are aromatic with fried onions and hamburgers, loud with old rock music and packed with locals and tourists looking for a junk find or a souvenir, or just a bit of voyeuristic fun watching the human charade. They vary from the more prestigious, like the Friday morning market held in Bermondsey (see Bargain hunting page 204), where fine china and interesting old jewellery rub shoulders with manky old clothes and kilims punched with interesting holes (see Restoring old rugs page 85) to the fairly indiscriminate flea markets, like my local Brick Lane (see Bargain hunting page 204) held on Sunday mornings, where the stalls throw up anything and everything. The atmosphere has a Cockney 'knees-up' vitality, but watch your purse and pockets carefully just in case of pick-pockets.

AUCTIONS

If you have time to spare and a dogged temperamental mix of hopefulness and perseverance, check out regularly held sales at auction houses: it's almost certainly the thriftiest way to fill the biggest gaps in both your hard and soft furnishing. Auctions are chancy, a lottery from start to finish, but on a lucky day you may land a real snip. Opinions vary as to whether big town salesrooms or smaller provincial auctions offer the richest pickings; in the towns the sheer volume of stuff is in your favour, but in my experience local salesrooms are more likely to turn up hidden treasures: fine bits of water gilding slathered in paint; Arts and Crafts chairs with the rush seating gone; a Deco vase in need of cleaning.

Viewing is one of the most important elements at auctions. Auctioneers I spoke to agree that the best strategy for amateurs (which means most of us) is to view and then leave bids for items that take the fancy, rather than attending the sale itself. This way you can cool-headedly decide on the top figure you can afford instead of being coaxed into a sudden extravagance by the drama and tempo of the occasion. The auction house sale catalogue will provide guidelines of estimated prices for the lots on view; these are usually on the generous side. As ever you need to weigh up the situation – what you think the item is really worth, what it is worth to you, and what you can afford – then hit on a sensible compromise bid. You may (in fact you probably will) lose out the first few times, having underestimated dealers' interest, but it doesn't take long to acquire a feel for these things and the day will soon come when you triumph, your diffident bid comes romping home, and the lot is yours.

If you have time to spare, there is no denying that auctions can be entertaining affairs, attracting a motley but picturesque crowd, especially in the provinces: local tradesmen, poker-faced dealers, bored housewives, a few eccentrics. A good auctioneer can get the joint jumping, and a duel between interested bidders is both instructive and quietly gripping; you can almost hear the mental number-crunching. If you decide to enter the bidding yourself (as newcomer and outsider) make your intentions clear, waving your sales' catalogue decisively – the lifted forefinger and raised eyebrow code is for the old-timers.

Country house sales are great fun, but usually so well publicized, the dealer mob turns up in strength. However, waiting till the end, when the job lots come up, can be rewarding since the important booty tends to be auctioned earlier on and the pros will be itching to load up their vans and be off home. The most fruitful sales for small time bidders are less grand, local affairs, usually called by the heirs to some elderly person whose death creates so many problems that the swift solution seems to be an auction. A rambling old suburban semi can hold more surprises than the 'big house', especially if the event gets only a modest mention in the papers. The problem is to find out about these sales; local knowledge, insider chat in the pub, and much reading between the lines of the local papers is the usual route.

As a general rule, if bargains are what you seek, mark out the visibly 'faulty' lots (whatever is going to need time and money spent on it). Caned chairs with the caning gone are an obvious example, as are fine old curtains with badly tattered edges, rugs with holes, almost anything of quality which has been crudely over-painted. A dealer will most likely see their potential, but calculate that the cost of restoration will make them expensive, harder to sell and less profitable. If you have the time, the energy and the know-how to tackle these jobs yourself the same item can be a bargain.

A living room today combines many functions. It is where you listen to music, watch the box, flake out after a hard day at work. But it is also the room you show people into – friends, acquaintances, strangers even. It presents the public face of your home, so it seems to matter that it should reflect your taste and style as well as offering comfort and a certain orderliness. It should also feel lived in, with books, plants, and, ideally, a crackling fire in the grate in winter. Friendly, rather than wild colours, seem most appropriate.

PROJECT 1: THE SCANDINAVIAN LIVING ROOM

Here we have decorated a typical terrace house double room, once connected by double doors, long since gone, Small rooms, both, but catching the sun front and back, and retaining some impressive original features – fireplace surround, doors, cornice, and a generous bay window. The floor had merely been sanded and sealed to a glossy orange brown, shrinking an already small space. I decided to play the floor down, with a greyish wash of paint, and play walls up with a colourwashed finish, in a warm saffron towards yellow, applied over an ivory matt emulsion. We fitted bookshelves into the alcoves both sides of the fireplace. Filled with books, these anchored the room visually, making it look surprisingly larger. Painted cream the mantelpiece looked too large for its context, so this was changed to a spattered finish in subdued but warm colours, red, grey, black and cream on a beige base, for an effect suggestive of warm-toned granite. This worked a treat and delighted the owners. All woodwork was lightly dragged in silver grey and buff, applied over an off-white base. This toned it down to harmonize with both walls and floor, and again helped to make the rooms look more together, and spacious. Bay windows are tricky to curtain. We compromised on the simplest muslin drapes, using a limed reproduction oak table and a large lamp to bring a somewhat blank space into the room's orbit. The cool-looking 'Driftwood' floor, plus simple furnishings, added up to a charming but unpretentious effect with a strong Scandinavian feel to it.

Above and below
Woodwashed floorboards in a driftwood silver grey make the room look larger. The handsome original shutters and window frames were lightly dragged in two colours – silvery grey and buff – with mouldings emphasized by a second coat of buff.

Above and right A junk picture frame makes a good-looking mirror. The frame was chunky and a good shape, and demanded only a quick 'facelift' of silver leaf and mahogany stain. The fireplace is spattered in off-white, black, beige, and a dull red, over a coffee-coloured base to shrink it visually and add a period feel.

Above Here a showcase of travel ephemera blends well with plain floorboards and colourwashed walls of terracotta and pale yellow.

Right Rainbow stripes – an easy effect to copy thanks to masking tape – transform a plain chest of drawers into a vivid eye-catcher.

Opposite A stripy throw, a simple lampshade and a colourful floorcloth all take their cue from a lively print, plainly framed.

Above There is no easier, quicker way to 'lose' an ugly sofa than by wrapping it in a swathe of unbleached calico. But what makes this look 'meant' and effective is the row of matching cushions stencilled with a wreath of ivy. Twinned lamps, side tables and wall plaques either side give a sophisticated look which balances the 'deconstructed' sofa.

Right Simple matting, plain wood furniture and a plethora of checks give a Scandinavian feel to a living/dining space, which has the uncluttered look that suits present day living. A dresser-bookcase displays a nice mélange of books and ornaments, and its blue lining picks up the colour theme in fabrics and china.

Left Photocopies of old prints linked and embellished with rope stencils make an imaginative and thrifty decorative feature over a plain blue, Shakerish fireplace.

If a whole print room seems over-ambitious, this is a clever way to turn a few attractive images to good account. Use good quality paper and wallpaper paste.

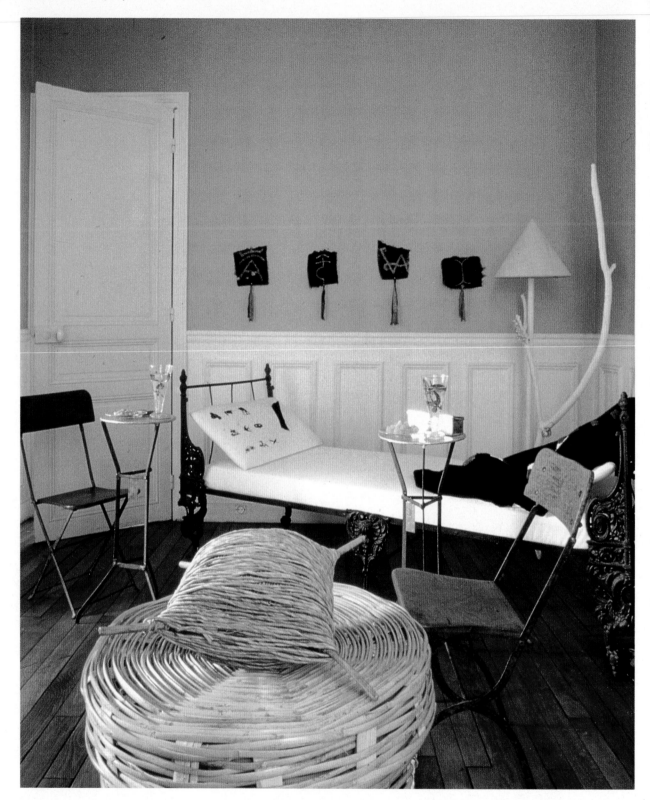

Very much a designer's room, this, but with ideas we can steal and recycle. Walls are brown-papered, making a background to black and white and natural textures like wicker, string, 'found' wooden shapes. A black iron *chaise-longue* is softened with stencilled canvas cushions, and a plain café-type chair assorts well with a round rattan table. Try beachcombing at low tide for sculptural pieces of driftwood.

ANTIQUE GALLERIES AND SALVAGE YARDS

Both these strike me as something of a recent phenomenon: old roomy industrial premises now housing a petrified forest of 'old' going on antique furniture, plus a few knick-knacks, for as far as the eye can see. They have sprung up in many big towns. I know at least half a dozen in London, a few outside London and I have been introduced by a dealer friend to one or two in France. The intake is fairly indiscriminate, since the turnover is mainly with foreign dealers who buy up vast quantities for shipment abroad, and aren't too fussy about quality. Most of the items will sell as old and British, both of which are still selling points in Tokyo, Australia, North America, or wherever new money seeks old goods.

The immediate impression these places give is usually depressing: acres of unlovely pieces smothered with old, glutinous French polish, their intrinsic worth hidden under this once popular finish. But because of their sheer size (the one I am thinking of occupies four floors in a shed the size of a small factory) all sorts of things come to roost – marble pillars from a demolished bank, old school furniture by the ton, exotic foreign pieces. I visit my local gallery (see Bargain hunting page 204) whenever I want something that's big and solidly built but not too special, and when I'm hoping for a choice of style and price. Recently much of the stuff on display seems to have come from France: armoires, *bergère* chairs, curly metal café furniture. Most of these places will arrange for large pieces to be delivered to you, but check the cost of this beforehand.

Architectural salvage outfits grew out of builders' yards where the odd choice remnant from a demolished building was pounced upon by someone with a good eye. I often think of the builder who bragged (when he saw me examining a fine but dilapidated fireplace surround) of all the fireplace surrounds he had tossed on to bonfires over the years. I imagine him moaning as he realizes that if he had just put them all into 'archisalvage' he could be a rich man by now. Architectural salvage is a good business now that any scrap saved from demolition work has its price, be it a brass light switch, finger plate or entire church pulpit. If you want something extraordinary, and enjoy the challenge of working it into your home, these are definitely places to visit. Prices tend to be top whack, but now and then an item turns up that is affordable, because it is so enormous (I have a huge bathtub with chromed fittings from a demolished mansion) or so eccentric or broken up that no sane shopper would take a chance on it. One of my favourite architectural salvage haunts is housed in a Victorian church (see Bargain hunting page 204), an immense shadowy pile of a place bursting with visual surprises: carved oak screens, heaps of marble, pulpits and pews galore, stained glass windows, doors of every shape and size and period, stacked like books in a reference library. Looking around is instructive if nothing else – you will never pass a skip again without checking the contents – and the whole experience is mindblowing and entertaining even if you spend a whole afternoon there and emerge with nothing more than a fireplace tile for a future patchwork wall.

CHAPTER 2

WALLS

The state and colour of your walls and ceilings can have a profoundly depressing effect on you when you move into your new home. To transform the wall colour or re-paper may take a little time, but it is a relatively inexpensive procedure compared with buying furnishings. And the sight of softly coloured or crisply papered walls will not only elate you, but establish the decorative theme for the rest of the room.

Prepping

This is the decorative painters' phrase for the preliminary work that has to be done on interior surfaces before you *begin* decorating. In the highest standard of work, prepping usually takes longer than the final painting. How lavishly you 'prep' is optional in your own place but there is no question that decorating looks better, goes on more smoothly and lasts longer if the undercover work is done properly. If walls are painted, start by wiping them over with the sponge and cleaning solution, paying special attention to areas that get fingermarked, round light switches for instance. Clean woodwork down at the same time, dusting the top of door frames, window architraves and picture rails. Ceilings usually only need a quick brush with a soft broom. When surfaces are dry, start filling the cracks, dents and nail holes with a well-stirred creamy mix of filler. Fill shadow cracks and holes 'proud' with a filling knife or spatula. Deep cracks and dents need to be filled in two or three stages to level them up. Leave all this filling to dry whilst you tackle the cracks that usually run along the top of skirtings, round doors and window frames, or between built-in furniture and walls. For these mix up a sloppier mix of filler and apply with a brush, for speed, working it well in, then wiping flat with a damp rag. This is tedious work but makes a great difference to the sleekness of the final result.

Wear old clothes and plastic gloves for rubbing down filler, and tie hair up in a scarf. Fold papers to get into curved mouldings and wrap abrasive paper round a small block to help with sanding large patches of filler. Use a medium then finer grade of paper to get a smooth surface. You may find you have to 'fine fill' in certain places; there are finer ready-mixed fillers available for this. If the woodwork is painted and in a reasonable condition, then sand this down too – this gives a 'key' for the new paint. Filler is more absorbent than painted plaster so before going on to the painting proper, 'stop out' all filled areas with acrylic primer or the same emulsion you are using on the walls, or undercoat on woodwork. Just brush on enough to seal the filler in.

The usual system when re-decorating is to start with the ceiling, then tackle the walls, and finish with the woodwork. If you want a special finish, do this

Above Wallpaper strippers and spatulas for filling cracks, and a lambswool paint roller, which produces a slightly textured effect

after undercoating the walls, but before the woodwork. If some glazes or Colourwash splash onto the ceiling, it is quicker to paint these out later with more ceiling paint than to wipe them off as you go along. However, it is a good idea to wipe splashes of colour off woodwork as they occur because it is harder to paint these out later. If the woodwork is in such a grungy state that it is going to stand out (thick with layers of old paint, chipped or cracked) it should be stripped off with a hot-air gun or blowtorch at the start of the job.

Papered walls may present different problems. Paper that is loose, torn or stained with damp is best removed altogether. It may be worth your while hiring a professional gadget that steams the paper off. Otherwise sloshing water over it and scraping with a steel stripping knife will eventually remove it. The wall surface beneath will almost certainly require extensive filling. If you uncover old lime plaster (not uncommon in houses over one hundred years old) you may feel it needs repairing with more lime plaster (see Suppliers page 202). Otherwise fill as above, stop out, then size the wall surfaces with diluted glue size and paint with home-made distemper, or a commercial brand. This not only looks beautiful but allows lime plaster to breathe and dry out.

Wallpaper in reasonable shape just needs tidying up. Stick back loose bits with wallpaper paste. Where the plaster behind feels dodgy, slit the paper with a sharp blade, scrape out loose plaster, fill, sand and paste back. You can paper over a reasonable paper, or paint over it. If the existing paper needs a lot of work done on it, you may feel it makes sense to line it out with lining paper. This is hung like any other paper, and gives a tight, neat base for further papering or paintwork. A paper-hanger's table, like a flush door on trestle legs, is inexpensive, collapsible and speeds up any papering job. Use two brushes for paper-hanging: a wide brush to get the paste on, and another dry wide brush to smooth it out on the wall. A little brush is useful too, for getting into corners or round cut-outs for light switches.

Removing that pimply Artex finish from walls or ceiling is a hefty undertaking; people often ask for solutions to this inherited nasty. I really think the best bet is to camouflage it with Colourwash (see pages 36–38).

PAINTING OUT NASTIES

It is not uncommon these days to find the marks of the bodger imprinted, almost immovably, all over your new home, be it recent conversion or tumbledown cottage. Having acted as agony aunt in this area for some years, I know most of the objectionable legacies of both spec buildings and cack-handed amateurs looking for a quick sale: the job lot of tiling that looks like cold porridge; interior surfaces pimpled with Artex or scratchy with woodchip paper; unspeakable foam-backed vinyl flooring glued down over concrete; bathroom suites in babyfood colours – pea green, yucky yellow or lurid pink. Harmless fireplaces are invariably ripped out and boarded up, or worse, made into a little cave of sooty brick (they took out the old iron grate) holding an arrangement of dried flowers, or, sometimes, inappropriately converted into a 'ranchstyle' random stone hearth with a cubbyhole for logs. Nor am I forgetting the acres of melamine, in fumed-oak finish on fitted kitchen units, or stark white and clinical, for built-in bedroom cupboards.

Who was it said of Scott Fitzgerald, 'the style is hope, the message is despair'? Well here it's the other way round: the style is desperate but the message is hopeful. Most if not all of these decorating gaffes can be redeemed unobtrusively if you know the appropriate paint trick. I am of course assuming that you are obliged to make the best of them in the short term since their removal and replacement, right now, may be the straw that breaks the bank manager's back. For instance, not only are woodchip and Artex the devil to remove but they undoubtedly help (in older homes at least) to hold together the plasterwork behind them. Strip them off and you are probably looking at a re-plastering job, pricey in itself, before you even get to slap on the colour. I suggest we deal with problems and solutions in their most frequent order of appearance.

Artex and woodchip wallcovering

The same paint treatment does for both these uncharming surfaces, though they differ basically in that Artex is a ready-mixed form of plaster used to create a range of textured finishes, mostly prickly and unpleasant, while woodchip paper is simply a super-tough paper which performs like Band-aid on a grand scale, binding dodgy old plasterwork, covering cracks, flaky bits and so forth, and contributing its own ineffable scritchy-scratchy texture. Architects tell me that both (but Artex especially) are popular with the refurb fraternity owing to their cover-up qualities: with these techniques in place cracks from resettlement or plaster drying out quickly will not be visible to the eye of prospective purchasers. (In fact, if used subtly, and spread out thinly with a steel spatula, Artex can add interesting texture to standard plasterwork, and it is easy to apply.) If you have either in your home this does *not* mean that your place is on the verge of collapse. Buildings move subtly without falling down and cracks along the ceiling line or down corners are normally unimportant and non-structural. The ones to worry about seriously are diagonal rifts across exterior brickwork.

But to return to our interior problems, I have discovered that one of my own products, Colourwash, which is a water-based equivalent to the oil glazes

which dominated the paint effect scene during the eighties (oil glazes now being phased out of trade and DIY markets due to their noxiousness), works like a dream over both Artex and woodchip wall surfaces. Colourwash comes in ten colours, from hardly-there antique white and buff, to quite strong blue, green and terracotta, and is designed to be user-friendly in the sense that it will go over existing matt emulsion paint (but clean this down first) or woodchip, in a neat, fast way.

Tip some of the colour – concentrated, but do not dilute – from its plastic keg on to a decorating sponge and simply wipe this rapidly in all directions over your lumpy and scratchy wall finish. I reckon (having tested this out in my mother's Essex cottage, a bodger's delight) I can civilize one of these wall finishes with Colourwash in less time than it would take to spring clean the walls with a solution of Flash or sugar soap. This transparent wash of colour subtly softens the brashness of these wall textures, making them less noticeable while adding enough colour to make a pleasant background for your bits and pieces. The bumpy surface becomes an asset, enriching the final effect which looks old and friendly instead of cheap and makeshift. If the initial Colourwash is too watery for you, leave the paint to 'cure' (not *dry* – it is touch dry in minutes – but *harden*) for 48 hours, so subsequent sponging will not lift the first coat. Then wipe a second coat over.

In my experience one keg of Colourwash will give an average sized room 3×4 m (10×13 ft) two coats. Anyone who has tried painting in watercolours knows that a 'wash' is a fast, transparent layer of fragile colour. I mention this because US customers frequently phone from Dallas or wherever, hysterical because they have already used three kegs of terracotta in one room and only got two-thirds round the walls and the local supplier is out of stock. I *know*, without seeing their handiwork, that they are using our wash like paint, i.e. thickly, brushed on, in flagrant contradiction to the printed instructions. It is a very normal, natural, almost incorrigible, human tendency (we find this in our studio classes) to believe that if a little of something is good, a fat splodge of it will be better still. But now you all know better I hope. Let 'sensitive' and 'painterly' be your watchwords. This fragile-seeming finish looks best without further treatment and lasts pretty well under normal conditions. But there are certain situations – kitchens and hallways – where the occasional wash-down may be needed, in which case I suggest you touch it up with a coat of matt, colourless, near-to-non-yellowing varnish (see Suppliers page 202). Thin this with one-quarter white spirit, well mixed, before applying.

Incidentally, while paler Colourwash shades look fresco-ish and subtle over a white matt emulsion base, the darker shades – blue, green and terracotta – gain richness from a coloured base, for example a matt emulsion in a paler tone.

Radiators, light switches, power sockets

As every interiors photographer knows, objects like these in their inglorious factory finish jar on the eye once their surroundings have been imaginatively decorated. Mostly, in my experience, they are dingy white. Painting them to match their surround – wall or skirting – makes them inconspicuous, and doesn't take long.

This said, the standard gloss finish that covers most radiators does not complement the sort of water-based emulsion many people have on their walls. What does work is to coat them with a tinted oil glaze (see Recipes page 200) which matches your wall colour, since heat seems to affect oil-based finishes less, though they may darken gradually over a few years. To do this, turn the heating off before you start, then rub the surface down, if it looks flaky, with wet-and-dry paper dipped in water. Prime with a standard oil-based undercoat then mix up a glaze tinted to match your wall colour to be applied once the undercoat is dry. If this seems impossible, there are colour matching services which will analyse your colour formula if you can provide a swatch. But messing about with a few tubes of artists' oil colour or Universal Stainers may produce a close match. The result doesn't have to be *identical*; anything near to the wall colour is going to be less obtrusive than plain white. If your wall colour is a straightforward solid tone then paint the glaze over the radiators evenly, but if the walls are ragged or sponged or colourwashed, try to reproduce this effect (see page 59).

Switches and light sockets should be treated in the same way. Use the wall-coloured glaze for switches and a colour that matches the skirtings for the sockets. Switches do get a lot of handling so give them a coat of matt varnish, then they can be wiped down frequently without the paint wearing away.

Special Paints

Commercial alternatives

Most people still opt for the main commercial brands when choosing paint – emulsions for walls and silk vinyls for woodwork. These are adequate and available in wide colour ranges, but for some tastes 'plastic' paint applied in the standard way looks flat and lifeless; the colours need modification, the texture revitalization. It is useful to know that there are many ways to remedy these defects, such as applying a Colourwash on top of standard emulsion (when newly applied or already there) or 'distressing' emulsion paints on furniture and woodwork. Two other developments are worthy of a pauper's attention. Water-based paints, mostly acrylics, are fast taking over from the old-style oil-based paints. A coat of the new water-based eggshell paint, painted over an acrylic primer undercoat sealed with acrylic varnish, will cut drying time down to an absolute minimum and leave no smell. And you can wash your brushes in water afterwards. Speed is of the essence in DIY decorating these days, and the new water-based 'high tech' paints and varnishes address this problem with dispatch.

The other complementary technique is using primitive, make-it-yourself paints – distemper and limewash (see Recipes page 200). Aside from cheapness, the attraction of these 'old' paints is their beauty, colour and texture, and their ability to 'breathe' – an asset on old walls with damp problems. The materials are all readily available (see Suppliers page 202) and they get top marks for being environmentally friendly.

For tinting your own colours, or modifying commercial colours that don't quite hit the mark, invest in a basic range of cheap tinting agents: Universal Stainers for ready-mixed paints, cheap school-grade powder colours (dry colour) for distemper. Keep to earth colours for limewash. For stencilling, or decorative work on furniture, use artists' acrylic tube colours for speedy drying, or gouache tube colours in gum arabic for a nicely flowing transparent watercolour paint. Don't buy too many colours: get the primaries, red, blue, yellow, plus raw umber and black for 'dirtying' or softening. Normal matt emulsion is fine for painting white.

DISTEMPER

As well as being the name of an unpleasant canine disorder, distemper is a term used to denote a simple, beautiful and primitive type of wall paint, made from whiting or chalk, animal glue size and water. Made and used all over the world for centuries, distemper dropped out of use with the post-war boom in plastic-based emulsions.

Interestingly, with the revival of 'historic paints' for special conservationist situations, distemper is once again being made commercially – at a price (see Suppliers page 202). But to cut costs and create a greater variety of shades, I have devised a recipe (see page 200) which can be seen coloured a pure and singing blue-green on the walls of the bedroom shown on pages 145–47.

Making distemper requires effort; sturdy arms are needed to mix and stir the ingredients to the requisite smoothness, as is a powerful command of one's own brush when spreading it over the walls. The high content of whiting (a chalky substance) in distemper makes it unusually heavy and thick. However, on the plus side, one coat is all you need and the look of it *in situ*, with its ineffable texture and bloom, will make you burst with pride. There's no doubt, crude old-fashioned distemper delivers a look that people love today – a touch rustic with soft and clear colours, and a gentle, earthy texture to which brushmarks lend a patina no convenience paint can match.

The old cavil about distemper, or whitewash, was that its powdery surface 'rubbed off'. According to historic paint expert Peter Hood, the powderiness was due to cheap glue size being used in both commercial brands and by housepainters making it up on the spot. (Cheap glue size has less binding power, hence the friable nature of distemper made with it.) Our distemper shown in the rose bedroom (page 145) was made up with the best glue size available: rabbit skin, sold in granule form in good artists' supply shops (see Suppliers page 202). I can vouch for its effectiveness; a good rub left only a trace of colour on my fingers.

Distemper is a bulky paint, so if you are following my recipe on page 200 make sure you have plastic buckets and sink bowls in which to do the mixing and stirring, plus outsize wooden spoons, rolling pins or lengths of broom handle. A large wire mesh sieve (gauze is too fine and fragile for this job) is good for breaking up lumps in the whiting, prior to soaking or 'fattening' overnight. An electrically powered cake whisk can help in the final mixing stages, when you are blending the size solution and tinting colour with the soaked whiting. The finished paint should be smooth and thickish, like heavy cream or cake batter.

The complete distemper kit: whiting, rabbit skin glue, paint pigments, a large sieve, buckets, pans, and broom handle for stirring

Above To make your own distemper, sieve the whiting into a bucket of cold water, and place the glue size in another bucket with water to cover, leaving both to 'fatten' overnight; then heat the glue size until fluid, then add gradually whilst stirring to the whiting. Dissolve the powder colour in water and stir this in too

The natural colour of distemper, untinted, is a warm creamy white. With the addition of pigment this tints up into a beautiful range of light to medium shades. Traditionally earth pigments made from dried and pulverized natural clays were used for colouring distemper, and lamp black was made from soot; these were cheap, more easily available and yielded a range of gentle, sympathetic shades, from pearly grey to deep Suffolk pink. Earth pigments include raw and burnt sienna, yellow ochre, raw and burnt umber, a subtle muted green, terre verte and a less brownish pinky red, terra rosa. Traditionalists may prefer to stay within this colour range, especially if they live in old cottages in a rural area like Suffolk, which is strongly associated with a particular earth colour. But with the large range of pigments now commonly available, there is no reason to feel bound by the earthy palette. Our aquamarine green, for instance, was made up from the following pigments, in Universal Stainer form – blue, yellow and red added to white distemper. These are crude but inexpensive and mixable in both oil and waterpaints.

Distemper colours dry considerably lighter than their wet colour suggests, so test samples on paper or card, drying them off with a hairdryer. This takes a minute or two, but you will almost certainly find you need to add more dissolved colour to your mixture if the wet shade is closer to what you want. It is possible to make darker, stronger colours with distemper but only by adding extravagant quantities of pigment – enough to overpower the chalky white base colour which gives the paint its opacity.

Preparation for a distemper coat is straightforward. Walls should be clean, cracks filled, loose bits of wallpaper stuck down firmly. Distemper can be applied over a matt emulsion or acrylic primer, or over existing wallpaper or lining paper. It can also be applied to bare plaster, either new (allow plaster six months to dry first) or old, but brush over a weak solution of glue size first to seal the pores, so that the walls do not soak up too much paint. Use a large, wide, standard brush to apply distemper. The correct way to apply it is in regular vertical strips, brushing one way as evenly and smoothly as possible. The paint dries with a perceptible texture and is matt with a soft bloom and faint ridges from the brush marks. This is characteristic and attractive.

MY OWN COLOURWASH

If you want the colourwashed effect of airy dappled colour, but are not
prepared to repaint your walls with distemper, you might consider my Paint
Magic Colourwash which is designed for use over matt emulsion. We used it for
the walls in the yellow living room on pages 25–27. To get this warm but not
too bright yellow I mixed together the buff and yellow tones from the range and
applied this over a cream emulsion base.

Paint Magic Colourwash is a high-tech paint compared with distemper. It has
many of the properties of an oil glaze, like transparency, but it is a water-based
product, drying to a completely matt finish. Think of it as a convenience paint
– with it you can wipe a coat of colour over a room in a couple of hours.
Instead of using a brush or roller we recommend you use a large decorating
sponge, tipping the colour straight on to the sponge from its plastic keg and
then spreading it out fast across the walls as if you were washing them down. It
is handy to keep a small brush in your pocket: if the colour builds up too
strongly in one spot use the brush to thin it out again. The idea is to spread the
Colourwash out as thinly as possible to give a veil of soft sheer colour, not to
use it thickly like a conventional paint.

What is great about Colourwash is that you can use a shade of it to liven up
an emulsion colour you've grown tired of, thus flattering the plain emulsion,

Paint Magic Colourwash is best
poured straight from the container
onto a sponge

Apply Colourwash with broad,
generous strokes

which to me looks blank and lifeless on its own. The paler shades in the range
of washes are pretty over white (preferably a soft rather than brilliant white)
while the richer colours look best over a mid tone of the same colour.
Terracotta over salmon pink, sea blue and lettuce green over a light chalky
blue, for instance, produce truly singing shades. The colours can be intermixed
as in the honey yellow, or you can wash one colour on top of another, for a
subtle in-between shade. Make sure you allow the first layer of Colourwash to
'cure' or harden for the time stated (48 hours) before applying the next.

When you have just applied the wash it will look wet and shiny but it goes
quite matt as it dries, settling down before your very eyes. I reckon that one
keg (or litre) of Colourwash is enough to give an average sized room (say 3×4
m [10×13 ft]) two coats, if the colour is used sparingly. To varnish or not to
varnish? This depends. I give a colourwashed wall one coat of extra pale dead
flat alkyd varnish on surfaces I think will get a lot of wear – built-in cupboard
doors, for instance, or halls and stairways. Some people colourwash over
painted furniture, kitchen units and bedroom suites. Here I would always
varnish the finish for protection, but on ordinary walls, like our yellow ones, I
would leave the Colourwash unvarnished.

Special Paint Effects

Although paint effects have become associated with designer interiors, I first became interested in them when I realized what a really cost-effective way they were to add colour and individuality to my own home.

STENCILLING

Bold stencilled borders, in scale with a room's proportions, can add drama and definition to plainly coloured, or colourwashed, walls. But the stencilling approach I find most satisfying is where an overall pattern is created. Granted, this takes longer, but there is no obligation to complete a room at one go, though once you begin it is tempting to do just one more stretch of wall, and then another to see the final effect.

Overall-stencilling can be very rich, and polychrome, like old embroideries or brocades, or the intense decoration one finds in some High Victorian churches. Alternatively, it can be a simple one-colour repeat, on a regular grid, giving the look of early nineteenth-century wallpapers. The first effect is slower and more demanding; it requires some artistic talent to build up a rich overall design in several colours. But the result can be sumptuous. The second idea is one any patient stenciller can achieve, maybe sponging the design – or designs – for a more textured, quicker result. The simplest *fleur-de-lys* stencil, repeated over walls, will look like an expensive wallpaper and is especially effective worked in a metallic paint (see page 201 for a simple metallic paint recipe). Or use two separate stencils, alternated on a grid (see illustration) to create a different look – either dramatic or low-key.

Above Stencil brush

Left Coral stencil taken from a Swedish design

Two separate stencils – a flower design and a leaf design – alternated on a grid

We stencilled a stand at an antique fair with large and small leaf shapes, in a dirty bronze colour on a buff colourwashed background (so as not to clash with the antiques on display). It looked handsome and appropriate as a drop to some immensely distinguished furniture. In Sweden I have seen the most interesting and varied use of stencils imitating wallpaper. The fashion for wallpaper in Sweden pre-dated printing technology, so many professional painters and home owners re-created the admired effects and motifs of imported French or Swiss wallpaper, and the designs, using stencils. Now that wallpapers are ubiquitous, and inexpensive, these hand-painted imitations look all the more special. One of my favourite designs, discovered in a small provincial museum in central Sweden, is a twig of coral, repeated at quite wide intervals – at least 30 cm (12 in.) apart in all directions (see illustration) – on a plainly distempered wall. I would guess that this dated back to the 1830s, just before the Victorians went colour mad with the discovery and commercial use of aniline dyes.

Intensive stencil effects are best reserved, I think, for a special room. It could be a kitchen, or a living room, or perhaps a small study, or – and here is a thought – a tiny hallway with lots of doors leading off that needs a visual lift. Painter Emma Hardie, whom I often work with, made a cubicle of a hallway in her North London flat into a charming sort of ante-chamber, by painting walls and doors with the same soft creamy yellow, then stencilling a white *fleur-de-lys* design over the lot. Instead of feeling like a spec builder's lame solution, the space is charming and feels like a hat-box you can stand up in.

Something hand-made and hopefully exceptional, like stencilling on the scale of Emma's room, must be protected against unnecessary damage. In a small space I would coat the lot with extra pale alkyd matt varnish; in a larger room I'd varnish over the bits that get handled – chiefly doors. If you have a dado rail, paint the area below the dado a plain colour, and varnish, reserving the stencilling for the walls above the dado.

Fleur-de-lys stencil

Above Repeat pattern stencil designs make effective picture rails or dado borders. There are many stencil kits available today, but with a little care you can easily cut your own

SPONGING

Sponging colour on to walls is so quick and easy that I think people have decided anything so simple must be less satisfactory than more elaborate paint effects. This is a real pity because sponged-on colour can look delightful – innocently rustic or subtle and sophisticated – depending on the colours you choose and put together. It is an excellent choice for rough-textured walls, whether Artex or simply crudely plastered; the imperfections get 'lost' in the matt, blurry flow of transparent colour.

The simplest sponging is a one-colour job, done with standard matt emulsion, or Colourwash, which is more transparent. Test whichever paint you choose on some spare paper – white or pale to get the hang of the 'prints', how much paint to use or dilute (this applies to emulsion, not Colourwash, which should not be diluted) and how lightly to sponge to get the effect you want. White paper gives you the clearest indication of how sponging works, but it can of course be done over coloured walls too, preferably matt painted. Choose a colour or colours that enrich the existing tone. Again, a little experimentation plus your own instinct is the best way forward.

The essential tool for sponging is a genuine sea sponge because its irregular shape and porous nature automatically create soft and interesting prints. A size that sits comfortably in your palm is the one to buy. They're not cheap, alas, but undoubtedly effective.

With one-colour sponging the interest comes from the random build-up of colour where 'prints' overlap. Start with a light scatter of prints, leaving about 30 per cent of the base showing. Go over this with a second layer of prints, aiming for the maximum colour range in your chosen shade, from pale and hardly there, to decisively coloured. Try this out on paper first to get the hang of it. It can be attractive to leave some base colour showing; sponging doesn't have to build up a uniform texture, like knitting or tweed.

Duncan Grant and Vanessa Bell used a lot of sponged texture to add variety to their decorative schemes. A visit to Charleston, their high Bohemian farmhouse in Sussex, will give you a wealth of ideas. They often sponged stencils, for a pretty, broken colour. One of their characteristic decorative flourishes was a stylized column – a simple vertical shape topped by a round disc – often sponged, quite casually, like spongeware pottery. These appear both on walls, and reduced, on fireplace surrounds.

Sponging on several colours adds richness, and can build up an effect not unlike fossil-stone marble, especially if you use transparent colours. For colour combinations that work well you can't do better than examine pieces of fossil stone, or other marbles. This will give you several colour swatches as well as a good idea of the overall shade they create when combined. Effects like this look particularly good in hallways and bathrooms, and are excellent if you want to 'lose' a run of fitted units, by sponging them to match the walls. A slight sheen improves this type of sponging, so I would finish it with a coat or two of mid-sheen varnish, alkyd over pale colours, polyurethane over deep ones. The sheen brings up the colours in an interesting way. For transparent colours choose Colourwash, or tinted oil glazes (see page 201 for how to mix up your own oil-glaze colours).

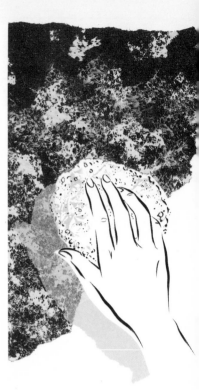

Sponging on colour. Use a genuine sea sponge to create soft, muted tones

OIL GLAZE

Once part and parcel of the decorative painter's range of special effects –
dragging, ragging, rag-rolling – oil glazes are being eased out in favour of
water-based equivalents because of their possible injurious qualities when used
over a long period and in confined spaces. It is not the oil, but the solvent, or
white spirit which is noxious. This is not to say that DIY decorators, rag-rolling
a room now and again, are putting their lives at risk, though it is sensible to
cut down on fumes by opening windows and doors as you work. The people at
risk are professional painters who might be working with these materials daily
over many years.

Having said this I should add that anyone at all seriously interested in
decorative techniques should at least try their hand at oil-glaze work because
being slower drying and more pliant, oil glazes allow you to produce effects
which are at once more precise and more subtle. Oil-glazed finishes take longer
to dry hard, but once dry – which is a gradual process, hardness increasing
over weeks – they are tougher and more durable. On the other hand (and this
can be a disadvantage) the oil content makes them liable to darken and yellow
which is fine when it suits the colour but not so good if one's using an ethereal
pastel blue or pink.

On page 201 you will find three recipes for oil glazes. The beginner's recipe
uses commercial scumble-glaze liberally, the professional recipe uses hardly
any scumble, but instead a high proportion of standard oil-based undercoat.
This is tricky to handle, 'going off' or setting hard faster and somewhat
unpredictably owing to factors like the thickness of the walls, the room
temperature, the time of year. If you can handle it (and this should be given a
dummy-run on boards rather than walls) you will find it gives soft and elegant
effects which make the scumble-based glaze effects look a bit obvious and
brash. The third recipe is for a glaze to make yourself without scumble, and
easier to manage than the professional recipe. None of the ingredients is
particularly expensive, so it could be time and money well spent to mix up and
test all three glaze recipes on painted boards, or on the inside doors of
cupboards.

The proper base for all glaze work is an oil-based eggshell paint applied over
the usual primer and undercoat. Professional decorators generally specify two
base coats or one base coat and one split-coat: eggshell mixed fifty-fifty with
undercoat. Eggshell is the least porous, or absorbent, paint, allowing the glaze
more time before it becomes too dry to manipulate, leaving unsightly streaks of
solid colour on our softly-ragged wall. If this should happen to you, the solution
is to dab white spirit over the dry patch or 'edge' to see if you can reactivate
the glaze. Prevention is better than cure, however. Try to work with a partner
and divide up the work, one person applying the glaze and the other distressing
it with rags, brushes or whatever. This involves much running up and down
stepladders, and is hard work, but exciting and quick as these things go. Don't
break off, for whatever reason, halfway across a wall. Stop when you get to a
natural break: a corner, or at a pinch, a door or window frame.

Tinting a glaze gives much more interesting colours, and is cheaper than
buying a ready-mixed glaze, or having one mixed up for you, though both these

alternatives are possible (see Suppliers page 202). Painters use artists' oil colours, or Universal Stainers, to tint glazes. Try mixing up a small amount first, using pigments in solvent only, to establish the colours used and, roughly, the proportions. Then carry on as described on page 201, adding the tint (dissolved in solvent) cautiously to the glaze, stirring well and testing as you go. Wet colour looks different from dry colour so use a hairdryer to speed drying and then check the results.

You may be lucky and arrive at the perfect shade in ten minutes, or it may take all day. Professionals usually allow at least half a day for colour mixing, so don't begrudge the time spent experimenting beforehand; one gets more certain and intuitive about colour mixing with practice. On the whole avoid using black to soften or dirty a colour; raw umber is a mellower means of softening and can be used with almost any colour. Mixing in a little of the opposite shade on the spectrum, bright green into bright red for instance, also has a softening effect.

Having arrived at a suitable glaze colour, and decided which of you does what, Painter One (the one who applies the glaze) begins at the top left-hand corner of the wall and brushes on a strip approximately 50 cm (20 in.) wide (the 'ell', or distance from elbow to fingertip, was the traditional span) all the way down from ceiling or cornice to skirting. Painter Two now runs up the stepladder and begins working over the wet glaze with rags and brushes, starting at the top and working down. Don't worry about colour straying on to cornice or skirting – this can be touched out or cleaned off later. *Do* worry about a build-up of colour along the top and bottom of the wall, especially when dragging. This is a dead giveaway, and one reason why I advise beginners to avoid dragged finishes. Ragging is much easier to control in this respect.

While Painter Two is doing the artistic bit, Painter One has applied a second strip of wet glaze just overlapping the first. It is this overlap where the aforementioned problems can occur, such as the wet edge 'going off', hence the need for speed and teamwork, and if possible, two stepladders, or at a pinch one stepladder and a stool. And so it continues, right round the room, working as a team until the walls are entirely covered.

Oil glazes are traditionally manipulated in one of the following ways – ragging, dragging, stippling – all of which give noticeably different results in close up though at a distance one is mainly conscious of subtle, controlled texture and colour with depth.

Ragging

Use a soft, lint-free rag bunched up in the hand to make a folded petal shape (see illustration above). Dab fast and lightly over the wet glaze, varying the angle of your hand and re-arranging the rag from time to time, to avoid monotony. Don't 'print' in rows, like postage stamps, but keep the pattern loose, flowing and multi-directional, like a shot silk. Don't leave patches of glaze un-ragged either; these show up in the ensemble. Chuck the rag and replace it when it becomes stiff with glaze. Some people use chamois leather, mutton cloth, J-cloths, even plastic bags, instead of rags, for a different texture. Try them for fun. I still prefer the torn-up old sheet.

Ragging – bunch up your rag in your hand and dab fast and lightly over the wet glaze

Rag-rolling

A larger piece of cloth is rolled up loosely to make a little roly-poly sausage – maybe 30 cm (12 in.) long – which is rolled either from the top to the bottom of the glazed wall, or from bottom to top, whichever you find easier. This leaves a nicely textured strip. Overlap the second 'roll-up' by 1 cm ($\frac{3}{8}$ in.) or so, to avoid a stripy look. There is a slight directional flow about rag-rolling. which you may like and which does have a stronger look than ragging.

Rag-rolling with a sausage-shaped piece of cloth

Dragging

Dragging means making deliberate brushmarks – which are easy on a small piece of furniture but pretty difficult when drawing a brush down a 3-m (10-ft) drop of glazed wall without wobbles, swerves or interruptions. Practice makes perfect and a rock-steady hand helps. So does a wide paper-hanging brush, rather than a standard paint brush – you can drag a wider strip each time (see illustration). Dragged walls look very subtle, like pinstriping, and are especially handsome in colour – dark over light blue, red over buff, etc.

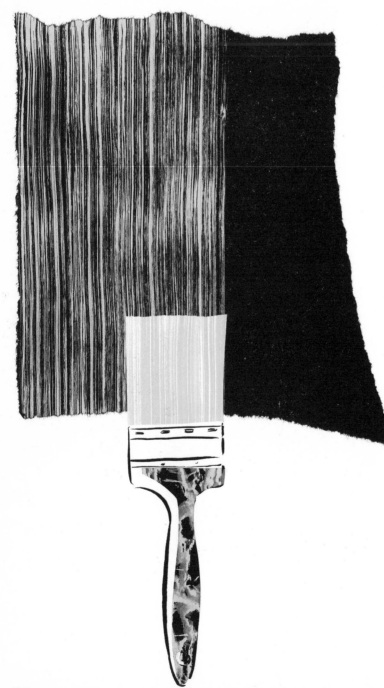

Dragging – deliberate brushmarks in a paint or glaze – creates a handsome yet subtle pinstriped effect

Stippling creates a surface of micro-dots in colour. Use a stippling brush on walls or a painter's dust brush on furniture

Stippling brush

Specialist varnish brush

Stippling

Easy but arduous, stippling gets rid of brushmarks and breaks a wet glaze surface into micro-dots of colour. The result is a soft, uniform, bloom of overall colour. Professionals stipple layers of glazes, one on top of another, when aiming for a deeply-coloured, high-shine 'lacquered' look, where evenness of colour and no brushmarks is important. I mostly stipple furniture because it is quicker (a painter's dusting brush will do this quite well). For walls you need a pukka stippling brush (see illustration) which is costly.

Note:

Wipe glaze off skirtings, door frames, etc. as you go along, with a rag dampened with solvent. Paint out stray colour afterwards on cornices or ceiling – strictly speaking, cornices should be coloured in with walls rather than ceilings. Varnish where necessary: on cupboard doors treated to match walls, on dados, kitchen or bathroom walls. Use non-yellowing alkyd varnish preferably or a gloss if you want a lacquer finish, remembering that glassy smoothness is a requirement here, so rub down between coats, leave to dry hard before varnishing, thinning the varnish coats slightly with solvent. Soak the brushes in white spirit and scrub clean in hot soapy water after use.

DISTRESSING

When you are new to DIY decorating, the thrill is all in the 'new lamps for old' syndrome: imposing a sleek new layer of fresh paint on the knackered surface you inherited. But there is a further subtlety to be explored, perhaps later when the occasion or need presents itself, which is to deliberately work over the paint surface, with various materials and techniques, making it look old and time-worn or 'heavily distressed'. New paint looks fresh and clean, for a while at least; it also looks impersonal, blank, even characterless. This is not a disadvantage on walls, perhaps, because you will humanize these with pictures, posters and souvenirs of one sort or another. But on furniture, old or new, or small items such as picture frames, a 'distressed' finish can make all the difference, adding a weathered softness of colour and texture that suggests graceful ageing. These deliberate imperfections suggest a whole dimension of family history that adds charm and character to almost anything painted, but especially perhaps the mongrel pieces issuing from modern workshops, made of softwood, MDF or even melamine. They may aspire to the style and proportions of their period prototypes, whether Georgian or Shaker, but if the finish is wrong, they betray their 'neo-ness' and look both mass-produced and boring.

I don't think 'distressing' should be overdone. It should not proclaim itself loudly, but it can add a delicious softness and warmth when used properly. Almost any painted piece coming from a professional studio today will have been distressed in one way or another, not so much to ape an antique, as to set it apart from the standard factory-sprayed items displayed in the department stores and furniture emporiums.

'Distressing' and 'antiquing' overlap. Antiquing usually involves rubbing over flash new paint and decoration with subtly dirtying glazes or washes of paint (raw umber or burnt sienna being useful colours), the aim being to blend painted decoration (flower garlands, painted lines, whatever) into their background paintwork. Rubbing off a little of the new decoration with wire wool pads is another wheeze that can rescue a crude effect, leaving it slightly threadbare. Any beginner in the field should experiment with this because it – together with an antiquing glaze – will make wobbly painted lines and heavy decorations look old, fragile and mysterious.

Another antiquing trick is to flick a spatter of tiny dots of colour – raw umber, burnt umber, black – on to a newly painted but antiqued finish. This takes no time, but lends surface interest.

'Heavy distressing' is, however, different, more rustic. It is suggestive of friendly pieces (I think of dressers, corner cupboards, hanging shelves) that have acquired a complex surface over the years, like layers of different paint colours, worn through and blended to create something unique, an in-between shade or texture – the closest paint can get to the 'noble texture' of grander materials exposed to wear, light and weather.

The most controlled way in which to create a heavily distressed finish on any surface is as follows. You need two contrasting paint colours in matt emulsion or Woodwash (see Suppliers page 202), plus a wax candle, brushes and wire wool. The charm of this distressing technique is that it goes where you want it to; wherever the wax candle makes its mark is where base colour will surface.

First paint over your piece solidly in the base colour you have chosen. This may take two coats. Leave this to dry. Smooth the piece down lightly with wet-and-dry paper or wire wool. Using the wax candle like a pencil, scribble over the areas where you want the base colour to surface. The realistic way is to keep the distressing to areas where a paint surface would get worn away naturally – round handles, down the front edges of cupboard doors, along shelves and worktops. To do this just rub the candle firmly along these edges leaving a visible deposit of wax. For a more overall, decorative type of distressing, rub the candle laid on its side over the whole area so that the wax lands on it lightly but more uniformly. Next paint over the entire piece with your chosen top colour, which can be a complete contrast with the base coat or a harmonizing shade in the same colour family. Leave this to dry, then with wire wool pads (first medium then fine grade), rub over the painted surfaces, going with the grain. You will soon find that wherever your wax treatment landed, the base colour surfaces (cleanly but quite realistically) through the top colour. At the same time the wire woolling raises a discreet sheen on the painted surface, which looks remarkably like an old paint and varnish which has mellowed over time. This surface can now be stencilled, lined, or decorated in any way you think suitable. I would finally protect it with a coat or two of mid-sheen varnish, at least on a kitchen piece, because water-based paints, though fast drying and quick to apply, are not as tough in use as their oil-based equivalents.

Penny-wise Papers

Papering your walls can be an expensive procedure, especially if you have high ceilings or big rooms. Here are four suggestions which show you how to paper a whole room for about the cost of one roll of commercial paper.

BROWN PAPER

It is not a new idea to paper walls with common brown wrapping paper; indeed, I first read about it as part of the decoration of the study of the nineteenth-century littérateur and poet, Lionel Johnson, where it was offset by curtains of grey corduroy and, doubtless, a fine collection of books. Somehow, though, it is one of those decorating brainwaves more talked about than seen. So when the chance arose to re-decorate a small study/office in North London, I thought we should put the brown paper idea to the test. You can see the results on pages 178–179. The general consensus is that it looks mellow, distinguished and in a word, excellent. We sharpened it up with black paintwork for contrast, a spot of 'easy graining' to blend in the panelled door and radiator, and a dash of the ethnic in the form of a 'tamba cloth' (see Suppliers, page 202). This gutsy African print was draped round a pole in lieu of curtaining, which was reckoned too enveloping for the quaint Arts and Crafts window which is a standard feature in this particular street of turn-of-the-century terraced housing.

Wallpaper brushes – the one with the handle is for applying paste; the comb-shaped brush is for smoothing the paper

A medium-weight brown paper was used, the sort with one matt and one shiny side and an almost imperceptible stripe. It is wider than a standard wallpaper – 90 cm (36 in.) – and the total cost for a room this size (3×2.5 m [10×8 ft]) was a trifling amount. That is the good news. The bad news is that like so many cheap packaging materials brown paper is sold in a minimum quantity of a 75-m (245-ft) roll. This provides, and therefore costs, twice as much as the room required. But there are ways round this. You could paper lots more rooms en suite, bearing in mind that brown walls are coming back into fashion along with other recycled seventies notions. You could go shares with friends enthused by our brown study picture. You could sell off the surplus at a discount to a local business that wraps parcels. Or, at worst, you could have enough surplus paper to wrap up parcels and presents (chic with black tape ties) till the end of time.

Now for the how-to, which differs marginally but significantly from standard papering procedure. Due to the extra width of the paper, where possible use a table wider than the standard paper-hanger's folding table and protect the table surface with plastic sheeting (available from all builders' merchants and most DIY stores). Measure and cut your 'drop' or wall length sheet, off the roll. If the paper edges are not perfect (a touch bashed about) use a wallpaper trimmer or Stanley knife and new blade, and with a steel rule, trim off a fraction each side. Use the paper matt-side out for a classier look.

This weight of paper is a touch translucent, but pasted over the lining paper, as in our case, or over a pale emulsion, this is a plus since it gives a certain quiet glow to the overall honey-brown tone. It does, however, mean that you should avoid slapping it up over a violently printed existing paper, or a vivid wall paint. If in doubt Blu-Tack a strip up and check. If the paper or paint fights back, you need either to re-line with lining paper, butt-joined, or to paint the pattern out with off-white emulsion, applied with a roller for speed. Next paste the brown paper sheets, one by one, on the back, using standard wallpaper paste. Take extra care when handling the sheets, both whilst getting them to the wall and whilst smoothing them out *in situ*, because the paper is stretchy and needs deft and thoughtful positioning and smoothing out. We went for a fractional overlap of sheets in case of shrinkage as the paper dried, rather than butt joins, where the edges merely butt up against each other. Use a clean soft cloth to spread out and smooth the paper surface on the wall, chasing out air bubbles by applying gentle pressure towards the sides, or in obstinate cases, by making a tiny pinprick. Try not to get too much paste on the front of the paper, and wipe off dribbles and smears with a clean cloth or kitchen paper, as you go.

I like the texture of this humble off-the-roll wallcovering, but I know that many readers will fret about how to protect it once it is up. (I get interrogated far more about protective finishes than I do about esoteric matters like colour mixing.) The answer is – it depends. If your office/study/room is your own civilized sanctum, brown paper needs no final protective seal. If you risk the invasion of tinies with felt pens, or pets with muddy paws, then by all means brush on a quick coat of matt acrylic varnish. Do make sure the varnish is acrylic, *aka* water-based varnish, since an oil-based varnish will make the paper itself transparent.

Clever and witty use of photocopied images makes this small dining corner special without costing an arm and a leg. The large screen features big and little versions of a wire egg basket and antique cooking pots, while paper placemats show antique plates and cutlery neatly laid out. All going to prove that ideas count far more than cash in today's dining spaces, which are usually tiny and ad hoc, as this neat eating corner.

PROJECT 2: THE SCANDINAVIAN DINING ROOM

Left It makes sense to keep a small dining space simple, going for clean colour and minimal furnishings. By 'greying' plank flooring, we provide a calm context for painted furniture and a limed oak dropleaf table. A yellow dyed calico curtain picks up yellow colourwashed walls and pottery, without interrupting things visually as a print fabric would. The curtain is simply made from a stitched tube of double thickness calico (cut with pinking shears and machined down three sides), then edged with contrasting blue fabric. It is hung from a wooden dowel, that simply threads through the top of the tube. A table, chairs and one substantial dresser is all the furniture this space needs, plus maybe a marble-topped table or washstand with drawers for storing cutlery and serving food.

Far right Canvas 'pinafores' piped in blue cost next to nothing to make and give a svelte appearance to a set of cheap reproduction chairs. Losing all those legs tidies the space visually. Oak furniture, 20s–30s period, in solid wood, is still a bargain. Strip and lime it for a radical facelift. The dresser is streaked with dilute woodwash applied over a cream base for a rustic version of dragging, before being coated well with matt alkyd varnish for protection.

Right Plates and glasses live in the dresser cupboard. This isn't a true dresser, incidentally, but a set of shelves married to a cupboard of the same width and given the distressed paint treatment. We kept the design simple, but rows of hooks provide catchment for cups and jugs whilst shelves allow you to display unmatched but colourful finds in the plate and saucer line.

Left A few select furnishings and sponged apricot walls here lift an otherwise plain room. A bold laminated check cover makes a practical no-fuss tablecloth whilst according with a Shaker-blue chair and striped blue crockery. Note the interesting frames for two little pictures. This is an artist's dining corner and the quirky little painted corner cupboard is a *spécialité de la maison*, as it were.

Above A forceful colour contrast of slate and cream paint on a pretty old pine dresser offsets an attractive and often-changed display of bright china, bowls filled with fruit as well as plates, a boldly framed flower print and a jug of fresh flowers – always better than dried flowers. Note the little electrified candle sconce to be lit for soft light on special evenings.

Above A carefree use of vivid colours on wall and furniture, with an acid green chair cover thrown in to lift and complete the palette. The boldly patterned *armoire* is an artist's *pièce de résistance*, but anyone could paint doors in deliciously coloured stripes and give table legs a few vivid spots and *arabesques*.

Right The crisp stencil border in black and yellow stands in for a cornice and draws attention to a culinary still-life hung from an iron metal bracket in this country dining room. A large pine table and painted chairs may well be country saleroom finds.

Opposite This dresser is obviously the owner's pride, with shelf edges adorned with zig-zag cut prints to dramatize a vivid clutter of china. Note the simple but striking wheatsheaf stencil on the rough plastered wall over the neat table.

A splendid old chimney piece, blackened by use, gives a real feel to this busy dining corner in a big kitchen. Sparse café-type chairs are light, inexpensive and popular seating today, fun to paint and sturdy to use. The wide shelf above the fireplace is the ideal place to display favourite pots and pictures. Melon-yellow walls, ornaments and rugs tie the whole bundle together and make the room warm and friendly.

PRINT ROOMS

It takes a leap of the imagination to realize that black and white prints, etchings, engravings, and later mezzotints, were to our forefathers what photographs are to us today. They were in some cases the equivalent of holiday snaps, showing the celebrated views and buildings young gentlemen visited on their Grand Tours. Others were black and white representations of equally celebrated paintings. At some point in the mid-eighteenth century a craze arose for pasting collections of such prints on to walls to make a print room. Fashionable ladies spent happy hours planning how best to display their prints, linking them with garlands, columns, urns and other neo-classical 'ornaments', to make elegant arrangements that filled the wall space above the dado rail. A soft yellow was a favourite background colour for print room walls, contrasting well with the prints themselves.

Print rooms are undeniably decorative, and this has led to their revival in recent years, along with so many other 'Ladies'' Amusements, such as découpage. Some decorators, mainly in the United States, specialize in making print rooms today. I am told they use genuine old prints and charge vast sums for a single room.

I am doubtful whether it is justifiable to use genuine prints in this way today, whatever eighteenth-century practice might have been. Even where the process is reversible, and the prints can be removed again, they are liable to discolour and generally deteriorate. Now that photocopying has made it so simple and inexpensive to reproduce black and white images, this strikes me as the best way to set about making a print room. The photocopier puts the idea within reach of a limited budget. Most libraries have an illustrated book section with suitable plates, together with photocopying facilities. Don't forget that small prints can be considerably enlarged, though there may be some lessening of fine detail. Having amassed a good collection of likely subjects, enlarged where necessary, the next step is to have them photocopied on to suitable paper. The charge for this varies, depending on size (if you supply your own paper). Standard photocopy paper is too glaringly white to look right. Firms will photocopy on to parchment-coloured paper if you specify this, either buying from them or supplying your own. Choose 100 g paper in weight (heavier than standard) because this takes pasting and varnishing better than the usual 80 g paper. Most old print rooms surrounded prints with a black and white printed border, usually reproducing some classical moulding like egg and dart or scrolling foliage. This looks attractive and helps to link a variety of prints together visually. The National Trust sells sheets of suitable borders, or you might find something elegant in a wallpaper border; but it must also be black and white.

The print room idea could make something special of a small hallway, or a landing; the smaller the room the fewer prints you will need. Prints also look good decorating screens. Most colours are enhancing as a background to prints: dull red, ochre, yellow, buff, mulberry, even black. Brown paper is an equally good choice. Print room walls can be either painted or papered, but keep the background plainly coloured; the effect here lies in the prints and the way they are arranged (see illustration for ideas). Symmetry is important when laying out

prints; round and oval prints, like decorative urns, swags, sphinxes, and the like, help to vary the arrangement and set up their own attractive patterns.

It is probably helpful to set out your prints temporarily first using Blu-Tack, or a tab of Sellotape. When you are satisfied with the lay-out, paste them down with wallpaper paste, smoothing them out carefully with a soft clean cloth and both hands. Don't rub them too hard once damp or you might dislodge the printing ink. Add borders, mitring corners neatly, and ornaments in the same way. Once dry, varnish with gum arabic (see Suppliers 202) adding a drop or two of raw sienna or raw umber gouache colour to 'antique' the prints slightly.

A *faux* yet fun print room created from photocopied prints and a little wallpaper paste

NEWSPAPER

A bit much for live-in rooms, perhaps, but newsprint walls are a neat and thrifty refurbishment for a cloakroom, loo, or somewhere you rush through. All you need is an *ad hoc* wallpapering of old copies of your daily papers, tidily pasted on with the best stories to the fore, and then sealed with a glossy yellowing varnish to bring it to the ripe hue of a pub ceiling. A variant on the theme suitable for City types is to use the distinctively pinky sheets of the *Financial Times*. For application, follow the advice on sticking up brown wrapping paper (see page 56), bearing in mind that newspaper sheets (avoid tabloids) are going to need patchworking to cover an average wall drop. Here, the varnishing will make all hang together. For a fast drying nicotine yellowing, try button polish (unbleached spirit varnish) diluted two parts to one with methylated spirit. Brush on evenly; this will dry in 20 minutes with a patchy sheen. For an even shine, repeat.

MARBLED PAPER

You can have a lot of fun making your own marbled paper to hang on walls, line a trunk or cover books with, using heavy-duty lining paper and artists' oil colours. The paper will look decorative as it is, but as the inspired stencil artist Althea Wilson has discovered, this swirling, cloudily patterned paper makes a stunning background to stencilling, either dark and crisp or gorgeously heightened with metallic paint. The marbling process is done in your bath tub, three-quarters filled with water. Start by marbling manageable lengths of paper – enough to line a trunk perhaps – and cut to size.

Mix artists' oil with white spirit to make a watery consistency, keeping the fluid colours separate in a plastic tub. Use an artists' fitch to mix the colours – it disperses paint more efficiently than a decorating brush. Then tip some colour into the water, give it a good stir with the fitch, and wait for the paint to float up to the surface. (Start with just one colour – the tonal variations are highly decorative. Let the paper dry, then repeat with second or third colours if desired.) Have a bucket and a strong cardboard box nearby to house the wet marbled rolls of paper. The tricky part is to make the swirling pattern continuous over a sheet, keeping the colours even at the same time.

Roll your sheet up so you can hold it in one hand, stand over the bath with the rolled paper in one hand and with the free end in your other hand, then let the paper unroll to float on the water. You will see the paint soaking into the paper. Lift the end near you and roll it while you lift and float the next width, and so on. The first width will be more intensely coloured than the next. If this looks wrong to you, add more colour and stir as before, between each print out.

When each roll is done, stand it to drip in a bucket, then stand the rolls in the box till you are ready to hang them out. Handle the wet paper carefully, trying not to stretch or wrinkle it up as it is fragile and tears easily. Hang completed rolls somewhere outside to dry, out of the wind – a plastic clothesline would suffice or maybe a towel horse. When dry, hang or paste on the wall, lining any other paper already there. For a shiny surface try brushing on a coat of shellac.

CHAPTER 3

FLOORS

Floors tend to be the biggest headache confronting a new home owner. The sheer extent of them, and their condition – gappy, crudely patched, blotched with old stain – is enough to chill the most ardent do-it-yourselfer. Or perhaps you have inherited with the fixtures and fittings, wall-to-wall carpet of such naff and lurid design that any colour scheme you might have dreamt up is shot to pieces. The first thing to do in this situation is to prize up a corner of the carpet and see what's underneath. We found quite decent parquet flooring under the pub-style carpet laid throughout my mother's cottage. Cleaned up, with a few rugs for warmth, the place was transformed. You might find quarry tiles, a document lino (see page 108) or perfectly sound boards. One justification for not chucking out a hideous carpet could be that you plan to use it as underlay for something better.

Bare floors can look bleak at first sight but much can be done to civilize and upgrade them without spending a fortune on carpeting, underlay or professional fitting. Until you have settled into a place and have a clear picture of how you want it to look, it's much better to sort out the existing floors, in some of the ways described below, and buy a few attractive old rugs for colour and cosiness.

Painted Floors

There is no cheaper way to smarten up floors than by painting them. Don't groan. This can be a slow, perfectionist's undertaking, if that's your style, or it can be little more trouble than a once over with a squeegee mop. Painted floors have come a long way since the 'three coats of flat oil followed by ten coats of varnish' approach of the early eighties, or for that matter the 'sand and seal' craze which left so many common deal floors burnished to a strong shade of marmalade. The problem with deal is its yellowness; oily varnishes turn this to orange. Current thinking is that floors should 'lie down' meaning that they should keep to their place in a room scheme, as unobtrusive underpinning for more colourful happenings above. Nothing looks more serene than the traditional Scandinavian floors of white pine, scrubbed, silvery pale and quite matt. The only way to make yellow deal look like white pine is with paint.

THE SCANDINAVIAN LOOK

This is a fairly rapid treatment as floor painting goes and gives a cool, pleasant greyish tone to deal planks, which looks well with most furniture and decoration. It is a treatment I envisage extending over a whole house, creating

A chequerboard design of dark painted squares over light woodwashed flooring is a striking treatment, especially practical for areas of heavy wear, such as halls

a calm unified look underfoot. Whilst masking the deal yellowness, the light grey wash should have enough body to even out knots and create a unified tone without obliterating the wood grain completely. With two coats of varnish this treatment will be quite durable and can be warmed up with attractive rugs in living rooms and bedrooms. In areas of heaviest wear – halls, stairs, landings – paint dark chequers over the greyed finish, to make a light and dark chequerboard effect. This looks crisp and handsome and shows wear less than plain grey. Scandinavians often paint floors in checks, using water-based paints with a matt finish; they carry the chequers right across the boards, cracks and all, usually setting them on the diagonal (see illustration).

Preparation

For a thinned paint to penetrate the boards enough to 'grey' them, they must be thoroughly cleaned of anything that might prevent absorption such as wax, seal, varnish or paint. Floors throughout a home will often present several of these conditions at once. Hiring a sanding machine for a few days is likely to be the quickest way to deal with these problems. Sanders are not too expensive to hire; they make a fair amount of dust but they do a great job of smoothing the boards (the larger models have an automatic dust extractor which helps though does not entirely lay the dust). One snag with sanders is that the heavy duty models don't sand right up to the skirting, so tend to leave a narrow tide mark round the edge of the floor which must be cleaned off, either with a varnish or paint stripper or a small hand sander. When boards have been sanded the floor can sometimes look patchy due to different coloured planks – often white fir is used which shows up more in its raw state. The grey wash will tone these down to some extent but if they are very noticeable, tint them to match the others before beginning the greying treatment. Use artists' acrylics diluted in water to do this and apply with a rag.

Before sanding a room, clear out as much furniture as possible, including the curtains. Masking tape across the bottom of any doors will help keep the dust from infiltrating the rest of the house. Knock down protruding nails and secure any loose boards. It is sensible to wear a mask while sanding (chemists' shops sell cheap ones) and make sure that anyone in the family with respiratory problems keeps out of the way till you have cleaned up afterwards.

Materials

Any standard matt emulsion in a pale grey, or greeny-grey shade can be thinned with water to make a driftwood colour. I use one of my own paints, Woodwash, in the 'driftwood' colour because it has greater staining power. A plastic bucket or bowl is best for holding your diluted paint. You'll need a squeegee mop, or an outsize brush to slop the thinned colour over the boards and a bunched up rag to even out the colour and work it into the wood surface. Wear slippers while you apply the paint and take them off when you leave the room or you will tread grey elsewhere. Conversely protect the 'greyed' planks as soon as they are part dry with plastic bags or a dust sheet; until the wood is varnished it will be easily marked. For varnishing I use a coat of eggshell varnish first, for toughness, followed by a coat of extra pale dead flat varnish which dries perfectly matt to give a scrubbed-plank look. Alternatively, if you can get it, use one of the new acrylic floor varnishes, which dry in up to two hours and are odourless.

Application

To achieve the right colour, tip some of the paint into a bowl or bucket, then add water (making a fifty-fifty mix) stir and brush on to the wood in a discreet corner. Wipe with rags till the grain shows through but the wood is noticeably greyish. Dry the patch with a hairdryer to check its final tint. Depending on the paint you are using you may need to dilute one part paint with up to four parts water, so experiment before taking off across the whole house. Rubbing the paint in with rags seems to give the tightest control of the colour transparency

Woodwash is best applied with a large brush or squeegee mop. Wipe off excess with a clean rag and, when dry, seal with matt varnish

grain balance; it is however fairly back-breaking, so don't attempt more than one floor at a time. The squeegee mop is quite handy for getting the grey wash over the floor quickly, but you need to go over with rags to even the colour out. Use a small brush to cut in round skirtings and cupboard doors.

Let the boards dry out thoroughly, then apply two coats of varnish (mentioned above). Thin the eggshell varnish with 5 to 10 per cent white spirit and brush on the floor starting in the furthermost corner and working with the grain (keep windows open to let out any fumes). The eggshell varnish dries to a mild sheen. Let it harden for a few days, then apply a coat of the dead flat varnish, thinning it a little, and stirring it very thoroughly to distribute the flattening agent. The floor will dry without shine after this treatment; if you have missed a small area apply the varnish again, then leave to dry. Acrylic varnish is simply brushed on as directed. Apply two coats for strength. *Colour note*: For a subdued colour underfoot, with the grain still showing, wash a thinned-down green, or blue emulsion over the grey before varnishing.

CHEQUERBOARD FLOORS

It is no big deal to convert a greyed floor into a chequered one, and the effect is charming. The colour you use for the dark squares can be charcoal (more subtle than black), dark green, blue or chocolate brown. Use a matt emulsion or Woodwash (see Suppliers page 202), diluting it enough to give a distinct but still just transparent colour applied over the greyed wood. *Important*: If you are adding dark checks, leave any varnishing till these are in place.

Marking out

Marking out the squares is not difficult once you have decided on the size. This will depend to some extent on the width of the floor. On the whole I like chequers over-scaled rather than standard floor-tile size: somewhere between 40 to 50 cm (16 to 20 in.) would suit a narrow hallway. Set the squares diagonally for a more dramatic perspective which also makes cracks less conspicuous (see illustration). Few halls or floors are geometrically precise with right-angled corners and parallel walls, but my approach to marking out is the simplest I can contrive.

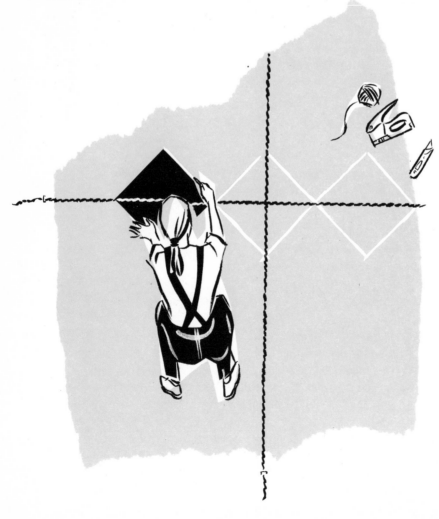

Marking out a chequerboard floor. Use a square template on the diagonal and mark round it carefully with a pencil. Horizontal and vertical guidelines ensure the design remains symmetrical

Make a template of stiff card cut to the size of your chequer, ensuring it is square and right-angled at the corners. To mark out the chequers you need a measuring tape, a long straight edge (a wooden batten for example), a sharp pencil, Stanley knife, ball of string and staple gun. Stretch the string from one end of the floor space to another and find the centre of this, checking that it *looks* central, then staple both ends down. Do likewise across the room, forming a cross. Use these markers to keep your chequers in a straight line. Slip the template under the string as shown opposite, pencil round it, and continue until you have pencilled squares on the diagonal the whole length of the floor. Use the straight edge or batten to extend these lines across, as shown, and the template to fill in the chequers. Don't worry when chequers are cut off irregularly by sloping walls or stairs set at an angle. As long as the central positioning is correct the effect will be convincing.

Outline the alternate dark squares with a narrow brush, filling in later with broad strokes

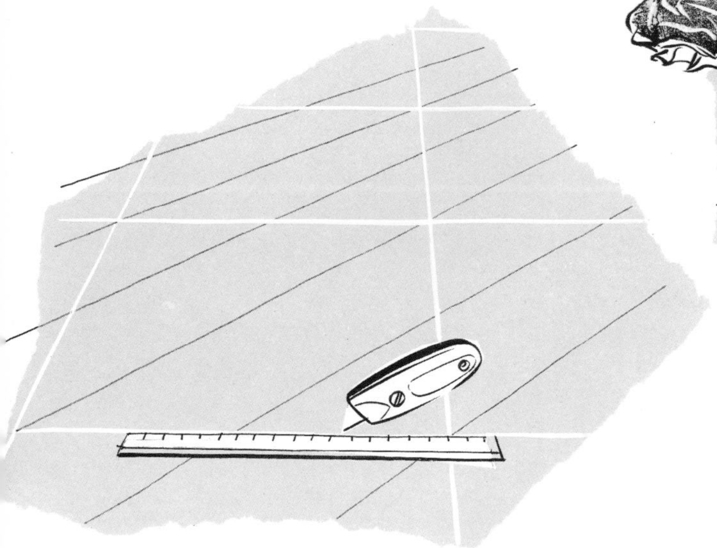

Score over the pencil lines with a Stanley knife to prevent paint seepage from dark squares to light

When the chequers are all pencilled in, use the Stanley knife to score over the pencil lines lightly; this helps prevent the dark paint from bleeding into the grey squares. I use a small 12-mm ($\frac{1}{2}$-in.) brush to outline each dark square neatly, filling in with a wider 6-cm ($2\frac{1}{2}$-in.) brush. Use rags as much as possible to smooth out the dark colour, leaving some grain visible, but take care not to brush into adjacent grey squares. Leave the completed floor to dry thoroughly, then varnish as described above. The best time to varnish a hall floor (no time is ideal) is on the way to bed, closing the doors to keep pets and children out, leaving a window open if possible and the heating on. The longer you can leave the varnish undisturbed the better (within reason). You might like to use one of the new water-based acrylic varnishes which dry in two hours and come in the usual shiny and matt finishes. They are also odourless but expensive, and remember that any sheen tends to wear off fairly rapidly in a hall anyway due to the volume of foot traffic.

The finished chequerboard floor opens up a small hall with its extending, geometric motif. Continuing the design or extending the colour scheme up the stairs and on to your landing is the ultimate in drop-dead chic

Stairs

If your hallway is chequered it is a good idea to extend the look up the stairs (or if not the chequers at least the colour scheme). A greyed finish on stairs and risers, followed by a dark motif stencilled on the risers will tie the whole visual package up nicely. Small chequers look splendid but are arduous to paint; a bold angular motif like a Greek Key might be a good compromise.

Risers tend to get kicked and scuffed so a contrast pattern makes this less obvious. Contrary to recommended practice, leave stairs (at least the treads) unvarnished. The reason for this is that any surface treatment wears away faster on stair treads and needs periodic re-touching. This only takes a moment on unvarnished wood: wash the surface down with a solution of sugar soap, rinse, then re-touch. If the wood were varnished or waxed this would need to be removed first.

SOLID COLOUR FLOORS

Painting floors a solid colour takes longer because more steps are involved, but it is the best disguise for sub-standard floors: badly stained planks, vinyl flooring in a colour or pattern that sets your teeth on edge, even a concrete screed. Going for a solid paint colour could encourage you to be daring. Consider a vivid emerald green like architect Edwin Lutyens used on his own study floor, with black walls and white woodwork. Or red-oxide red (use red-oxide metal primer) which is a friendly brownish red. Or denim blue. Plain white, *à la* Bridget Riley, lightens a dark room dramatically. Plain black (use blackboard black) has a Japanese designer look you can enhance with simple mats. Any dark colour makes an effective background to stencilling, either as an all-over pattern or a border.

Contrary to popular belief, wooden floors can be painted successfully with standard matt emulsion paints, though these need two or three coats of varnish to protect them. Emulsions are much easier to apply, relatively odourless (a big plus when you are working away on hands and knees) and non-shiny – don't use a vinyl silk emulsion, this paint has poor covering power. For best results prime the floor first with fast-drying acrylic primer. When it's dry follow with one or two coats of emulsion; these can be applied with a roller for speed. When this is dry, varnish the floor with eggshell or matt varnish, using a wide brush and following the grain of the wood.

Oil-based paints have greater covering power and are more durable so need less varnishing. I like red oxide and blackboard black because they are cheap and exceptionally good at covering, though both need a couple of coats of varnish. These paints give off solvent fumes, so work with doors and windows open and wear a mask if the smell makes you feel queasy. An acrylic primer is an adequate base for an oil-paint finish. I would recommend an oil-based paint for covering up vinyl flooring or vinyl tiles, because it has more grip on a smooth surface. Make sure you clean the vinyl surface down very thoroughly beforehand, scrubbing down with a sugar soap solution, then rinsing and leaving until completely dry.

There are floor paints specially formulated for use on concrete (ask at a reliable paint shop). These are extra thick and tough. The colours are not exciting, but you can intermix them for more interesting shades. Alternatively, seal concrete floors with a coat of PVA, diluted with water, leave to dry, then paint with acrylic primer followed by an oil-based paint. Sealing with PVA will prevent the concrete soaking up paint, which means you can get away with fewer coats. Don't expect painted concrete to last and last, but it will look a lot better in the short term.

FAKE PARQUET

Fake parquet sounds, and indeed looks, swanky, as our picture demonstrates. And so it should since most fakes originate from the strictly palatial interiors of Versailles and Italian palazzi. But where the originals are complex jigsaws of rare hardwoods, the fakes consist of nothing more than standard deal plank flooring, scribed, stained and varnished. Given you have a board floor in reasonable condition (not too obviously patched, previously stained, or wormy and splintered) this is a grand effect which is eminently affordable. What is needed most to attain the effect is patience, a methodical turn of mind, careful execution and the possibility of leaving the floor undisturbed for up to ten days. I say possibility since this is the time taken for the finish – an acrylic varnish – to harden and develop its proper resistance to walking feet.

Fake parquet is a dramatic and effective floor treatment which looks equally at home in a hallway, dining room or bedroom.

The preparation of a wood floor for fake parquet is as for the Scandinavian look on page 70: a thorough sanding (by machine), the punching down of loose nails and planks and the discreet filling of obtrusive holes and cracks with plastic wood in a 'pine' shade. Don't worry about the cracks between the boards; the broad geometric designs of parquet 'lose' incidental details very effectively.

A selection of fake parquet designs based on Italian Renaissance patterns, with a dash of M. C. Escher incorporated

Geometric designs, many of them based on Italian Renaissance patterns which would have been executed in marbles of different colours, are the most effective form of parquet on old uneven floors as the busy nature of the patterning will hide many a bump and irregularity, visually evening out these imperfections (see illustration). If you decide to expand a design based on an original pattern, make sure your floor space is large enough for the scale to be effective. You really need to see a large pattern from a distance for it to work.

Marking out the pattern needs some time and thought. You'll need chalk or a hard pencil, a straight edge or a long batten for ruling, plus a steel tape for measuring. Use the method described on page 73 for setting out your design. Find the centre of all four walls and mark this first with chalk or pencil. For a design which goes right across the floor – not a border – begin marking out from the pencilled guidelines. This is more reliable than working from the walls inwards, since walls are frequently irregular. If the floor shape is extra complicated – there are alcoves, bay windows, a staircase – you might first plot the design on squared paper on to which you have drawn the floor plan to scale.

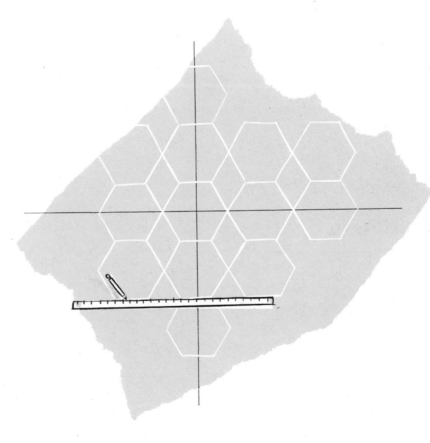

Once you have marked out the centre of your floor, pencil round your template for an all-over pattern. Work from the centre of the floor out towards your walls. This is more reliable than working from the walls inwards

Having pencilled in the design over the whole floor, the next step is to score over the pencil lines with a sharp Stanley knife, using the straight edge to ensure a straight cut. Cut to a depth of 2 mm ($\frac{1}{16}$ in.) or so. The idea behind this is to prevent the stains or paints from leaking outside their boundaries.

You can use either water-based wood stains, in contrasting shades (dark oak, mahogany, light oak) or acrylic tube colours (obtainable from artists' suppliers see page 202) diluted with water, and mixed to give appropriate shades, to colour in your design. The idea is to achieve distinct but transparent colours, which let the wood grain show through. Keep the colours subtle. Experiment first on a spare piece of wood or ply. I find a fine artists' watercolour brush best for brushing colour tidily round the margins of your pencilled shapes, then I move on to a fatter brush like a 5-cm (2-in.) standard paint brush or a 'glider' to fill in the central area rapidly.

Colour the squares with a layer of wood stain or acrylic paint, making the mixture dilute enough for the wood grain to show through. An artists' brush is best for delineating your pencilled shapes, and a standard paint brush for filling in

Once the design is complete, let it dry thoroughly overnight, then seal it in, using either an eggshell varnish, or the acrylic varnish mentioned above (see Suppliers page 202).

STENCILLED FLOORS

Stencilling offers a simple way of jazzing up painted floors. Unless you are very dedicated I would restrict it to smallish rooms. A friend of mine, stuck with a vinyl tiled loo in grisly colours, painted them out with a creamy emulsion, then stencilled over in Greek vase colours with a red and black Greek Key border and red rosettes at all intersection points for a stunning effect. The result is unusual and pretty. A small kitchen might take a similar treatment, but note that existing tiling in the room you are painting will establish a regular grid which makes locating the rosettes easy. All-over stencilling looks great; it is the marking out which is difficult. In a larger room a bold stencilled border looks very effective and is easier to handle if you simply follow the walls round.

Nowadays there are a great number of pre-cut stencils available, reasonably priced, in both plastic (mytar) and stencil card (see Suppliers page 202). Plastic is considerably tougher than stencil card – a point to bear in mind if you're planning to cover a large area. If you want to cut your own design, both card and plastic are available from artists' suppliers but card is much easier to cut by hand since plastic has a tendency to split. In either case use a craft knife with plenty of spare blades; cutting with a blunt blade is time-wasting. Use carbon paper and a pencil to transfer designs on to card, and a Rapidograph pen for the plastic. The ideal is to cut out the design with a smooth, flowing motion, moving the card or plastic when a cut changes direction, not the blade. Experts can achieve a bevelled cut, which is helpful because it discourages paint from seeping under the stencil. Cutting mats are great to cut out on, but quite expensive, so I generally use several sheets of newspaper, changing them when they get tattered.

Spraymount, available from graphics' suppliers, is very useful for attaching your stencil to the floor whilst you paint. A quick spray on the back of the stencil provides just enough glue to hold the stencil firmly in place whilst you wield your brush, but allows the stencil to be peeled away afterwards without lifting any paint (the stencil will also stay sticky for a long time so you don't need to re-spray it for each re-positioning).

Most people use acrylic colours (artists' variety) in tubes for stencilling since they dry so fast – more or less on contact – and the paint is very tough. Dab the acrylic colours round the edge of a paper plate, with a bigger blob of white emulsion in the middle, for lightening and softening the tones. You can use emulsion paints, collecting matchpot-sized tubs, but the disadvantage of these is that they dry more slowly and the high filler content rapidly clogs up the stencil. It's best to use a soft bushy rounded bristle brush (see illustration page 44) with a circular movement as opposed to an up-and-down stippling one, which makes work slower and more tiring. Whatever paint you choose, use the least amount of it on your brush, to avoid smudging and to create a clear but soft image. The trick is to work the colour up into the bristles by pounding the brush on to newspaper first; this soaks up water at the same time. Start applying the paint when the brush seems almost dry and you can't go wrong.

Some people stencil one colour at a time, others like to complete a stretch in several colours before moving on. I think there is something to be said for the latter approach, because the better something looks the more you push yourself to finish the job – but don't feel compelled to complete a stencil scheme at one sitting (or should it be crouching?). Give your back a break and spread the job over several weekends. When the stencilling's finished you will undoubtedly want to varnish your handiwork for protection. Rather than applying this immediately, you may want to walk over it for a week or two, to 'distress' it slightly before varnishing. Two coats of varnish – eggshell, matt or both – will buffer your floor under reasonable traffic for a year or two. When the wear and tear gets too bad, wash the surface with a sugar soap solution, rinse well then leave to dry and re-varnish. Polyurethane varnishes will gradually darken, which isn't a problem on a dark painted floor but a possible nuisance on a light one. Alkyd varnishes yellow and darken less, but are not quite so hard wearing.

PLYWOOD TILES

Using plywood tiles for flooring struck me as a brilliant notion when I first hit upon it, some years back: instead of working on one's hands and knees across a floor, the whole floor covering can be dealt with off site, sitting comfortably at a large table. I have met a few people who pursued the idea, and they seemed enthusiastic. One alternated black and white squares, the other used blond wood (the natural ply finish) alternated with tortoise-shelled squares.

Most floors will need levelling off first with sheets of hardboard or MDF, glued and tacked down to make a flat, smooth base for the tiles. These are made of sheets of 12-mm ($\frac{1}{2}$-in.) ply, usually sold in large sheets, which a timber yard will cut down for you into smaller squares. The edges will need smoothing with medium abrasive paper. Plot out the floor plan on squared paper before deciding on the tile size then mark out your tile positions starting from the centre of the floor, using the method described on page 72 for the chequerboard floor. It will save much time if you make your tiles as large as possible – up to 60-cm (2-ft) square. Then divide up the tiles into light and dark, or plain and stained, or whatever you fancy. Dark stained squares alternating with natural ones gives a quick marquetry effect. For these use wood stain, followed by a couple of coats of polyurethane varnish. Or you could paint half the tiles a pale grey, the other half a near black, in which case use primer, oil-based undercoat, then tinted undercoat for grey, and blackboard black warmed with a little burnt umber oil colour.

Tiles can also be marbled, stencilled or decorated with fake marquetry designs. Whatever colour you decide on, varnish them at least once off site and leave them to dry hard. To install, coat the back of the tiles and floor with a good adhesive, press the tiles into place and tack them down with thin tacks at each corner. When the floor is all laid – cut a plain border if you get left with gaps round the walls – re-varnish once, starting at the far corner and brushing your way out of the door. Leave the whole floor to dry for 48 hours.

Rugs and Matting

FLOOR CLOTHS

Floor cloths, made of painted and varnished canvas, were a cheaper and popular alternative to carpet in the late eighteenth and early nineteenth centuries. People liked them because they were a neat floor covering and were easier to keep clean than heavy carpets, which in those pre-vacuum-cleaner days, had to be swept and beaten. A smooth floor cloth needed only an occasional clean with a mop. Floor cloths were made of single widths of sail canvas, sometimes cut to fit a particular room wall-to-wall. Stencilled designs tended to be based more on costly types of floor coverings, imitating marble flags, tiles, matting, even Turkish rugs. Production was slow because of the lengthy drying time of the many coats of oil-based paints and varnishes used, but a good floor cloth was surprisingly durable. I have seen examples over a hundred and fifty years old, worn but by no means threadbare. However, with the advent of linoleum on the roll – linoleum was like a floor cloth bonded to a resilient cork backing – the old hand-made floor cloth faded out, though some thrifty American farmers' wives continued making their own, till the end of the nineteenth century.

Practical and hardwearing, traditional floor cloths are ideal for kitchens or bathrooms. Designs are generally influenced by Moorish tiles or American patchwork motifs

Recently there has been a revival of interest in this traditional form of floor covering, owing as much to its decorative potential as its thriftiness. The fact that you can have exactly the colours and patterns you like is a lure, as is the usefully short drying time of new-age paints and varnishes, which cut the production time drastically.

Materials

Firstly you need a length of cotton duck (see Suppliers page 202) in the appropriate width, allowing 5 cm (2 in.) all round for a turnback, and some PVA solution. For decorating the cloth you need acrylic primer, matt emulsion base colour and acrylic tube colours. Use a non-yellowing alkyd varnish over pale colours, and a tougher polyurethane varnish over the darker shades. Old floor cloths were given a gloss finish, but this is optional, bearing in mind that the glossiest varnish will soon become subdued by the wear and tear of passing feet. Make sure you have a clutch of brushes: a standard 5-cm (2-in.) for priming and base coats (or use a roller); a bushy stencil brush plus pointed watercolour brushes for applied decoration; and a varnish brush or glider. You will also need a sharp craft knife and steel rule, a sharp pencil, thixotropic adhesive (such as Bison), stencils or stencil board if you want to cut your own, and a staple gun or tacks to stretch the cloth while working on it. Have a supply of wet-and-dry paper in medium to fine grades to hand, and/or steel wool pads for rubbing down, and don't forget the solvent for cleaning the varnish off your brushes.

Making up

Cut the canvas to size allowing a 5-cm (2-in.) turnback round the edges. Coat it with dilute PVA to make the fibres less absorbent. When dry, prime the canvas front and back with acrylic primer, using a roller for speed. Two coats on the front and one on the back is the minimum amount; this fills the weave, levels out the surface and adds strength to the material. Drying time for acrylic primer is about 30 minutes a coat.

Below left Nick off a triangle after marking out the turnbacks

Below Plot out your design, allowing for a painted border, using a pencil template. Low-tack masking tape helps to define straight lines

Next apply a base coat of matt emulsion on the right side of the cloth, using a brush or roller. Make sure the colour is solid. Leave to dry then smooth lightly with wet-and-dry paper or wire wool. When this is quite dry, mark the turnback with pencil round all four sides, nicking off a small triangle at the corners as shown (see illustration). Score over the pencil lines lightly with a knife to make the folding easier. Coat the turnbacks and the underside of the cloth with thixotropic adhesive. Leave for the stated time, then fold cleanly and

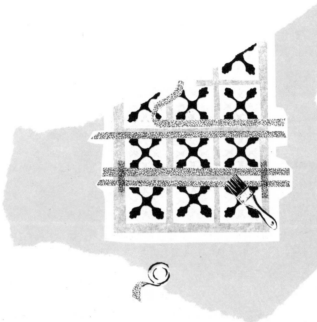

Using masking tape and a wider brush for painting borders

press flat. Your mat is now ready for decorating. Pencil the centre lines lightly (see illustration) to give your stencilling an accurate starting point. Plot out your design on the cloth, allowing for a painted border, and use low-tack masking tape to define straight lines or pencil and paint these in freehand. Stencil with the soft, bushy brush and acrylic colours using a round and round scrubbing motion. Use masking tape and a wider brush to paint in any borders (see illustration). When you have finished decorating your floor cloth, give it a first coat of varnish, thinned with a little solvent, then re-varnish it next day. Rub down this second coat of varnish lightly with wet-and-dry paper or wire wool, to smooth and clear any grit or dust, then brush well and re-coat. Leave this to dry for 48 hours so that the varnish hardens before putting the cloth down on the floor.

MATTING

Matting of one sort or another – sea-grass, coir, natural or dyed – has been everyone's favourite floor covering for some years now, owing to its modest good looks and one-time modest price. Though still cheaper than decent carpet, it is no longer the bargain it once seemed, and inherent defects have

come to light which might make you pause. Sea-grass, the toughest and
cheapest, which comes with a rubberized backing, is diabolical to cut, even
with the sharpest of blades – preferably a Stanley knife with a hook blade.
Other softer mattings are easier to cut, but are apt to fray and need turning
over at the edges. They all have a tendency to shrink gradually in centrally-
heated houses, and, unless Scotchguarded, stain ineradicably. I feel you
should add a professional Scotchguarding and laying into your budget when
deciding on matting, to get the best looks and performance out of your wall-to-
wall matting. This inevitably bumps up the price so obtain several quotations.
After cutting the matting leave it and walk on it for a week or so to counteract
any likelihood of stretching or shrinking; then stretch it and fasten it down.

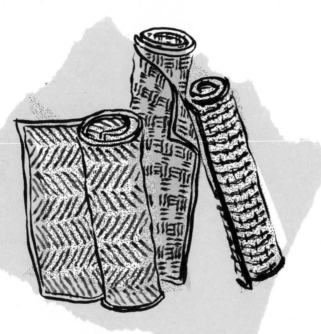

A selection of natural matting. Sea-grass, coir and sisal are all hardwearing alternatives to carpeting

For a cheap and cheerful solution go for the mats with bound edges which
come in a range of sizes and in a variety of finishes – coloured, natural or
chequered. These are genuinely cheap, add softness or bounce to bare floors,
and of course can be moved on to less exalted locations – bathrooms, kids'
rooms – when you get tired of them or find something more luxurious at an
affordable price. Remember too that the most amazing amount of household
dust and debris falls through openweave matting without a rubberized back. I
am not asthmatic, but I have sometimes wondered why the atmosphere in
matted rooms was fusty even after hoovering. Lifting up the matting reveals all
– there's usually a layer of soft powdery dust underneath which a vacuum
cleaner cannot lift. With smaller mats the solution is obvious: chuck them
outside while you clear away the fall-out. A little rain will do them no harm
since most matting comes from the tropics, where a damp atmosphere and
absence of central heating provide their ideal environment.

RESTORING OLD RUGS

As nomadic tribes like the Bedouin and Mongols have long known, a scattering of finely coloured rugs can make tent or yurt immediately hospitable, even luxurious. Plus, when you up sticks and move on, you can roll them up and take them with you. A few pleasantly faded and worn old rugs, of whatever provenance, do equally nice things for our own less romantic and peripatetic lifestyle. As more people latched on to this simple strategy, the price of appealing rugs, flatweave kilim, flowery Bessarabians boomed during the last couple of decades. Nevertheless, it has always been possible – and I speak as a rug fancier – to pick up a pretty old rug for a modest sum. It may have a hole or two in it, fribbled edges and unravelling fringes, but don't be deterred. My usual repair technique – basically freestyle embroidery with coloured wools on a canvas or hessian base – works best for flatweaves, like kilims, or on pile rugs that have worn close to the woven base. I cut a piece of embroidery canvas or jute sacking big enough to cover the hole, with 5 cm (2in.) or so extra all round, and fasten this down on the back of the rug with a light coat of PVA fabric glue, like Copydex. This is just to keep the thing in place while I move on to the next stage, which is to stitch the patch in place using linen thread and a sharp stout darning needle (wear a thimble, even if you never have before) all round on the back.

Rugs can be unwieldy objects to work on, heavy, hot and with a will of their own. Lacking the frames used by professionals, I make do by supporting the bulk of the rug on a table or sofa, with the damaged area supported on my lap. Most rug holes have a ragged fringe of frayed jute or string. In my best work I pull these straight and stitch them down on the patch; this feels more solid, because the subsequent stitchery binds them down. Sometimes I just trim them off so I can start with a clear space. I work my wools by eye, but you may prefer to draw the pattern on to the canvas with coloured felt pens as a guide. Don't worry too much about creating an exact copy; the design of many rugs meanders and varies like most hand-crafted objects. The main thing is to match the original colours or faded original – there is a difference – as closely as possible. I use tapestry wools which come in a splendid colour range and double them up or separate the strands, as needed. Restorers, of course, use untreated wools dyed with vegetable dyes, but we cheapskates can't be quite so fussy.

I cannot claim to use a clever variety of stitches, I simply try to replicate the rug pattern as boldly, or finely, as the original, using a form of tent stitch worked over twice as a rule to fill the pattern out clearly. What does not look convincing is for any of the base fabric – jute or canvas – to show. Wherever possible, I work over the perimeter of the original hole with the same wools in order to bind down any loose edges, and integrate the patch with the original fabric. When the patch is entirely filled in with colour, the loose edges have been secured and the whole piece has come together physically, you will be surprised at how much more handsome and satisfying your bargain buy has now become.

CHAPTER 4

WINDOWS

Once your walls and floors have been transformed, the next thing to concentrate
on is windows. A bare window frame, however nicely painted, may look cold
and unfriendly in a living room, and be too revealing in a bedroom or
bathroom. Blinds give a clean uncluttered look, whether simple split bamboo
blinds (stencilled for added decoration) or more formal Roman blinds, which
require only a small amount of fabric. For a softer, more luxurious look, you
can't improve on curtains – beautiful hand-sewn and interlined ones, swathes
of simple plain fabric, or cleaned-up and re-vamped second-hand hangings.
With a little ingenuity, a deft hand with a needle or a scout round junk shops
or curtain exchanges, you can cover every window in your home for a fraction
of the cost of buying ready-made.

Making Your Own Curtains

VASTLY SUPERIOR CURTAINS

The very best curtains, the kind you see swathing the windows of stately
homes, are still almost entirely stitched by hand (main seams apart). This
hand-work includes not only hems, but pleating and gathering, any fringes or
braids, plus a great deal of internal stitchery, not visible from the outside but
serving to weld together the three thicknesses of fabric – curtain fabric,
interlining and lining – so they handle and hang as one, in heavy sculptural
folds. Curtains made to these specifications seal off draughts as effectively as
double glazing (one reason why they have always been *de rigueur* in stately
homes), look wonderfully luxurious and hold together till the actual fabric is in
tatters. If you were to order a pair from one of the leading specialist firms, they
would set you back the price of a foreign holiday, *exclusive* of the cost of fabric
and trimmings. The small outfit up the road will charge anything from a third of
this price for making up, but will cut down on the hand-stitching, using
rufflette tapes for instance, rather than hand pleating on to a hand-sewn tape
with hand-sewn hooks.

It takes time and perseverance to complete a pair of 3-m (10-ft) curtains to
such exalted standards. It also requires an extra-large work table where all the
layers of fabric can be laid out flat (paper-hanging tables or trestles are good
value and ideal for this). Given you've got all this, you can have yourself

Relieve the plainess of humble curtain fabric by adding a border of cotton rug fringing or herringbone webbing

splendiferous curtaining for the cost of the materials. This will not be negligible, owing to the vast amount of fabric involved, but you can re-coup on the curtain fabric itself since quite humble cloth, such as cotton ticking, denim, twill or anything in natural fibres with some body to it, looks very good with this sort of treatment. To relieve the plainness, you can add a border of cotton rug fringe dyed to match, a striped webbing, or a wide border of contrasting fabric. I cheat on the hand-sewn tapes, using a sturdy rufflette tape, machined in place, and a lavish amount of hooks, one every 7.5 cm (3 in.), since heavy or handsewn curtains sag if they are not properly supported.

Two to two and a half times the window width is the usual amount of fabric needed, with 30 cm (12 in.) added on to the length, so the curtains trail or 'puddle' on the floor, enhancing their sculptured effect. Curtains like these look good hung from an outsize pole – a dowel 7.5 cm (3 in.) in diameter, from a good timber yard, stained – but you will need to look out for big wooden rings, and large knobs to act as finials. Wooden rings of this diameter are almost unobtainable new, but batches still turn up in salerooms, antique markets, even boot sales. Another alternative is to go for the standard track sold in most good department stores, and hide the rather unsightly workings with a pelmet. The shape illustrated looks handsome, or you might prefer a simple flat pelmet (see page 109) fringed or trimmed with braid to give it consequence.

A pelmet needs to be at least one-eighth of the total curtain drop (excluding the trailing bit) to look right, so allow a bit more fabric to be on the safe side. The most effective pelmets have a buckram or tailors canvas, lining, stiffening, plus a layer of interlining (a fluffy blanket-like material available in the same good department stores) to add richness to the look. Measuring up accurately will certainly save you money in the final analysis.

Most furnishing fabrics, together with interlining and sateen linings, come in

1.2-m (48-in.) widths. Interlining is also sold in a 1.3-m (54-in.) width. If you are using a dress fabric (like denim) check out the width before making your calculations since these tend to be narrower. If you need to economize somewhere it could be on the lining fabric; cotton sateen is relatively inexpensive, but at a pinch you could substitute calico, sheeting, even old but not threadbare sheets, dyed some unobtrusive colour. But don't skimp on the interlining because it is this that makes the difference.

Measuring

Measure your window from top of track, or bottom of pole, to the floor (or sill, for sill-length curtains) for the *length*, and the length of the track or pole, for the *width*. Multiply the *width* by 2 or $2\frac{1}{2}$ (as desired), then divide by the width of your fabric. Round the resulting number up to a full number (if necessary) to give the number of fabric widths needed. Next multiply the *length* by the number of fabric widths to give the full length of fabric needed.

   If you are using patterned fabric you will need to measure the pattern repeat in order to allow for matching the pattern across the fabric widths. Divide the *length* by the pattern repeat (rounding up to a full number, if necessary), then multiply this number by the pattern repeat to reach the full length needed. To the full length add 30 cm (12 in.) for the hem and heading.

Making up

Cut fabric and lining to the previously measured length. The interlining can be a few centimetres (inches) shorter as you don't want a bulky turnback at the hem or heading. Any lengths of fabric which need to be joined to make up the necessary curtain width should be machined together with a 2.5-cm (1-in.) seam, matching any pattern. Make sure the tension is just right; if it is too tight the seam will pucker when hung vertically and spoil your curtain. Iron seams open and flat. Now lay the curtain fabric on the table, right side down and lay the interlining on top, making sure both are lying smooth and flat. What you then have to do is loosely catch both fabrics together, using a large herringbone stitch, down the length of the curtain. How many lines of this invisible bonding the curtains need depends on their width and the weight of all the materials used. Once about every 20 cm (8 in.) is usual.

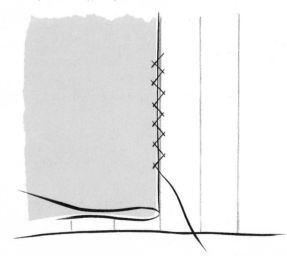

Secure the interlining to the curtain fabric with herringbone stitch. Herringbone is an unusual stitch: whilst your hand moves from right to left as you take up threads from each layer alternately, your sewing progresses from left to right

This wonderful battered painted meatsafe, now host to a clutch of jugs and pots, sums up the look many people are striving to achieve in their kitchens today. Tattered paint, or 'heavy distressing' is just a means to an end. Weathered pieces of furniture such as this evoke generations of use, and introduce a much-needed human dimension in an often sterile environment of melamine and factory-finished units.

Left The joinery here is not beyond a patient amateur carpenter, with a modest range of tools. Measurements are critical in such a tight space. Most of the pieces were cut to a given specification by a timber merchant, but we had to spend some time trimming and adjusting on site. Blackboard paint was used on the sewing machine's curly iron base and protected with a coat of varnish.

Right A red ladderback chair (which I painted and rushed myself) partnered by a junk shop table, stencilled with designs taken from my *Paintability* stencil book – *African Bedroom*. I chose a sludge grey and deep red for the motifs, stencilled over a neutral 'smoke' woodwash coat. Two coats of matt alkyd varnish make the surfaces durable as well as enhancing the colours. The Chinese canisters are souvenirs from one of Jason's travel-writing trips.

PROJECT 3: THE ETRUSCAN RED KITCHEN

Jason Goodwin is a travel writer, and lives with Kate in an urban cottage. A two-up, two-down with a back extension in London's East End. He is also my son, so decorating their kitchen was a project in which I had a special interest. They both have a keen eye for a bargain as well as firm ideas about kitchen planning. The oven and hob were bought separately at knock-down prices, one from a small 'ad' in a local paper. Unit doors are tongue and grooved, battened for strength. Tiles are Victorian, from a salvage company, fixed and grouted by Jason. Note the tiny shelves for cookbooks and tapes inserted into an otherwise wasted space. Their one extravagance was the solid mahogany work top, which a friendly joiner cut to fit the gas hob and ceramic butler's sink. A stable door leads out into a small backyard, giving a feeling of space and light to a small north-facing room. An old sewing machine base, painted black, supports a narrow wooden table top (it needs to be narrow – the kitchen is barely three metres across). We worked out the colour scheme together, choosing light Etruscan red, a historic colour in a full-tone emulsion, specially mixed in my shop for the walls. Woodwork is painted with slate woodwash, applied directly to bare wood and sealed with a matt alkyd varnish. But the chequered floor is the real *coup*. Sheets of ply were laid over sub-standard boards for a smooth surface and then treated to a coat of driftwood woodwash. The diamonds (better than squares for increasing perspective and giving an illusion of extra space) were pencilled on top, and every alternate one was painted in the same slate-grey used for the cupboards. This was sealed with two coats of fast-drying acrylic floor varnish. The whole thing looks crisp and dashing, and the cost was peanuts.

Left The kitchen/dining area on the left has a charmingly 'retro' atmosphere, due to the generous use of a flowered cotton for café curtains and bench cover and for covering a typical kitchen gloryhole.

Above Symmetrical tiers of massive wood shelves look handsome and practical – providing storage for favourite jars and jugs as well as hooks. Note the clever use of uplighting and the cushioned concrete plinth making a handy bench-seat.

Right Old tiles and a huge window add charm to fairly basic kitchen equipment. Note the narrow trestle and stool with its chic clip-on angle-poise lamp, space enough for meals à *deux*.

Left A delightful freehand-painted wall treatment definitely stars in this exceptionally attractive, but essential orthodox 'Aga Saga' country kitchen. Inspired a little by Dufy and Bloomsbury, the owner has decorated pink colourwashed walls with witty and pretty illustrations of kitchen basics – plates, jugs, mugs, fruit bowls and teapots. All lovely shapes to play with. Wisely, Aga and wall cupboards are simply white as a foil to all this exuberant colour. The overall effect is as friendly as it is memorable.

Above right Once again we see those stylish props of the thrifty kitchen: the table supported by an old treadle sewing-machine base and the invaluable plate rack.

Right Wood planks sturdily battened together to create rustic kitchen units, individualized with black iron hinges and latches; vivid 'rosmaling' painted decoration adds to the folksy effect.

Overleaf Small and chic, this kitchen is characterized by Art Deco influence notably in the austere black, grey and cream colour scheme and glossy lacquered surfaces. The eye-catcher is of course the mural, trailing round from wall to wall and counterpointed by a small gallery of black framed fashion photographs, casually propped on top of the units. Note how a bowl wall light is painted in with the mural.

When you have worked out how many you need – the first comes 20 cm (8 in.) from the side hems, as these are efficient bonding in their own right – it is a help to mark the lines out on the back of the curtain fabric, using coloured chalk and a long ruler. They should be as straight as possible. Do the centre line of stitching first because this will make the bulk of material more wieldy. Pin the fabric and interlining together alongside the first chalk line, then fold back the interlining down its length, half-way across (see illustration).

Start at the top and work downwards when stitching. Your herringbone stitches (see illustration) should be quite long, 8 cm (3 in.) or so, but the actual stitch which catches up the curtain fabric should be tiny, taking up a few threads only so that it will not show on the right side. Don't pull any of the stitches tight, for the same reason – they should lie a little slack. When you have come to the bottom of the interlining, end off with a few stitches caught securely in the interlining.

Now spread the curtain and interlining flat over the table again, and fold back the interlining above the next chalked guideline. Sew as before. Repeat till you have finished that half of the curtain. The other half is done the same way except that you will have to sew in the opposite direction, i.e. from bottom to top, unless you are ambidextrous. When curtain fabric and interlining are stitched together you can trim the sides, heading and bottom of the interlining to the correct width and length of the curtain. Fold in 5 cm (2 in.) of the fabric at the curtain sides, 10 cm (4 in.) at the heading, and a double turning of 10 cm (4 in.) at the hem, back over the interlining, mitring the corners (see illustrations). Smooth to make sure they are lying perfectly flat, then pin to hold the thicknesses together while you tack the folded-back edges to the interlining with large stitches (see illustration).

Tack the folded-back edge to the interlining with long stitches

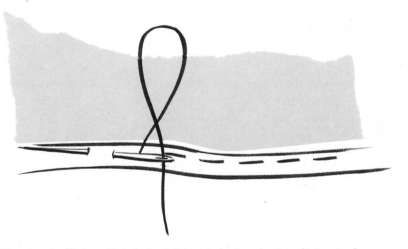

Now for the lining. This is invisibly stitched to the interlining in the same way. Once the bulk of the curtain is stitched together and manoeuvrable, it is simpler to sew all the lines of herringboning from top to bottom. To reach the outermost chalk mark, fold the curtain in half before laying the lining out on top. Fold back the lining and sew as before, catching in the interlining only. Take the lines of herringbone to within 8–10 cm (3–4 in.) of the top and bottom of the curtain.

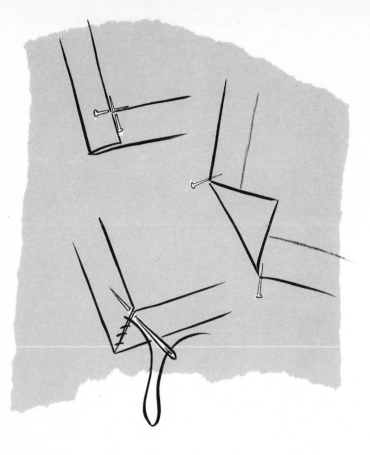

To mitre a corner, turn under side hem, press, and open out, then fold under bottom double hem, press, and open out second fold of hem, so that first turning remains. Fold in the corner of the fabric at the point where the two vertical pressed lines cross, checking that the corner forms a true right-angle by aligning the pressed lines on the triangle with those on the fabric. Then turn under the side hem and second part of the double hem, to form a neat join over the triangle, and slip-stitch together

When the herringboning is completed lay the curtain out flat, and fold under the sides, hem and heading on the lining, mitring the corners. Hems on the lining should be set about 2.5 cm (1 in.) in from the edges of the curtain all round, except at the top where they should be nearly up to the edge. Pin at intervals. Then stitch the lining down all round, making large hemming stitches (see illustration) so that the stitches are largely hidden underneath. Stitches 2.5-cm (1-in.) long are about right, but do not pull the thread too tight.

Attach the lining to the curtain fabric and interlining with large hemming stitches

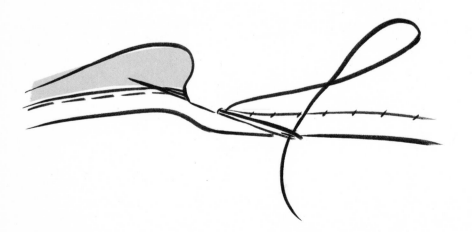

The real perfectionists will also sew the curtain tape on by hand so that there are no rows of machining visible to mar the smooth flow of the curtains on the right side. You may find you *have* to handsew them on because some machines balk at stitching through so many thicknesses. Rufflette tape should be sewn 5–8 cm (2–3 in.) down from the top, to give a bit of a heading, unless you are having a pelmet. Deep-pleat tape is sewn flush with the top. Handsewing is a nuisance because you have to catch in all three thicknesses of fabric every inch

Sewing on curtain rufflette tape with small, close stitches, securing all three thicknesses as you go

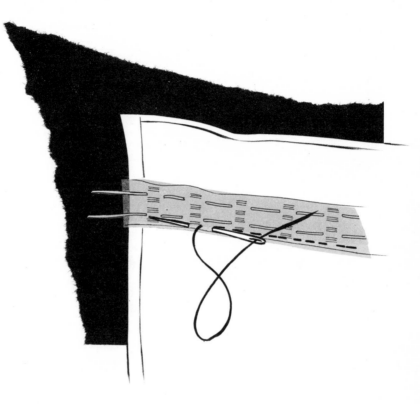

or so, if not with every stitch, otherwise the lining will be taking the whole weight of the curtains when hung. Use small, close stitches for strength, and stab right through the curtain every inch or so, taking a tiny backstitch to make sure the sewing doesn't slip. Sew along both sides and one end of the tape, leaving the end where the rufflette cords emerge, unsewn.

To sew on fringe or webbing, first pin the fringe or webbing on at intervals on the right side and then stitch in place using fairly large stitches inside and little ones on the surface (ordinary running stitch with a back stitch now and then). Webbing has to be sewn on along both sides, and the corners should be neatly mitred (see illustration).

Contrasting borders

These look very attractive, though they are a good bit more trouble to do. A wide border should be machined in place round the edge of the main fabric before interlining and lining are sewn into place. A contrasting band, set some way in from the curtain edges, as with webbing, can be hemmed in place along both sides after the curtain is completed.

QUILTED CURTAINS

If your windows are elegantly proportioned, high and slender as in many old houses, it seems a pity to smother them with voluminous curtains. The eighteenth-century treatment for windows like these seems often to have been narrow curtains of stiff material with just enough fullness to give a little gathering when drawn. The prettiest modern equivalents I have seen were made of the cheapest cotton available (curtain lining), quilted over old curtains which had been cut down to the right size. (Two thicknesses of fabric in these are best, i.e. fabric and lining. If the old curtains are too bulky, the new ones will look like eiderdowns.) All the quilting was done by machine, a swing-needle model with zigzagging and various fancy stitches, so parallel bands of plain stitching were varied with fancy ones. A fair labour, it must be said, but the quilting gives just the 'body' narrow curtains need if they are not to look meagre and droopy. These were finished with a narrow fringe and little tie-backs looping them to the window-frames, and looked quaint and charming.

Though there is a lot of machining involved, these quilted curtains are very easy to make. Measure the length and width of the windows. The curtains should be 5 cm (2 in.) longer than floor level because quilting shortens them, and allow 5 cm (2 in.) or so as a heading above the curtain rail. They should be $1\frac{1}{4}$–$1\frac{1}{2}$ times the width of the windows, depending how wide these are (narrower if the window is very narrow, wider if the window is broad). Cut the fabric and lining of a pair of old curtains to the size of the finished curtain, plus 5 cm (2 in.) either way, then cut the fabric to cover these with a 4–5-cm ($1\frac{1}{2}$–2-in.) turnback all round. Lay fabric over the backing materials, making sure they lie squarely and smoothly over each other, pin here and there to hold them securely, and then run a few lines of large tacking stitches through all the thicknesses to hold them together while you are machining. Fold the hem allowance on the curtain fabric back over the linings all round and tack down.

Quilting gives instant 'body' to narrow curtains, ensuring they never look meagre or droopy

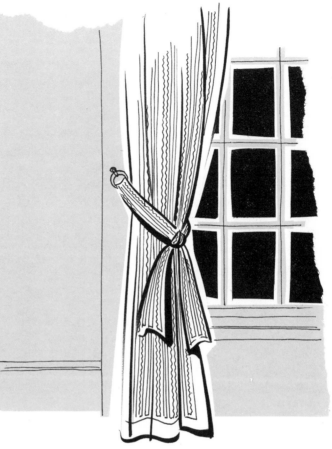

Simple quilted tie backs made with narrow strips of curtain fabric are an elegant finishing touch

Choose a sturdy sewing cotton in a matching colour, or one of the extra strong synthetics (bearing in mind that your biggest outlay will be on thread, so don't fly too high). It's not fatal if the thread breaks, but it wastes time. Now decide how you want your quilting lines to run. If you don't have a swing-needle machine, you can vary the effect by bands of stitching very close together, alternating with more widely separated ones, or bands of plain fabric. But the more closely you quilt your curtains the better it will look – large unquilted areas tend to sag after a while. If you have a really up-to-date machine, you can work out any combination of plain and fancy stitching that appeals to you. You can either machine straight up and down the curtains, or follow the curtain rectangle, filling the oblong centrepiece with any arrangement you like.

Try to keep your lines of machining reasonably straight if not mathematically parallel (a little irregularity looks attractive). You can run your first lines of machining near enough to the edges to take in the hems, or hem them by hand later. Use a rufflette tape, machined on, to hang them and plenty of hooks to prevent drooping. Tie backs can be made with narrow strips of the curtain fabric, quilted to match and looped through rings attached to the frames, or hooks (see illustration). A narrow, fringed edging about 4 cm (1½ in.) looks pretty. Or you could make a narrow frill of the same or contrasting fabric and machine that round the edges. A pleated frill can be turned out quickly if you have the appropriate sewing machine attachment.

PLAIN FABRIC CURTAINS

Cheap and cheerful fabrics for curtains are getting harder to find all the time though imported Indian furnishing cottons, mostly in stripes and checks, still represent good value compared with designer fabrics whose cost makes one blench. If you are desperate for curtains, can't find anything suitable second-hand, and can't afford to spend too much, then that old decorator's standby, unbleached canvas (which comes in many weights and widths), is almost certainly your best bet. It is solid enough to hang well without interlining, the creamy colour is easy to decorate around, and the texture is pleasantly gutsy. Canvas curtains look good with the sort of low-key, going-on-minimalist schemes currently in favour with younger designers, brown papered walls, metal furniture, neutral floors – 'greyed' boards or matting – and strong blocks of black, lacquer red or verdigris.

If you make canvas curtains generously full, they will not even need lining: a considerable saving in both time and cash. Bind the curtain edges with a plain colour, or black, for contrast, and hang them from canvas loops (see illustration) threaded over a metal rod. These are available in black, with spear-head finials like the ones on cast-iron railings. Curtains like these are primarily for show, 'dress' curtains to camouflage ugly windows, and need a bamboo blind behind for privacy. If you want curtains to draw easily you are better off with a curtain track.

Canvas curtains are ideal for stencilling, should the day come when their tasteful neutrality gets on your nerves. Go for a bold, shapely image; this is not the place for dinky flower borders (see illustrations for ideas). Use matchpot sizes of standard matt emulsion, or acrylic artists' colours, to stencil with, plus a bushy brush.

Below left Canvas curtains present an ideal surface for decorative stencils. Go for strong colours (black is ideal) and simple lines

Below Finish canvas curtains off with restrained yet chic loops and a cast-iron rod with spear finial

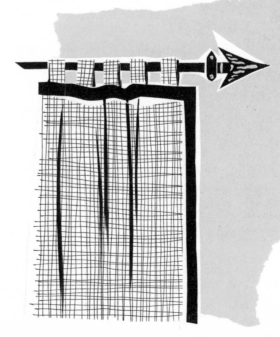

Surprisingly these plastic paints stand up quite well to washing, and they are easier to handle than dyes, bonding fairly immovably with the fabric surface. Alternatively, you can use special fabric paints which are ironed on the back to set the colour.

Hessian

Hessian is almost as cheap as canvas, and comes in a sensational colour range. It is coarse in texture, but not unpleasantly so. It won't drape as well as canvas

Above Simple muslin curtains threaded over a metal rod look serene and classic

Above right The Scandinavian touch: finish off muslin curtains with a little theatrical panache, by looping another swag of muslin around the rod, allowing the ends to drape voluptuously down either side

because it is always stiff with dressing, but used again in 'dress' curtains, pulled back either side of the windows, this wouldn't matter. Stencils work well on a hessian surface too. Stencil a strong red hessian with big paisley motifs in dark green and yellow, for a spectacular look. I wouldn't bother lining hessian curtains although the edges need to be bound to stop them fraying. I think of these as temporary, stage-prop curtains, so I think glueing tape or binding round the raw edges with a PVA adhesive would be quite suitable.

Cotton muslin

If you want to lose an ugly view without blocking out too much light, drifts of sheer cotton muslin, in white or cream, look serene and classical, and are an acceptable update on nets and lace flounces. The simplest way to make these is to machine a hem along the top edges wide enough to thread over a metal rod (see illustration). Machine the bottom hems to prevent fraying, but there is no need to seam up the muslin widths; the material hangs more prettily without. In Scandinavia muslin curtains are traditional and are often finished with a swag of the same material looped around a rod, with the ends hanging down either side of the curtain (see illustration).

Tamba cloth, saris, batik

Because they are intended to be worn, these cloths are sold by the piece rather than by the metre, but worked out at their cost per metre they are surprisingly cheap, the designs and colours available are impressive, and the quality of the fabric itself is often very fine. I think it is a mistake to treat any of these like conventional furnishing fabrics; they look best casually looped or draped and floating free. We use a tamba in the brown paper study as an instant pelmet. Tambas come in striking patterns and unusual colour combinations; saris are an obvious choice if you favour the twinkle of gold or silver on jewel colours; while Javanese batik prints are as pretty as a tropical fruit salad. But the most distinguished batiks for my money are indigo and white, a wonderfully strong colour combination of which one never tires.

Blankets and bull-dog clips

My London neighbour, textile artist Polly Hope, came up with an ingenious and thrifty idea for instant, no-sew curtains for her studio windows. She conscripted some old-fashioned woollen blankets, creamy wool with contrast stripes on the borders, and herringboned hems (increasing use of duvets has created a glut of these on the market) and converted these into curtains with bull-dog clips, attached to curtain rings by means of diminutive butchers' hooks. The clips grip the top of the blanket (fold the top over as shown above if necessary) and the hooks pass through the top of the clip and the hole on each ring.

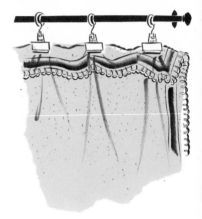

Blankets pinned up with bull-dog clips – a highly effective if slightly eccentric way to cover your windows

Second-hand curtains

New fabrics are mostly expensive, and curtains use up an awful lot of fabric. Old fabrics tend to be considerably cheaper unless we are talking about antique velvet, handblocked linen or toile de Jouy. For my money the best buys occur in the old but not antique category: pre- or post-war printed union, cotton velveteen, corduroy, cotton lace. The curtains shown on page 146 are good examples, working out at a very cheap price by today's standards. Old curtains usually need some alteration, so expect this, but it can't be bad to solve a curtain problem for around the price of a restaurant meal for two.

There are many venues where such bargains are on offer, from swish antique fairs (see Bargain hunting page 203) to baskets full of bundled-up sets, often found under stalls at junk markets and boot sales. So many variables are involved in choosing ready-made curtains. Are they the right size (too big is no problem, too small can be)? The right colour? In reasonable condition? Can you live with them? As ever, keep a list of measurements handy, plus a tape measure. If you do slip up (curtains that are too short and a little narrow for a large space, can be extended with an add-on border) I have suggested solutions, but I tend primarily to think of second-hand curtains as a cheap source of fabric, to be recycled in all sorts of ways. I have drawers packed with odd bits and pieces: a wonderful piece of old crimson silk velvet, worn, but

Carry a list of measurements and a tape measure when hunting for the ideal pair of second-hand curtains

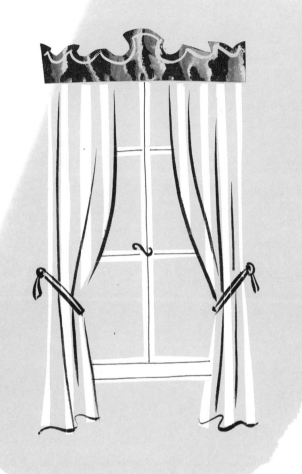

A decorative pelmet will successfully extend a pair of curtains a little – this may make a crucial difference when making the most of nearly-new curtains

trimmed with a wide, matching silk braid; a pair of cream velveteen curtains, short, but wide enough to re-cover a chair; some bright pink silk stately-home cast-offs; a thirties handblocked indigo print on linen, and a variety of other fabric lengths just waiting for the right window.

Anyone with a magpie instinct will understand this collection. The main problem with it is storage – lined and interlined curtains take up a massive amount of space. An old steamer tin trunk, peppered with mothballs, is probably the most practical solution to the problem, provided you can get at it easily.

CLEANING OLD CURTAINS

Old fabrics age differently: velvet goes bald, silk 'cuts' into tatters along leading edges, unions acquire a nicotine-ish hue. Fragile fabrics are best left alone unless you feel their rarity merits expensive specialist cleaning. All cleaning is costly, because of the sheer bulk involved, so I tend to use a washing machine wherever possible, especially on sturdy fabrics like unions. Simple washing splendidly refreshes the colours and texture of cotton/linen mixtures, plain cottons and some velveteens. Obviously don't put a lined and interlined curtain into a washing machine; interlining is a felty material which shrinks drastically, whilst linings tend to disintegrate with washing, because they have taken the brunt of sunlight (a great fabric destroyer) for so long. Both can be replaced but only you can decide whether the game is worth the candle. If you plan to alter your curtains or recycle them, it's best to unpick hems, side seams and rufflette tapes first to minimize the contrast between hidden, unfaded bits and the rest. Remove all hooks. Use a non-fast colour setting to be on the safe side, or even a delicates setting if you are worried about the effect of spinning. Usually with old curtains unpicking as such is unnecessary; the original thread is so weak you can often pull gently and the whole lot disintegrates in a moment, but go easy till you are sure.

If old curtains are oversized, badly worn strips can be cut back to sound fabric (make sure you cut along a straight edge). Do this before washing or cleaning, to prevent damage spreading, then turn the new edges in and stitch along the new hem. Replace tattered linings with cheap cotton lining, cotton sateen or even calico (pre-washed to shrink).

RE-LINING AND EXTENDING

Re-lining is a simple enough process, worth considering if the original lining has collapsed into tatters but the curtain fabric is still sound (which is often the case). Remove all trimmings, lining, tapes and hooks, pre-wash if necessary, then lay the fabric out flat and measure up. Choose a suitable, inexpensive fabric for the new lining, noting that strong colours will shine through the curtain fabric with light behind, so go for neutrals. Machine stitch the lining together, then hand stitch it to the curtains, or machine. Replace the rufflette and hooks and hang.

Extending is a pain, but worth doing if the curtains are wonderful in every respect but their scale – too short or too narrow to meet when drawn. If the curtains are simply too short, you may be able to cheat by constructing a decorative wooden pelmet board painted to tone in and deep enough to allow you to add several inches at the top of the curtains which will be concealed by the pelmet (see illustration page 109). One-eighth of a curtain drop is a good rough guide to the proportion of a pelmet to the whole window.

A flat add-on border in a toning or contrasting colour and compatible fabric can extend curtains lengthways by up to 15 cm (6 in.), and looks intentional and decorative to boot. I used 3 m (10 ft) of a neutral-toned cotton sateen to extend the curtains for the yellow dining room on page 58, matching the strips down, then slipstitching the border to the lining on the back. Mitre the corners neatly, so it all looks professional. The borders can carry on round three sides (minus the top), if you need to increase the width of the curtains more than the length. Make tie-backs to match and no one would guess that this window treatment had such humble origins.

NEARLY-NEW CURTAINS

Curtain Exchanges (see Suppliers page 202) are a relatively new phenomenon now that the merits of designer rejects (the colour didn't please when hung, the client just had a change of heart) have been thoroughly publicized. Certainly you can acquire luxurious curtains, lined, interlined and generously cut, for much less than the original estimate – around half-price is my guess. But this will still work out pricey by thrifty decorator standards. As with special lines in the sales, one can see why such curtains were rejected in the first place; for every acceptable set, in a pleasant colour and texture, there must be half a dozen in the no-no category. However, having made my point, I still think these exchanges are well worth checking out. You could strike lucky and find bargains, but remember to subtract the cost of lining, interlining, trimmings and your own sewing time, when trying to estimate the real value.

A selection of antique fabrics – some of which turn out to be highly prized 'documents'

Salerooms and auctions

The curtain stock at salerooms and auctions is very varied and ranges from the real antiques to last year's Laura Ashley fabrics. You could strike lucky first time or you could spend days in research, viewing, leaving bids, losing your favourites to a dealer who just topped your bid at the last minute. To the initiate it's the chance element of auctions that's half their attraction, but if time is short and you want results pronto, they may not be your scene. Most of the larger auction houses hold regular textile and soft-furnishing sales: the gala goods will be pounced upon and fetch their price, but you might pick something up towards the end of a sale, especially if it looks frayed, pieced, faded or plain dirty.

Antique curtains

Antique curtains (a much less precise category for dating than antique furniture) tend to be snapped up by the trade, even when considerably worn. Antique (let's say pre-First-World-War) fabrics are usually of a superior quality altogether, worth recycling into cushions, especially when they come lavishly trimmed (trimmings are almost more sought after than curtains today). There is another factor that can also be exploited by someone with a shrewd eye and some sense of textile history, which is the value (to a manufacturer) of forgotten, but attractive old designs and prints, usually in chintzes and cottons. A rarity in this field can be sold to a manufacturer, who will re-launch it in many new colourways, and often clean it up in the process. Designs of this commercial potential and historic interest are called 'documents'. A document does not have to be a large piece of fabric; one repeat of a design is enough. If you think you have come across a document print, don't rush around showing it naively to a group of textile people (some are decent, many are ruthlessly exploitative) but seek advice from an impartial source with textile expertise such as the Victoria and Albert Museum or some local museum with a reputation in this area. They will be able to advise you on your find, and maybe on what you should do with it if it has commercial possibilities.

Old trimmings

The only affordable modern trimming which I can abide is cotton rug fringe, which is usually sold in a natural string colour, but can be successfully dyed in the washing machine. Choose washing machine dyes, intermixing them like paints if you want a special colour. Put the fringe into an old cotton pillowcase to prevent it getting too snarled up, then dye according to the makers' instructions. The fringe will probably need some tidying up before you hang it out to dry: shake it vigorously, undoing any knots, till it is once again straight, with the fringes hanging properly (a quick comb through with your fingers will help) then loop carefully and peg out.

Fringes, tassels and braids – look out for lovely old trimmings in thrift shops and markets and rejuvenate them for a second life

Pelmets

Compared with the patient stitchery involved in curtain making, knocking up a pelmet is quick but decisive; rather like the difference between undertaking a complicated frock and making a hat with a few odds and ends. Like a hat, too, a nifty pelmet, well designed, well proportioned, tricked out with imaginative

A decorative cut-out pelmet board and a fabric-covered pelmet. A decorative board is made from a sheet of ply or MDF, from which a pattern is cut with a jig-saw. Side pieces project the fascia clear of blind or curtain fixtures. The pelmet board can be painted, decorated and varnished. A fabric pelmet is made from shaped pieces of four layers of fabric – curtain fabric, lining, interlining and stiffening (buckram or canvas) – stuck together and either attached by Velcro to a wooden pelmet board or hung by hooks from a bendable pelmet track.

trimmings, adds considerable style to the ensemble. The more elaborate-shaped pelmets do need a solid core of some stiff material – buckram or canvas – to hold their line crisply (and although flat pelmets can dispense with this, it does always look better added).

DECORATIVE CUT-OUT PELMET BOARDS

I first came across these in Early American interiors and liked them for their perky and upstanding upper profile (see illustration). Basically, they consist of a decorative cut-out fascia of ply or MDF (medium density fibreboard) fixed with brackets, or glue and tacks, to side pieces (see illustration) to make a pelmet box that can be fixed to window frames or walls with mirror plates or small brackets, as shown. Their special charm is that they lend themselves to improving existing window proportions. Also, being wooden, they can be painted to match the window dressings – curtains and blinds – which may seem easier than the stitchery involved in making fabric pelmets.

How do they improve mingy windows? Let me explain. I have two standard casement windows in my bathroom which are rather square and rather small. By setting the pelmet boards a good 15 cm (6 in.) above the windows, and filling in the gap with a frill that matches the curtains (a pelmet in other words), an illusion is created of windows that are better proportioned and more generous, because the actual window surround is nowhere visible. This is a pretence, certainly, but it works.

Blinds

BUNDLE BLINDS

This is by far the easiest blind to make yourself; it's just a strip of fabric the width and length of the window frame which rolls up manually and is secured with simple ties. Bundle blinds are the ideal choice if you want to keep your windows partially screened most of the time – for privacy, or because the view is depressing, or simply because filtering the 'headlight' on tall windows makes the room look cosier and more inviting. The height of a bundle blind can of course be adjusted, and either let down fully or rolled up higher when the sun shines, but you will find you won't want to do this too often as it obviously takes a little time to get it right.

Made in the cheapest natural calico or fine canvas, and tied with contrasting red or black tape perhaps, blinds like these can look handsome in an understated Japanese style. If you choose one of these fabrics, put the length through the washing machine first to pre-shrink it, and check that the colour ties are colourfast (you will probably need to wash a fabric blind regularly). To make removing blinds easier use Velcro to attach them to the window frame. Bundle blinds made up in colourful prints, stripes or checks can look attractive in quite a different way, but always hold the fabric up to daylight before deciding on it; a print that looks fetching in the hand can be lurid when the light shines through it. Bundle blinds can be lined or unlined: a flimsy fabric like calico would be better lined, a heavier canvas fine on its own.

Making up

Make sure you have enough fabric to cover the windows, measuring from the outside edge of each frame and allowing a little overhang at the bottom, plus 5 cm (2 in.) for hems to length and width. You also need tape, ribbon, braid or contrast fabric strips for ties. For the latter choose something sturdy, preferably a webbing or grosgrain ribbon which won't look like a bootlace when stretched. Buy enough sew-on-type Velcro to stretch across the windows and a 2.5 × 2.5-cm (1 × 1-in.) batten the same length as the Velcro for each window.

Trim the fabric to the correct width and length and if you are using lining, cut this the same size. Turn under a 12-mm ($\frac{1}{2}$-in.) double hem on sides and bottom of blind, and slip-stitch in place. Position the ties as shown, and machine them firmly in place. Turn the top edge under to make a hem the depth of the batten, and machine this down. Now stitch one side of the Velcro strip across the top, tucking the ends under neatly. Screw the batten to the top of the window frame and fix the other side of the Velcro strip to it with glue and tacks. Press the two Velcro sides together, stretching the fabric taut, roll up the blind to the required height and tie as shown.

Note: if you use a contrast fabric for the ties instead of webbing or ribbon, make the ties by cutting out lengths of material to double the width required, folding them in half (right sides together), machining them up from top to bottom, then turning right-side out and double hemming the ends by machine. Finally, machine through both sides to make them firm and crisp looking.

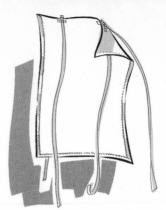

Machine the ties firmly in place on either side of the bundle blind

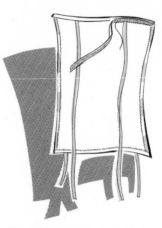

Sew Velcro to the back of the curtain where it will make contact with the batten

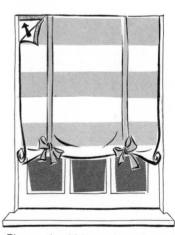

Glue another Velcro strip to the batten and then press the blind onto it. Roll up the blind to the required height and tie as shown

ROMAN BLINDS

Did the Romans invent Roman blinds? They are as architectural as a blind can be, and Romans – both classical and contemporary – did and do have a predilection for clearly structured accoutrements. If you need privacy but want a minimal, clean look, then I suggest Roman blinds; they look good on their own and are substantial enough to screen windows at night (though they do look better lined). Roman blinds are not simple to make, needing careful measuring and marking out, but you can cheer yourself on through the tedious bits with the thought that by doing it yourself you are saving big amounts of money. Because Roman blinds are a serious window dressing I feel this is the place for a moderately opulent fabric: a fine plain glazed chintz perhaps, or a checked Madras cotton, or a bold black and white print. Use cotton sateen or pre-washed and thus pre-shrunk calico for the lining and for the batten pockets. It is the rigidity given by these wooden battens, slipped into their pockets, that holds Roman blinds taut and hauls them up into such exact horizontal pleats.

Materials

Roman binds should span the window from architrave to architrave and the drop, when fully extended, should be from the top of the window to the sill. Make sure your chosen fabric is the correct width for your window, joining lengths if necessary. The lining fabric needs to be the same width and length. Allow 2 m ($6\frac{1}{2}$ ft) extra in the lining fabric for making up the batten pockets. Battens are set 25–30 cm (10–12 in.) apart, depending on the size of the windows, so divide the window height to find the number of 2.5-cm (1-in.) wood battens needed and ask at a timber yard for these to be cut to size. You will also need a head batten measuring 5×2.5 cm (2×1 in.) to the width of your blind. The bottom lap of blind is unstiffened so take this into consideration when measuring. A contrast binding looks smart; use fabric, coloured webbing or tape or ribbon for this. You will also need a tape measure, set square, small screw eyes (two to each batten) for the cords to pass through, and enough blind cord per blind to add up to double its length plus $1\frac{1}{2}$ times its width for the draw cords. A screw hook on the window frame allows you to fix the blind at the chosen height.

Making up

First cut the main fabric and lining to the measured window size, and run a couple of lines of tacking (see illustration) up the double thickness to hold fabric and lining together with right sides out (a tacking line round the outside edges is a great help). It is *important* that both rectangles of fabric lie smooth and flat with the warp and weft of both fabrics aligned throughout the blind making, or your precise pleats will pull out of shape and look clumsy. Next bind the sides and bottom, mitring the corners, then turn the top edge under and machine down for strength. The binding can be tacked in place, and machined in one go (see illustration), or machined on the wrong side if you are using a strip of contrast fabric, taken round the edges to the front, turned under and slip-stitched in place by hand (see illustration). Now you have a neat rectangle, double thickness, bound in contrast material on three sides.

For the next stage you need your measuring tape or ruler and set square. Leaving 4 cm (1½ in.) at the top of the blind to fold over the head batten (see illustration), start measuring off 25–30-cm (10–12-in.) intervals down both sides of the blind, using the set square and tape or ruler to make sure that these are strictly horizontal and aligned with the cross weave of the fabric. Pencil or chalk these on the lining, as guidelines for the batten pockets (see illustration). Cut strips of lining fabric the same width as the blind and 7.5 cm (3 in.) deep. Pin and stitch these down as shown (see illustration) through the centre of the blind, then fold the edges in and stitch together to make pockets. Slip-stitch one end of each pocket closed then insert the battens through the other and slip-stitch this end closed.

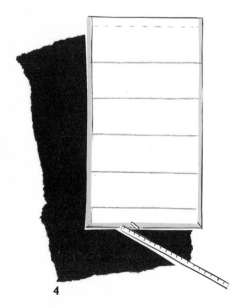

1

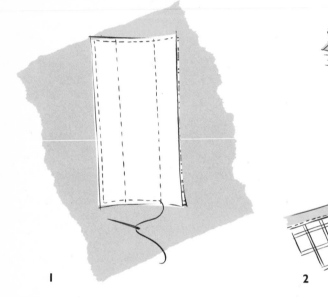

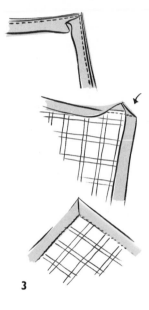

2

3

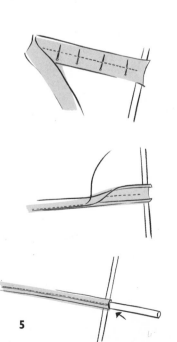

4

5

1 Tack the fabric and lining together

2 *Either* tack then machine the binding on in one go, mitring the corners (see page 98 for more detail), *or* **3** tack then machine the binding on the wrong side, take the edges to the front (with mitred corners) and slip-stitch in place by hand

4 Mark batten lines with chalk and a ruler

5 Make batten pockets from strips of lining fabrics

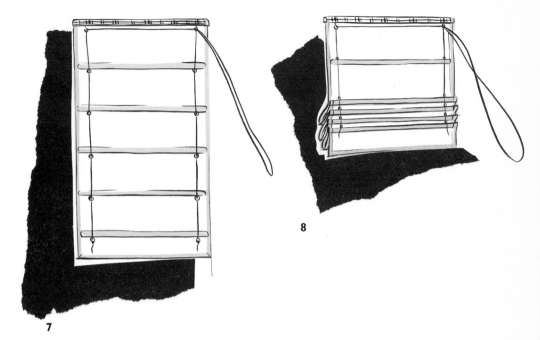

6

8

7

6 Attach the top batten and screw eyes to the blind

7 Thread the cord through the screw eyes either side, knotting both loose ends at the bottom and pulling the loop of cord through the top right-hand screw eye

8 Draw the blind up by pulling on the loop and secure the cord around a curtain cleat

You now have a neat rectangle sectioned off on the back by concealed battens. To position the screw eyes correctly on the batten edges (approximately 5 cm (2 in.) in from each edge) line them up vertically, batten by batten, measuring carefully and using a bradawl to help the screw bite into the wood through the fabric pocket. Thread the cord through as shown, knotting the loose ends to the bottom rings and taking the cords across to make a draw string (see illustration). For a wide window you will need three lines of screws.

Screw the head batten to the top of the window frame, inside the architrave, then staple the top of the Roman blind over this as shown (see illustration) making sure it is taut and smooth. Test the draw strings to see that it all pleats up at a tweak, then knot the ends together and screw a hook into the frame at a convenient height for securing.

JAZZING UP KIT ROLLER BLINDS

Kit roller blinds, complete with cords, roller and spring mechanism, are available in a good range of standard window sizes (instructions are included for cutting down over-scaled blinds) and are so cheap that it seems unnecessarily laborious to try and make your own. It must be said though that they look a bit mean, even with curtains hanging either side – the fabric is vaguely plasticized and the blinds end abruptly just below the batten with no shaped or scalloped edges. However they do make an excellent subject for stencilling, and a few hours' work with a stencil brush will give you an altogether different and more attractive window display, customized to suit your own tastes. The trick when doing this is to use the stencil paint very sparingly, so it remains transparent (otherwise whatever colours you choose will simply register as dark on light).

Materials

You need either home-made or bought stencils (see Suppliers page 202), acrylic tube colours, acrylic medium, a bushy brush, a paper plate as a palette, lots of newspaper for testing colours, masking tape, a ruler or tape measure and a pencil (see illustrations).

Roller blinds can be jazzed up with either free-hand or stencilled designs

Making up

Open out your blind flat. Do this before attaching it to the roller, but check first that the width is correct for your window. If it's not, trim it to size as instructed. Decide how you want the stencil pattern to be seen – as a broad strip down the middle, arranged in stripes (see illustrations) or as an all-over pattern. Remember that if you also have curtains, the sides of the blind will tend to be hidden behind folds of curtain fabric.

Below left All the materials you need for stencilling

Below Work from the bottom of the blind up, and use masking tape to keep your design straight

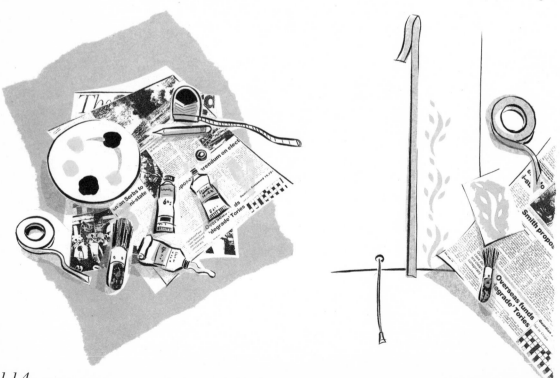

Squeeze the colours on to your paper plate with a little acrylic medium in the middle (this adds transparency to the colours and makes them easier to handle). Work a little medium into the colours and test them on the newspaper. When you have the tones you want, make sure that your stencil brush is not overloaded: a wet brush always makes a splat. The ideal is to work the colour up into the bristles while removing surplus moisture; do this by jabbing it repeatedly on to newspaper. When it prints a soft but distinct spot of colour (not a squidgy blob) you can start on the blind. If in doubt try it out on the top of the blind, which will hardly be seen in use.

Begin stencilling from the bottom of the blind, since this area will be the most visible. You can plot out the stencil locations before starting, making discreet pencil marks with the help of the ruler, but don't overdo this because the pencil marks will show up unless they're painted over. Otherwise work by eye, using masking tape (see illustration) to keep your plumb line straight.

Use the brush in a circular scrubbing motion for a clear but even print. Elaborate stencils may need to be fixed with tabs of masking tape while you work, but simple ones can be held in place with your free hand. To paint a coloured border round the three visible sides of a blind, position the masking tape inset from the sides, then brush colour up to the edge and leave to dry before peeling off the tape.

Note: If you can't lay your hands on a suitable stencil, paper doilies (the lacy cut-out kind) make charming patterns, rather like fancy china. Shades of blue on white give you a chic and instant blue-and-white china effect. You may need to strengthen the doilies with a lick of shellac or varnish, and a quick squirt with spraymount on the back holds open-work designs in place while you paint. Use newspaper to mask off the surrounding blind.

A split bamboo blind decorated with old Chinese characters is an impressive window treatment for a modern, minimalist room

SPLIT BAMBOO BLINDS

The roll-up blinds of finely split bamboo look well, but with a little tarting up (see illustration) they look better still. Binding the edges with coloured tape and glue doesn't take a minute but adds considerable class, while stencilling a few bold Chinese or Japanese characters, as shown, adds decorative punch. Use black and/or sealing-wax red for Eastern characters. To make stencils from these, simply trace round the characters, enlarge then on a photocopier to the required size, then trace off a copy with carbon paper on to a stencil card.

Materials

You need black and/or brown and red acrylic or emulsion colours, a bushy brush, masking tape, coloured tape for binding and PVA (Copydex) adhesive.

Making up

Set out the stencils either as shown or in your preferred way. Paint as described above. Fold the binding tape in half and iron it to make a central crease then coat it and the edge of the blind with adhesive, following the maker's instructions. Leave both for the time stated, then carefully stretch and press the tape round the edges and bottom of the blind, mitring corners neatly. A stitch at the corners will help hold these in shape.

CHAPTER 5

FURNITURE AND STORAGE

When you are starting out as a homeowner (which generally means skint) it is wonderful how little furniture you can manage with. A shop display-rail takes care of your clothes, wooden crates or stout cardboard boxes stand in for odd tables, heaps of cushions or a futon double up as your seating, a mirror propped on the windowsill is your dressing table. Improvization is the name of the game, and while the first glow of proprietorship lingers, nothing could be more appropriate or fun than such blithe makeshift furniture. Travelling light is one of the delights of being young.

One day, however, sooner or later, for whatever reason, you find yourself impatient with the ephemeral lifestyle. It suddenly becomes important to acquire furnishings, for comfort, for tidiness, for your own pleasure, and even, if you are honest, to catch up with your contemporaries. Travelling light is alluring but there is also a need to put down roots, get sorted in your domestic situation, declare your personal style via the choices you make.

In Getting it Together (page 8) I make suggestions on where to look for your first serious objects, large or small, old or new, pristine or dilapidated. In the next three chapters I will round out the 'where' with the 'how-to', in the sense of rehabilitating and refurbishing your finds, stripping off grungy old paint, varnish or French polish, re-caning or rush-seating chairs, re-covering upholstered pieces, adding decorative paint treatments that can make a piece of junk furniture look suave and covetable.

Equipment for restoring hardwood furniture

Revamping Wood

This section is not to do with paint finishes, but with reliable, not too technical ways of improving the looks of old-going-on-antique wooden pieces – chairs, tables, bookcases – of no great distinction but of pleasing proportions and sound workmanship. These may be lost to view beneath disfiguring grime, flaking French polish, ink stains, cigarette burns and other blemishes to which old pieces are liable.

RESTORING HARDWOODS

My remedies are of the simplest sort, but efficacious, when it comes to revitalizing old – say late-Victorian – mahogany and rosewood. These are superb materials, fine textured and richly coloured in their natural state. What often happens with furniture of this vintage is that it emerged glassy bright with French polish in its salad days, and this finish (which I do not despise, but consider over-used in the past) has suffered to the point where to the casual eye the honest timber beneath is almost unrecognizable. Remove the finish, with care and discretion, and what leaps to the eye as you work is the rich colour, distinctive grain, and fine texture of the original excellent hardwood. Nothing could be simpler or more rewarding.

The basic clean-up (removing the French polish and dirt) requires only methylated spirit, a brush to apply it, wire wool in fine grade (get a roll), rags and household gloves to prevent your hands looking as if they were pickled in nicotine. A plastic dust sheet for splashes is essential if working indoors.

Begin by wiping the piece over with a damp rag to remove ordinary dust and grease. Next slop methylated spirit over the piece, a section at a time. Leave for a few minutes till the old finish has softened and made a dark 'gravy' and then begin rubbing firmly but not brutally with the grain of the wood. You will be surprised at the speed with which your wire wool pads are saturated with dark gunk. Chuck them and repeat the process, but more cautiously now, because the ideal is to strip the French polish back to the wood surface but not to the point where the original wood filler (used to fill the pores of timbers before further finishing) is removed. This is not disastrous if it happens, but means that the wood may need more re-finishing for a fine surface.

A well cleaned piece of mature mahogany or rosewood is handsome and dignified. When the wood is of high quality, then I prefer to avoid further treatment, merely rubbing in a little linseed oil mixed with a little real (artists') turps to bring up the colour and a subdued sheen. The sheen can be heightened to a shine by regular buffing with a soft clean cloth. It is gentle rubbing which eventually creates the finest patina, not generous blasts of silicone polish or anointings with beeswax. These create a high shine fast, it is true, but the tendency is to use too much, which creates a faintly sticky surface which in turn attracts dirt and the whole cycle is poised to begin again.

Ink stains can be bleached out once the wood has been cleaned but do this before oiling or polishing. I use a proprietary bleach and stain remover which is very effective. Follow the maker's instructions and keep the chemical closely confined to the stain itself, dabbing it on with a fine brush.

Burn marks or scorch marks need more radical treatment as a rule. Superficial marks can be gently rubbed away with wire wool or a fine grade wet-and-dry paper. This will tend to create a slight hollow in the surface but this is less noticeable than a dark burn. Where burns have really scorched deeply into the wood the best solution is to plane off the entire surface till the damage is cleared. Unless you are skilled with a plane, this might be better left to a professional.

LIMING

In terms of value for money, solid oak furniture, mostly dating from the thirties, is the best buy around. This definition – solid oak – encompasses a considerable range of styles, much of it in the 'Tudorbethan' area (twirly-legged stools and tables, refectory tables with massive bulbous legs, throne-like chairs) but you may also find pieces with an Arts and Crafts look, and some later, plainer, stuff from the Utility furniture produced in the immediate post-war era. For what it is, sturdily made of solid wood, it is still underpriced, the reason being that it has not aged well and at first glance looks unprepossessing, dark, lumpish and clumsy, hard to imagine fitting in with the casual but colourful interiors people go for today.

The solution is to 'lime' it – a treatment that seems made to order for oak, though it can also be used on ash and chestnut wood. 'Liming' lightens and brightens oak out of all recognition, making a virtue of its grain and vigorous figuring, and giving it a cool sophisticated appearance that suits any setting. I put 'lime' in inverted commas because unlike traditional limewash which has a caustic action, our updated version uses a white pigmented paste which gives the same effect without risk of irritating the skin. Liming is hard work, physically, especially on a large piece, and the white 'fall out' is considerable, so I do urge people to do it out of doors on a plastic sheet. Tie a scarf round your hair and wear old clothes, or you will look as floury white as a freshly baked bap.

Strip the wood of its old finish. Most old oak (I take it as read that no one is going to lime *antique* oak, this would be sacrilege) has been French polished using shellac. Methylated spirit is the solvent for shellac, so start by brushing meths liberally over a surface, leave for a few minutes and then rub over with wire wool. If a sort of 'gravy' wipes off on the wire wool pad, leaving a patch of pale wood, you *are* dealing with French polish. Carry on dousing with meths and clearing the gunge away with wire wool, until the piece looks uniformly pale and clean without dark patches. You may need a pointed tool of some sort to clean out deeply carved surfaces. If the meths treatment is unsuccessful, then move on to varnish stripper, available in most DIY stores. Apply this following the method for methylated spirit.

Next, whether you plan to stain the piece or not, scour the grain with a wire brush. The type of brush we used is like a suede brush; not the great rake sold

You need only a small amount of equipment for liming: paint brushes, wire wool, rubber gloves and a small wire brush

in ironmongers which would damage the surface. To clean out the soft grain, swab the piece, one surface at a time, with cold water. This softens the fibres so that when you scrub the surface with your brush, going with the grain, you will find gunk appearing on the brush. Keep going (this is the tedious bit) until you have scoured the whole piece, and cleaned out the soft fibres. If you cheat on this bit the limed effect will not be so striking or handsome: more of a white smear than a sharply distinct graining showing white against the wood. You will need to clean the brush quite often, or even replace it if the piece is huge. I used three on one bookcase.

Liming directly on to this gives a cool, silvery tone. Another option, which suits some pieces and interiors better, is to stain the bare wood before liming it. This gives a subtly colourful finish. Dark blue, dark green and black are the best stain colours, being strong enough to mask the natural wood colour. When limed the effect is many shades lighter: deep blue and green come out as pastel versions of themselves, while black becomes a mid-to-charcoal grey.

Materials

We used colours from our Woodwash range, which are powerful stains, but you can buy similar stain colours in standard commercial ranges. Liming paste and wire brushes (see Suppliers page 202) are available by mail order.

You need a roll of medium, and one of fine wire wool. It is cheaper in the end to buy wire wool in rolls, because one finds so many uses for it. Also needed are a couple of standard paint brushes, methylated spirit or varnish stripper to clean off the old finish, rubber gloves and a plastic dust sheet. To seal and protect the limed finish I recommend bleached shellac, known as white polish, available from trade suppliers (see Suppliers page 202). Use a fine 'glider' brush to apply this. Clean in meths after use and reserve for the shellac work.

Method

If you're using stain then apply it now. Woodwash is usually diluted one part wash to two parts water. Check the makers' instructions for other stains. Leave this to dry completely. The piece will look very dark, but don't fret: all will be well. Now completely cover the piece with liming paste, brushed on and worked well into the grain (the piece will look as if it's been dipped in icing). Leave to dry completely, then with wire wool pads, working from medium to fine grade wool, start rubbing at the 'icing' following the wood grain. A snowstorm will cascade round your feet, but the reward is to see the wood surfacing again with the white 'lime' remaining in the grain. Don't rub *too* fiercely over stained wood otherwise you risk rubbing through the stain to the natural wood colour.

When your piece is done, wipe surfaces with a damp rag. Tip white polish (bleached shellac) into a jar, adding a little meths to make it more fluid. Stir, then brush fast and lightly over all the limed surfaces, flooding them rather than working the shellac in with the brush. This will dry in an hour, with a mildly shiny finish. If you want a completely matt finish, and the piece is going to be well-handled, reinforce the shellac with one coat of matt alkyd varnish, applied according to the instructions, slightly thinned, and very well stirred beforehand. My stained limed oak desk has impeccably survived almost three years of constant use and much elbow propping.

Note: Liming wax, a soft wax impregnated with pigment, is favoured by some for its ease of application, but I find it less satisfactory because it leaves the wood looking greasy and inevitably the fatty content brings up the gingery yellow colour of waxed oak. The paste method aims to suppress this colour. However, if you go for ease, it can be obtained from good specialist shops.

Paint as Cover Up

By no means all the surfaces crying out for some form of paint camouflage are going to be plain honest wood these days. Much cheap furniture, both free-standing pieces and fitted units, incorporates one or other of a range of wood substitutes such as MDF (medium density fibreboard), chipboard or blockboard. These are sold in large sheets which makes them a popular commercial choice for unit doors and shelves, and for larger pieces like fitted cupboards. Veneered blockboard is acceptable, but MDF and chipboard (often given a melamine finish) are intrinsically unlovely materials in need of clever paint jobs. A step up from these substances, but not necessarily lovable, come the cheaper timbers like knotty pine, deal and whitewood. Veneered pieces may fall into this category too, but *antique* veneered furniture is different and deserves proper repair and restoration. However, much twentieth-century veneered furniture is of no special merit, and may reach you missing large patches of veneer in which case you could do best to level up the scars with plastic wood and paint the lot.

Because of the variety of surfaces these materials present, from factory-spray lacquer to plastic-smooth melamine, the steps involved in preparing them for a paint finish are somewhat different. I will therefore treat them separately, indicating which paint finishes seem specially suitable in each case.

MELAMINE

Melamine makes a practical, easy-clean finish for the inside surfaces of furniture, shelves and drawers. As an exterior surface, however, it is less appealing, whether pristine white or given a tacky fake-wood look, and I would always paint over it where visible. The crucial step in painting melamine is to begin with an oil-based paint which grips the smooth plastic coating. Once the base-coat is in place you have the choice of continuing with an oil-based finish, or switching to a water-based one, faster drying and odourless.

First clean melamine well with a sugar soap solution to remove all grease and dirt. Next, abrade the plastic coating to give a 'key' for the paint: a pan scourer dipped in Vim, or a Brillo pad will do quite an efficient job of this, or use wet-and-dry paper dipped in soapy water. Don't exhaust yourself over this bit of the prepping – you need only scuff the plastic lightly. When dry, the surfaces are ready to paint. If you want to give the melamine a fancy glazed finish – dragged or ragged or stippled (see the rose bedroom photograph, page 145) – start with one coat of standard oil-based undercoat, followed by a coat of eggshell paint. This will give you an ideally smooth 'canvas' to decorate, especially if you lightly rub down the dry eggshell before glazing. To mix up a glaze see Recipes (page 201), tinting with artists' oil tube colours (Universal Stainers) to arrive at the shade you want. Our melamine fitted cupboards in the rose bedroom had a narrow applied moulding simulating 'panels', which allowed us to mix techniques, dragging the 'frame' and stippling the 'panels'. The drag painting mimics the way wood grain would go if the structure *was* made of wood instead of melamine, discreetly suggesting that it *is* made of wood. We then picked out the moulding lightly with a further coat of the glaze applied with a $\frac{1}{2}$-in (2-mm) brush. When dry this was sealed with a protective coat of extra matt varnish to blend the cupboards in with the ultra-matt distempered walls. On kitchen units, use two coats of varnish.

For a solid, dark-coloured paint finish, use a standard oil-based primer instead of white undercoat. Red oxide metal primer is cheap, widely available, and makes a good base for Shaker-type paint colours, or for rustic 'distressing' in two or more colours. You can please yourself as to which type of paint you carry on with, from this point, as the primer will take either oil- or water-based paints. I suggest you choose an oil-based paint from the Shaker, or National Trust ranges (see Suppliers page 202) if you want an interesting colour. If you fancy a 'distressed' finish, apeing generations of wear, you might go for Paint Magic Woodwash colours (see Suppliers page 202) which are fast-drying and water-based. The range includes twelve colours, so the permutations are endless. (See pages 54–55 for the 'distressing' how-to.) Note that this is a two-colour finish, with the top-coat predominating, but enough of the base colour showing through, depending how you wield your candle, to lighten or enliven the overall effect. If you match your choice of colours already in the room, you can't go wrong.

When rubbing through the top coat take care not to rub so hard you go through to the melamine. This is important because you don't want this plastic finish 'ghosting' through. Seal when dry with one, two or three coats of varnish, depending on how much wear and handling the surfaces can expect.

Note: A similar approach will allow you to paint over plastic with fair success. I have a pair of large black plastic plant tubs left over from planting pot-grown holly trees, which I primed and finished with a 'verdigris' stipple (see page 186) that have survived a year of outdoor life in reasonable shape. Those cheap white plastic urns on pedestals are immensely improved by this treatment.

MDF

MDF (made from sawdust compressed with resin) is not much cheaper than timber, but it has certain qualities that appeal to joiners and manufacturers: it is relatively stable, non-warping, extra heavy, and takes decorative 'routing' cleanly, without splitting or chipping. In its natural state it looks not unlike new gypsum plaster, only less appealing. It needs to be painted to tie in with timber framing, and to protect it from damp, its chief enemy. Damp can cause warping, and if it enters the end grain, the fibre becomes soggy and mildewy. So don't use MDF for kitchen surfaces or shelving where leaky taps or condensation are a likely hazard.

The prepping consideration with MDF is to pre-seal surfaces for paint (especially water-based paint). In workshop or factory situations, a spray sealant is used for this. I find a coat or two of standard orange shellac (or button polish) brushed over all the surfaces to seal the porous MDF makes a good base for further paintwork. Once the shellac seal is dry (this takes 20 to 40 minutes) you can use water- or oil-based paints. Because MDF is slightly frigid-looking – with no wood-like texture – a distressed finish gives it body. Alternatively, it makes a splendidly smooth surface for serene Shaker colours. Indeed, once suitably 'prepped', MDF lends itself to painting as for wood, so the options are endless. Remember to treat the end result with at least one coat of varnish to act as further insulation against damp.

BLOCKBOARD

This is a pleasant enough material, usually consisting of a rigid compressed sawdust and fibre core with veneers applied on both sides. It may be my imagination, but blockboard veneer seems to have an excessively 'open' grainy texture which looks its worst when varnished. If you want to retain the 'wood' look – and the veneers supplied are quite attractive – you could improve its appearance considerably by filling the grain with a proprietary wood filler obtained from any good DIY shop (see Suppliers page 202). If the veneer has been varnished or lacquered you should clean this finish off first. Varnishes are easily removed with a varnish stripper but lacquer is more problematic; cellulose thinners (as for car paint spray) are one solvent that could work, but wear a mask and work outdoors if possible, because the fumes are potent. Otherwise consult a friendly tradesman *or* abandon the wood finish and move to paint instead.

For filling follow maker's instructions, brushing the filler well into the grain, then rub back when dry with wet-and-dry abrasive paper to get a silky flat surface. Stain all over with wood-stain and apply one or two coats of fast-drying shellac, followed by a coat of semi-sheen polyurethane for protection.

To paint, prime with the above-mentioned primers or undercoats, or fast-drying acrylic primer, rub smooth, then use oil- or water-based paint.

KNOTTY DEAL, PINE, WHITEWOOD

These are all softwoods, which were traditionally painted to upgrade them from a cheap building material, and also to protect them to some degree against woodworm and other tiny creatures.

During the stripped-pine craze which swept the country a decade ago, much poor quality, knotty, porous and generally lowly softwood was made into dressers, kitchen units, chairs, tables and much else. The styling of these pieces can be pleasant enough; it is the materials which have suffered over the years. The spray-lacquer finish has worn away in patches, dirt has become engrained, the 'knots' look annoyingly spotty instead of sweetly countrified and there's a good case for a paint camouflage job. A suitable paint treatment, plain or fancy, will give such pieces new dignity and charm, as well as masking their imperfections and bringing them up-to-date. You can add stencils, lining, antique patina and many coats of rubbed-back varnish for a superior painted-piece effect. Or you can opt for a quick solution, like a transparent colour-finish which leaves the grain showing but softens the knots.

An opaque paint finish takes less 'prepping' and needs only a good clean and sanding to key the surface for paint. After this, prime, undercoat and paint as for MDF or melamine. Use water- or oil-based paints for the final surface, plain or distressed. Varnish with one or two coats of matt or eggshell varnish. 'Antique' with a rubbed-on mixture of artists' oil colour (burnt siennas, burnt umber or raw umber) diluted in white spirit. Apply with a rag, rubbing on, then rubbing away to create a shadowy patina, which is darkest in the crevices, lightest on the prominent areas. You can finish with boot polish for a soft shine and a suggestion of colour: dark tan is good over dark colours; light tan over pale shades; black over grey, blue and silver.

If you opt for a transparent finish through which the wood grain is clearly visible, make sure the wood is bare of any varnish, wax or, worst scenario, spray lacquer. Varnish is removed swiftly with varnish stripper and wire wool, wax comes off with white spirit and wire wool, but lacquer is a brute to remove. For this try a strong paint-stripper with a coarser grade of wire wool first. Cellulose thinners might work on some lacquers, but wear a mask and work in a well-ventilated space – the fumes are powerful. Finally, try vigorous sanding, or just resign yourself to an opaque finish. Alternatively, try the water-based dragged finish described on pages 132–133.

If the wood is clean and bare, apply transparent colour (such as woodwash) with a brush or rag. Try to keep the colour even. If, when it dries, you feel the colour is too pale, simply wipe another layer of wash over the first. When dry, varnish with one or two coats of extra-pale, flat alkyd varnish. When this is dry, pick out mouldings or add further decoration, and re-varnish.

Decorating Painted Furniture

Some pieces of furniture cry out for decoration beyond a special paint finish and painted lining. A visit to Charleston, the Sussex farmhouse where Duncan Grant and Vanessa Bell lived and painted, is the sort of visual treat which can leave you longing to splash colour on everything in sight. So too could a trip to the American Museum, or a guided tour of Pompeii. The sort of pieces that will be transformed by further applied decoration might include pine chests of drawers, blanket boxes, cots and other nursery furniture, corner cupboards, round tables and hanging shelves.

Simple sponging is very effective, especially if you stick to vivid colour combinations and use a natural sea sponge

SPONGING

I rarely see this technique used to decorate recent pieces though it was much used in the nineteenth century on rustic items such as long case clocks, washstands and chests. Yet sponging is as charming as it is simple to do. I have a picture of a little Scandinavian pot-cupboard, round, in metal, which has been sponged very simply in blue on white, and it looks perfect. The secret I think is not to overdo the sponge prints; leave lots of background colour showing for a look like spongeware pottery not fake marble. Choose vivid colour combinations: green on ochre yellow or creamy white (add dark red lining); bright pink on blue or white, chestnut on the palest blue.

Use a sea sponge. This is essential because it makes pretty, irregular prints. Acrylic colours are best for drying speed. You can add a little acrylic medium to them for transparency and variation of tone. Dip the sponge into the paint, pound it on to newspaper to work off excess moisture then lightly pat it over your painted piece. There is no rule for what looks best; just follow your instinct and know when to stop. Varnish the piece to protect it (see page 123). Lining in the same colour (see edge lining on page 129) will give coherence to your decoration.

VINEGAR GRAINING

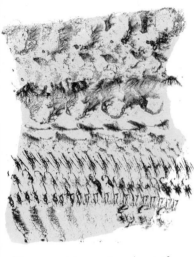

Vinegar graining – using a lump of putty and a vinegar glaze you can create these engagingly bizarre patterns, loosely based on figured hardwood

Another rustic effect, vinegar graining was popular with nineteenth-century provincial grainers, who worked up engagingly bizarre patterns loosely based on figured hardwood such as mahogany, walnut and maple. The patterns are made by dabbing, rolling or otherwise manipulating a lump of putty (or another material) into a wet glaze, made from ordinary vinegar coloured with powder colour, to which a little sugar is added for 'stick'. American painters used corn cobs, pleated paper or the side of their hands, to produce varied impressions, but putty seems to react with the vinegar to create attractive seaweed shapes. The nineteenth-century painters used woody colours, such as red, brown or black on yellow or iron-oxide red (black on iron-oxide red looks surprisingly like tortoiseshell) but I think the technique would look more fun in non-woody colours like green on yellow, or pale blue. Leave the glaze to 'set up' for a minute or two before you start making shapes. It will dry disappointingly flat, but a coat of shellac followed by gloss varnish will bring it up wonderfully. A touch of gilt cream looks good with vinegar graining.

POTATO PRINTS

Potato print designs – a square mosaic pattern and a leaf motif – effective, cheap and child's play

These look crude but feisty. See illustration for an all-over pattern done with a humble spud and consider variations such as stars, leaves (cut several sizes) or leopard spots. Use acrylic colours on matt emulsion. Wipe your potato cut from time to time, and to replace it when the prints go fuzzy. Varnish as above when dry, adding contrast lining if you like.

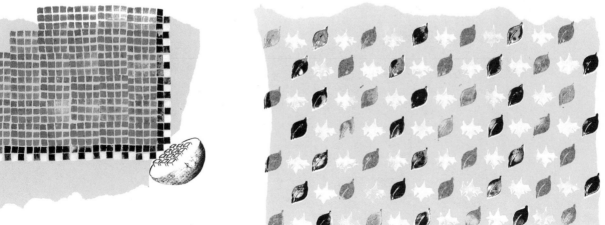

STENCILS

If too much creative freedom worries you, try stencils. There is a wide range of pre-cut shapes to choose from, from chunky ethnic designs to florals and non-classical swags. An Indian leaf motif, such as one finds on Kashmiri and Paisley shawls, would look great scattered in cream on a black table top, or in paisley colours on a cream background.

Use a bushy stencil brush, acrylic colours, and use the brush almost dry, for precision and a soft clear print. A whiff of spraymount on the back will keep your stencil stuck down while you work, and enable it to be peeled off easily and re-used. Rubbing off some of your stencilling with soft wire wool can give it a softer, aged look as will antique glazes. Varnish as above.

Above A small stencilled table adorned with a whacky paisley motif

Left Patterns can be transferred to furniture with carbon paper. Confident, lively brushmarks are the key to effective decoration

FURNITURE PAINTING PATTERNS

Furniture Painting Patterns are designed to look like freehand decoration, but this is a cheat really because the designs are supplied for you to trace off on to your surface via blue transfer paper or carbons.

This is an enlightened form of cheating because having exact patterns leaves you free to cultivate your brushstrokes, and confident lively brushmarks are the key to effective applied decoration, whether your subject is classic wreaths of bay, folksy birds, galloping horses, or romantic sprays of roses. (See page 202 for suppliers of these pattern books. They come with full instructions and tips like using gold pens for borders and gouache colours in gum arabic for delicate florals.)

A fern pattern created from a real fern, which has been sprayed to create a 'negative' image

FERNWORK

Another bright idea from the 'Ladies' Amusements' of a century ago is fernwork. Collect your ferns (fresh or plastic) and use as a template, stippled round in a dark colour so that when you lift the leaf, hey presto, there is its shape in negative. If ferns are arranged (use spraymount on the back) to make a lavish pattern on a cupboard or table painted a soft yellow or cream, and the stippling is done in black, or brown-red, the final effect is close to the elaborate inlaid work in coloured veneers. Fernwork can look spectacular, an antique of the future, so it is worth practising on small-scale objects, like trays, to get control of the technique. Though it is tempting to use spray paints for this work, I think hand stippling with a bushy brush and acrylic colours gives a crisper impression. Orange shellac will give the fern shapes a golden tinge and seal the work. Varnish repeatedly, rubbing down to give a really fine surface.

GRANITE-SPATTERING

One of the students in a furniture painting class brought along a problem for us to solve: a door unscrewed from the melamine-fronted kitchen units she has inherited in her new apartment. The units were faced in a sombre 'Jacobean oak' melamine and the overall effect, she said, was both gloomy and tacky – not her style at all. She wanted something cool, chic and modern. The finish we worked out was inspired (I should say) by a visit to Terence Conran's Docklands kitchen, which sported among much else that was covetable, a good swathe of real granite: grey, speckled and smoothly polished. We agreed on a grey granite painted finish on all the unit doors, starting with the one she brought to the class, with the surrounds to be painted matt black (see Suppliers, page 202, for blackboard black). Finished off with brushed aluminium handles, the formerly dark hole of a kitchen was transformed.

The point to note here is that we combined oil-based primer, and final varnish, for toughness, with water-based emulsion colours for the spattering, which gave us speedy drying and ease of application. Because the woody melamine was semi-shiny we rubbed it down with wet-and-dry paper, dipped into water – just enough to knock back the shine and give a key for paint. Red oxide metal primer is a cheap, tough and widely available primer which I use regularly. We gave the unit door an even coat of this, inside as well as out. Don't skimp by leaving out the inner face of doors: it makes any work look third rate. Melamine cupboard interiors and shelves are a different story: here the easy-clean aspect of the material comes into its own, so leave them be.

The next stage in granite spattering was to paint over the primer with a coat of light grey matt emulsion. A hair dryer speeds drying time and you may need a second coat of light grey, because the primer is there not for show but to strengthen the finish. Try to paint the light grey base smoothly, laying off brushmarks. Now mix three spatter colours: white, black and dark grey. Use acrylic artists' tube colours diluted with water to skimmed milk fluidity; a teacup of each will be ample to spatter an average run of kitchen units. Practise spattering for a few minutes on paper before launching off; it isn't difficult but you will feel more confident once you have the *knack* under control. Don't take up too much colour on the brush; it is a common mistake and leaves wild blobs of colours instead of a fine freckle. Tap the loaded brush sharply on a ruler or a piece of wood (it just needs to be rigid) so that a shower of specks of colour land on the surface to be spattered. You will soon find that

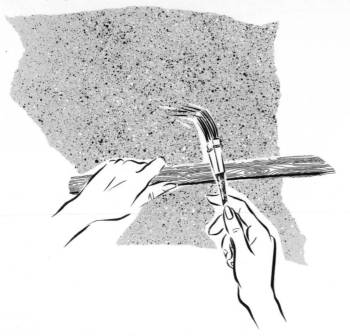

A spattered finish – tap your loaded brush against a piece of wood or ruler, sending a fine shower of speckled colour onto your chosen surface

by adjusting the distance you stand from the surface, and the sharpness of your tapping, that you can more or less direct the spatter where you want it, though it's a good idea to mask off areas you want left clear, using newspaper and masking tape. Another ruse is to unscrew doors completely and spatter them all in a row outside, propped against a wall. It doesn't really make much difference which spatter colour you begin with, though it is customary to have a slightly heavier white spatter than the other two colours. In each case just freckle lightly all over, leaving plenty of base colour showing. Compare with some real granite if in doubt. Spatter colours dry on contact so you can complete the sequence in one go. Varnish as with the cupboards already mentioned, and leave to dry whilst you paint the surrounds with blackboard black. Then re-assemble, adding aluminium or chrome or black handles. Kitchen unit doors might benefit from a second coat of thinned varnish, since they will need fairly frequent cleaning.

LINING

The ability to paint fine, straight, decorative lines on painted furniture is acquired by practice and to some extent by using the right brush and paint of the proper consistency. It is an enviable knack, since neat confident lining adds definition and quality to an ordinary piece. Fine lining following the outline of the chair back, drawer front or table top, is usually associated with period furniture of a certain elegance, while broad washy lines which follow the edges has a more rustic look suited to simple painted pine. A novel use of lining I noticed recently was a gingham check effect created by close, spaced lines crisscrossing over an entire piece, in this case a small table with straight legs (see illustration). This went with broader edge lines, and it all looked lively, attractive and up-to-date. The colour scheme used was sepia lining on a stone-coloured ground.

A small, square table is transformed from the mundane to the magnificent with a lined gingham pattern

Whatever type of lining you settle for, it is a sensible safeguard to cover the whole piece first with a coat of varnish or shellac. When this dries it will allow lines that veer from the straight and narrow to be wiped off cleanly leaving you to try again. If you are anxiously holding your breath, your lining will be hesitant, and the pressure of your brush uneven, spoiling the effect. The ideal is coach-lining, so called because craftsmen with a lifetime's practice could whip a perfect steady and even line round a custom-built car body, but few people today can match that. Anything that makes you feel more relaxed, like knowing your mistakes can be wiped off, is a confidence booster and the more confident you are the more smoothly your lines will flow.

A lining brush definitely helps, because the extra long bristles (see illustration) hold enough paint to complete a line in one movement. There are two lining brushes in general use: the long bristled type and the swordliner, which some people prefer for its compactness. Neither is expensive, so I suggest you try both, giving yourself plenty of practice runs on painted boards. For short runs of lining, a fine artists' sable is quite adequate. A professional tip when lining is not to look at the brush but just ahead of it; this makes for smoothness and control.

Let your two spare fingers slide along the outer edge to help you guide the brush for edge lining

Inset lining on a round table requires a little more practice. First mark out your lines with a compass or a pencil and string

Using a transparent medium for lining is another helpful idea. It looks prettier and allows you to get away with the odd swerve and wobble. Painters generally use oil-based varnish tinted with artists' oil colour for the lining, with a drop or two of white spirit added to make it flow smoothly. Don't make up too much lining colour; an eggcupful will go a long way. If you prefer to use a water-based paint, then acrylic medium or the new acrylic scumble glaze, both tinted with artists' gouache colours, would be a good choice, giving transparency with flow or 'slip'. If it is too thick add a few drops of water.

Edge lining is easier because you can use your two spare fingers (see illustration) to help guide the brush, letting them slide along the outer edge as you apply the paint. Inset lining is considerably more difficult, though a pencilled guideline will help. Try various methods on practice boards. Inset lining on a round table is the hardest of all; here, a fine pencilled guideline done with a compass or a pencil on a string (see illustration) is the answer.

'CHEAT' LINING

Freehand lining has a verve and dash all of its own, but of course there are ways of cheating to achieve a similar effect if such proficiency seems unattainable. Masking tape is a popular aid for painting straight lines. Choose low-tack tape if you can get it because it is less likely to lift paint. To line, simply set two strips of tape the required distance apart, running your nail along the inside edges to make sure they are tight to the paintwork, then run a brush – not too wet in this instance – along the top. When the paint is dry, peel off the tape. For an inset rectangle do the top and bottom lines first, leave to dry, then mark out the side lines and complete the rectangle. You will probably need to tidy the corners with a sable brush. Lining in reverse can be done with narrow car body tape. Let us suppose you want blue lines round a yellow table. Paint the table blue (you may get away with simply painting a broad blue band where the line is to go), then when the paint is dry, apply the tape where the line is to go. Paint over the entire surface with yellow paint, making sure the blue is covered. Leave to dry, then peel off the narrow tape. 'Narrow' here is around 6 mm ($\frac{1}{4}$ in.) and therefore not so fine as a hand-painted line, but useful definition for a tabletop or around drawer fronts.

Lastly there is the super-cheat method, which is simply to draw lines with coloured felt- or fibre-tip pens and a ruler. Metallic pens give quite impressive results if you want gold or silver lines. All this penwork should be 'fixed' with a puff of fixative from an aerosol. You can now buy environmentally-friendly aerosol versions, relatively odourless. After 'fixing', the lines can be varnished safely with the rest of the surface.

All cheat lining, plus less-than-perfect freehand lining, is improved by subtle distressing, so the lines look a little worn and faded. Use fine wire wool for this, making sure the lines are hard dry before rubbing them gently with the wire wool. On broad wash lines you can rub the paint to almost nothing here and there. A final antiquing glaze rubbed over the whole piece will help soften the lining and paintwork nicely and make it look both natural and professional all at once.

A cottagey set of chest of drawers individualized with a painted diamond motif. You can apply lines freehand or use masking tape to steady your edges

Stippling

Stippling into wet glaze gives a svelte appearance to a piece of painted furniture, with a rather thirties feel, especially if you keep to thirties' colours like parchment and ivory. Stippling gets rid of brushmarks, leaving a fine powdery layer of transparent colour. It also makes an excellent background for stencils and other applied decoration. A stippled finish would be a good choice for bedroom furniture, or something you want to look pretty.

Prepping needs to be extra thorough for a stippled finish, with two layers of eggshell base colour rubbed back to smoothness. Over this brush your tinted oil glaze, taking one surface at a time. With a soft painter's dust brush, lightly pounce over the glaze using the bristle tips to create a fine 'mist' of colour. Try to avoid a build-up of colour at the edges. Work out the sequence in which you will glaze and stipple so that you do not have to handle the piece – take out drawers, unscrew doors if possible and lay them flat. Remember to stipple the parts you don't see, like sides and back of doors, top of drawer-fronts – half-finished pieces look incompetent. When the stippling is dry, varnish with extra-pale alkyd varnish *before* embarking on further decoration. This allows you to wipe off experiments should you have second thoughts.

A DISTRESSED PAINT FINISH IN TWO OR MORE COLOURS

Easy and effective, this is one of the most currently fashionable finishes for country-style furniture, old or new. The idea is to mimic threadbare paintwork on old and much-handled pieces where paint tends to get eroded on all the leading edges, down door fronts and round handles and knobs. By using two contrast paint colours an effect is arrived at which is decorative in itself, with the base colour enlivening the top coat colour, and suggestive of aged, layered paint applied over generations of use. This gives country, especially kitchen, pieces a friendly, human dimension, even when – as often happens today – much of it is not wood at all but MDF.

The heavy distressing technique hinges on the use of contrasting paint colours (I use two, but you could try three) with an ordinary wax candle used as a 'parting agent' between them. Wherever you deploy your candle, the under colour will surface through the top coat, with an effect that can be either

Distressing furniture – spread a thick 'resist' layer of wax on areas where you want the undercoat of paint to show through

discreetly decorative, like flecked knitting wool, or boldly graphic. When
choosing colours it is useful to take some existing colour in the room as a
starting point. Remember that more of the top colour will show ultimately than
the one beneath, though the overall tone will be a mix of the two. As a rule of
thumb, dark colours over pale ones look cool and distinguished; strong over
dark colours (barn red on dark green) look folksy and a bit Shakerish; pale
colours used together give a soft pretty effect, unless they are vivid Provençal
shades like bright blue and yellow, when the effect is more Designers' Guild.

Woodwash paints are excellent for this technique because of their covering
power, but you can use standard matt emulsions. If you have odds and ends of
emulsion paints knocking around, try different combinations on boards or card;
the effect is rapidly completed so this could be time well spent.

First apply your base colour thickly enough to cover the entire piece. Brush
it out well, and make sure it gets into cracks, mouldings, the underside of
shelves, etc., then leave to dry (Woodwash dries in 30–40 minutes which is a
help). Now for the candle treatment. You can use the candle on its side,
rubbed over large areas, to create fine flecks, or you can use it like a pencil to
make strong gashes of colour showing through the top coat. Either way, rub the
wax on firmly, so you can *see* it against the light. Lay it especially thick over
prominent mouldings. Now re-coat the entire piece in the top colour, painting
over the whole surface, wax and all. This coat should be thick and opaque.
When dry, using pads of wire wool (first medium, then fine grade), rub away at
your top coat (following the grain if you're painting on wood). Quite soon you
will see the under colour surfacing, cleanly and distinctly. Carry on over the
whole piece. Woodwash and emulsions will 'burnish' up pleasantly under this
treatment. All these emulsion finishes need serious varnishing to protect them
from chips and scratches. Use a mid-sheen or matt varnish. You can rub over a
little dark tan boot polish as an antiquing dodge. When dry, buff this to a *low*
shine.

Apply the top colour over the
whole piece. Rub away at the dry
top coat with wire wool to reveal
the undercoat and amalgamate the
two paint layers slightly

DRAGGING

A dragged finish uses deliberate brushmarks, in a transparent glaze over an
opaque base, to create a discreetly textured finish, reminiscent of fine-grained
timber like old pine. Derived from standard graining practice, dragging can
look immaculate and formal, with the finest pinstripes of colour (from oil-based
paints), or blurry and rustic using casual brushmarks (from water-based paints).
Both are attractive in their different ways, the former being harder to execute
well than the latter. I usually dissuade beginners from attempting to drag entire
walls since it involves constant running up and down stepladders, and requires
both a rock-steady hand on the brush, and a light touch at top and bottom to
avoid darker build-ups of colour. It takes considerable practice and experience
to do a good job of dragging walls. However, dragging comes into its own as a
finish for flat, characterless surfaces like melamine cupboard fronts, veneered
doors, kitchen units in sundry non-woody materials. The 'game' that a dragged
finish sets up in these contexts is an amiable and flattering pretence that the
surfaces we are looking at *are* wood, or at least, 'woody'; the pretence wins
hands down over the anonymous reality.

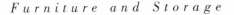

Dragging on perfectly flat doors, large or small, is heightened by an easily executed *trompe l'oeil* detail which hints at panelling by simply painting two pale lines and two dark lines. The 'panels' are dragged in a paler shade, the 'frame' in a darker shade of your chosen colour (shades of grey on white, blue on white, etc.) while the *trompe* lines are usually painted in off-white and sludgy grey. You can use masking tape to keep these under control, or boldly paint them freehand with pencil guidelines.

The trick is to drag the frame in a careful sequence, so that horizontal and vertical stripes cross slickly at right angles, as if joined in the traditional way from pieces of timber, morticed and tenoned. Oil glazes allow time for re-brushing and re-thinking, so this is not difficult provided you keep to the sequence of steps described here.

First pencil outlines of the panel: a 12-mm (½-in.) masking tape outline will keep areas separate. The panel can be dragged or stippled. Use a paler shade of glaze for this, adding more tinting colour when you come to drag the 'frame' (or rails and stiles if you want to be pedantic). If you are careful you can complete the door in one session, though if you have several to do – a run of kitchen units or built-in wardrobes – it may be easier to do all the 'panels' in one go, then all the 'frames' later when the first lot of glaze is dry. When the glaze is quite dry (after 24–48 hours) peel off the tape. This will leave an unpainted rectangle. Make up an off-white mixture of tinted undercoat, and a sludge grey one, with raw umber. Use a flat, hog's-hair artists' brush to hand paint the white lines and dark lines to suggest moulding. If you find it impossible to paint straight lines confidently – it is more difficult on a vertical surface – cheat by outlining the rectangle with masking tape on both sides. Reduce the 'tack' of the tape first (or it may lift off some of the dragging) by sticking down to another surface, then peeling off, or use low-tack tape. Mitre the corners of the lines neatly to give authentic detail. When all is dry, varnish the doors with two coats of extra-pale alkyd varnish, rubbing the second coat down lightly to remove any grit or hairs, which invariably float on to wet varnish.

Dragging with water-based paint produces a soft but rustic streakiness, rather than fine even stripes. The dresser shown on pages 58–59 in the yellow dining room was finished in this way. The base coat was Woodwash in the Driftwood colour, applied to cover opaquely, then left to dry. This was rubbed back a little to give a smooth finish. Then I mixed up two Woodwash colours, Midnight and Conifer, to give a blue-green wash, which was then diluted with water to a milky consistency. This was brushed on, following the dragging sequence described above, but without trying to keep the brushmarks precise; a more even tone was aimed at. The panelled door mouldings were picked out in a slightly darker shade. The whole dresser was varnished with extra flat alkyd, two coats, as protection.

Note: Colourwash, another Paint Magic product, can also be used to give a soft streaky finish over a painted piece. If you plan to colourwash walls (see page 42) allow a little extra to paint fitted cupboards to match, varnishing these as above for protection. This is a classic trick for making intrusive fitments 'disappear' into the overall scheme, thus making the room look larger and more cohesive.

Shelving

Shelving, as I have said elsewhere in this book, is a real boon in a start-up situation. Cupboards may be tidier, but shelves are quicker and cheaper to put up, and in the early days when you are not encumbered with possessions, it is pleasing to re-arrange their contents artistically from time to time. This holds true of kitchen clobber, make-up and cosmetics, tapes and CDs, but most of all, books.

SHELF PACKS

One of the tasks I faced researching this book was to find, install and decorate the best value ready-to-go shelf packs from one of the DIY sheds. I finally chose the B&Q shelving shown on page 179 in the brown study. This consists of deal shelves with supporting brackets, sold individually, though we used five in a stack. The timber was low grade whitewood, but decently cut and bevelled. We painted it all with blackboard black, two coats, followed by two coats of matt varnish for durability. Coloured stains would also look good, varnished for protection. Don't leave this sort of wood untreated; it is soft and porous and will soon pick up stains and look unsightly.

Fixings consist of screws in rawl-plugged holes, drilled into the walls. Use a plumb line and spirit level to locate the screw holes for brackets, making sure they are exactly placed one above another.

On interior or party walls, erecting solid fixings can be a problem. If the shelves are going to carry much weight you need to locate timber studs behind the plasterboard (or lath and plaster) into which you can then drill screw holes. Those with sensitive hearing can locate these by tapping along the wall surface; a solid clunk, rathter than a hollow one, denotes the presence of stud timbers behind (but double-check by boring with a bradawl to make sure). Stud timbers are usually sited a standard 34–46 cm (14–18 in.) apart, so once you locate one it should not be too difficult to find the next which will probably be at about the right spacing for these shelves. Use 4–5-cm ($1\frac{1}{2}$–$2\frac{1}{2}$-in.) screws depending on the load your shelves will carry; the screws need not be massively thick. Brass screws cost a little more but do not rust.

ALCOVE SHELVING

Most oldish houses have fireplaces, or at least the old fireplace flues leading to chimneys on the roof. These project out into the room creating recesses which are a natural and convenient location for built-in shelving on either side. The yellow colourwashed living room on page 26 presented us with just such a situation. The owners were happy to have them fitted out with symmetrical tiers of shelves for their books, but they wanted them to have an architectural look, finished with mouldings all round, and a false skirting at the bottom. Once installed and packed with books and other bits and pieces, everyone agreed that the shelving and contents not only added warmth and character to the room, but surprisingly made a small room look larger.

If you do have empty recesses like these, putting up shelves is a straightforward DIY project. You will need the usual handyman tools: drill, panel saw, hammer, screwdriver, spirit level, plumb line, but any friendly wood yard will cut the materials to size for you, provided you supply them with clear instructions and measurements.

We used MDF (medium density fibreboard) sheets for the shelves, in the standard 2.4×1.2-m (8×4-ft) size and 2-cm (¾-in.) thickness. With supporting battening beneath three sides of each shelf, 2 cm (¾ in.) is sturdy enough to carry books without sagging; if you have a wider span use 2.5-cm (1-in.) MDF instead. Either way wider facing battens are applied to shelf fronts to suggest imposingly weighty timber. Measure up carefully across the recess all the way up from skirting to picture rail or cornice to ascertain the width of each shelf. Old walls are often askew and wider at the top than bottom or vice versa. Take the maximum measurement as your module, resigning yourself to trimming smaller shelves to fit exactly, with panel saw or jig if you have one. If all the shelves are to be the same depth, then 24 cm (9½ in.) is a good size. The number of shelves you need depends on the wall height, the type of books you own (paperbacks need smaller gaps) and the room proportions. Big heavy books are best housed lower down in any shelving system. You might want a wider gap at hip height, or dado rail height, for some sort of display – model boats, pottery or whatever. Time spent drawing this up and checking relevant measurements (average height of paperbacks, etc.) will not be time wasted. We settled for seven shelves, at decreasing intervals as they went up the walls.

We added 20×16-mm (¾×⅝-in.) battening to trim front edges. For a false 'skirting' to fill in the gap below the bottom shelf and the floor, use your existing skirting as a guide. You will also need lengths of 50×12-mm (2×½-in.) battening, plus a decorative ogee or other moulding (timber yards, picture framers) to create the narrow frame which runs right round our shelving concealing battens and fixings as well as adding a finished appearance. Also a generous supply of screws and/or OBO or masonry nails to put up the shelf battens; we used a mixture to combine strength with speed.

Method

Mark up a vertical line, using a plumb bob, down the centre back of each recess (see illustration) using pencil or chalk. This allows you to mark off horizontal shelves accurately using a spirit level. When deciding on intervals between shelves remember to allow for the thickness of the shelves themselves plus their facing battens. Mark up the side walls to the 24-cm (9½-in.) depth of your shelves. A short cut here is to fix the back shelf battens in place on the walls, using screws or OBO nails (or both). Prop the shelves on these, lay the spirit level on top and mark the side walls with a pencil when the bubble is in the right place. This does mean that shelves must be adjusted first, to accommodate any irregularities, and marked so you know where they go in the final stack. It isn't disastrous if shelves don't fit the recess *precisely*; tiny gaps round the sides and back don't matter so long as the fronts line up. A panel saw or jig will trim slivers off where necessary.

The joiner's method is different. Having marked the side battens' positions on the walls, cut them to 12 mm (½ in.) and drill for screws or nails at

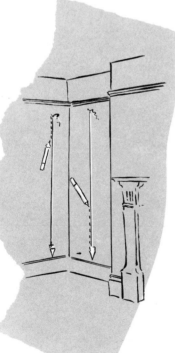

Mark a vertical line using a plumb bob down the centre back of each recess

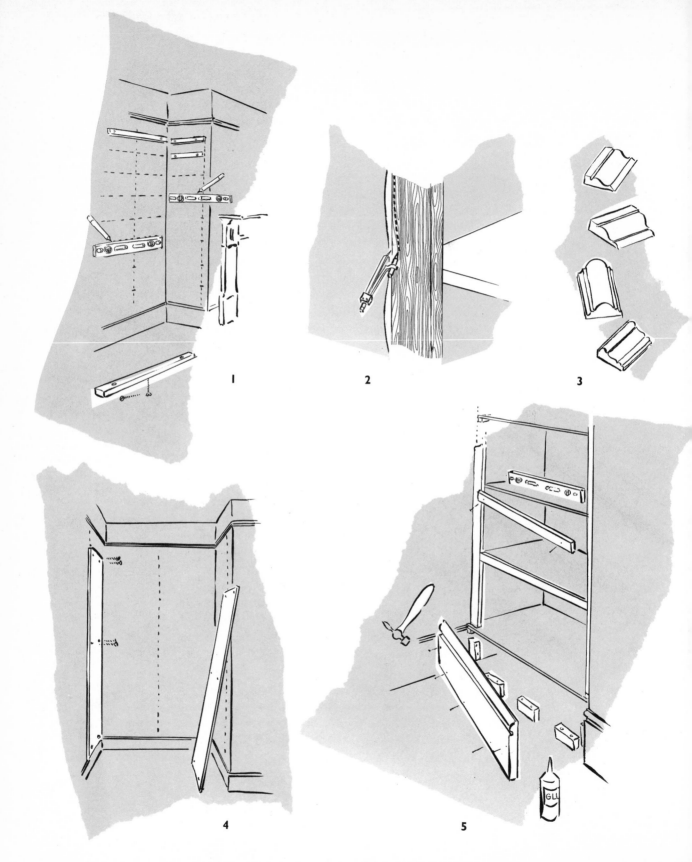

1

2

3

4

5

1 Attach the side battens to the walls using the spirit level to mark their places, then spring the back battens into position

2 Scribe uneven side walls using a pencil and compass in fixed position

3 Choose from a wide selection of decorative mouldings readily available at DIY stores, for the finishing trim

4 Vertical boards screwed to each side of the recess can be the answer if walls are in a very poor condition

5 Cut the false skirting and attach it to wooden blocks nailed to the floor and side skirtings. Cut the front trim for each shelf and glue and tack this into place

approximately the same spacing on each batten (see illustration). Fix to side walls over marked lines, using screws or OBO nails, or both, depending on the walls you are dealing with. Next measure and cut the back support battens and 'spring' these into place between side battens, nailing or screwing to secure at regular intervals. Start sliding the pre-cut shelves into place. Some will slide home snugly, others will need slivers cut off either side to fit irregular walls.

Note: If side walls are in a parlous state, it may be easier to screw vertical boards up each side to hold the side battens securely (see illustration). Because old walls lean about in all sorts of directions, expect to spend some time getting the shelves into place. There may be gaps in some cases and you may need to bang in tiny wedges of wood to hold the shelves firmly. Rest assured, the front battening hides these subterfuges.

Measure, mark and cut the false skirting to fill the gap between the floor and lowest shelf. Nail blocks on which to fasten the skirting, on both floor and sides (see illustration) then nail the skirting in place.

When all the shelves are cut to fit, mark them, remove and squeeze dabs of woodworking adhesive on to the battens and lower edge of the shelves. Wait for the time prescribed then slide the shelves back, and press firmly into place on the battens. Check the shelf levels with the spirit level whilst the glue is again workable, tapping in tiny wedges here and there to make level if necessary.

Remember: It is *critical* that the front edges of the shelves line up vertically so the 'framing' batten can be applied neatly. Check both sides for this using a spirit level.

Do the 'frame' next. If the side walls are uneven they may need 'scribing'. To do this press a batten up against a side wall (see illustration) then with a pencil and compass in fixed position, and the compass point kept firmly against the wall run the pencil up the batten parallel to the wall, to register bulges, etc. Use the jig to cut along the scribed pencil line, giving you an exact fit to the wall surface. Repeat on all verticals, then measure facing for the top shelf, as shown; this can be butt-ended to meet verticals rather than mitred since it is flat. But the decorative ogee (or other moulding) trim should be mitred at the top corners, as shown, before being glued and tacked into place.

Lastly measure, mark off and cut the front shelf trim, shelf by shelf, and glue and tack this into place along each shelf (see illustration).

Leave glues to harden off overnight, or for time stated. To prepare shelves for painting, sand off all surfaces, rounding off sharp splintery edges. Seal MDF shelves above and below with a quick-drying coat of shellac before priming, to prevent them absorbing too much primer. Prime with acrylic primer, which dries in half an hour or so. Smooth with medium grade abrasive paper. Re-prime, dry and sand then finish with one or two coats of alkyd or water-based eggshell, to achieve a smooth, opaque covering coat. Sand lightly and varnish when hard dry with at least one coat of mid-sheen or matt varnish, either alkyd or acrylic. Alkyd is tougher, but acrylic dries in just two hours.

Note: For a de luxe finish a professional painter would spend some time 'filling' any cracks round the shelving – i.e. between the front facing and the wall – with interior filler, sanded smooth when dry, then primed and painted as above.

Both wicker and Lloyd Loom are light and strong and can be rejuvenated by a new coat of paint

Wicker and Lloyd Loom

While superficially similar, with their densely woven surface, wicker and Lloyd Loom furniture are made of quite different materials. Wicker is a natural stripped willow shoot, while Lloyd Loom is a clever imitation made of paper wrapped round a fine wire core. Both make light, strong, attractive furniture which is much sought after in second-hand shops and junk markets. Older versions will have been painted (Lloyd Loom invariably so) but by now look decidedly shabby, not to say scabby. You might be tempted to strip wicker pieces back to the natural colour of the material, but it is truly laborious trying to clean old paint out of the interstices of woven wicker; as you scrape one surface clean you inevitably force more softened paint down into the cracks and crannies. If a wicker piece is thoroughly gummed up with old paint, and special enough to warrant extra outlay, it might be worth getting it cleaned up by a specialist firm, who use a non-caustic stripping bath. The piece will need to be in good condition. A local firm will advise you if you take the piece along. Alternatively, if the piece is large, like a three-seater sofa, they may send someone along to you.

In general, a good clean up followed by a new paint finish will rejuvenate both wicker and Lloyd Loom items, prolonging their usual life. I like wicker painted in a matt finish, with water-based primer and paint, followed by a matt varnish. Lloyd Loom, on the other hand, has a dapper thirties look about it, and on this a semi-sheen eggshell paint seems more appropriate.

Scrub wicker and Lloyd Loom out of doors using a sugar soap solution and a stiff brush. Hose down afterwards and leave to dry out completely. If old paintwork is at all glossy, rub over as much of the surface as you can reach with wet-and-dry paper in order to break down the gloss and give a key for new paint. Brush down afterwards.

PAINTING WICKER

A solidly applied matt paint colour looks distinguished in a dark shade like black or dark green, and pretty and fun in a vivid Mediterranean shade: bright yellow, vivid blue, emerald. White and pastels don't do much for these robust shapes. Either way you will need quite a bit of paint (and perseverance) to work it well down into the weave, so the colour looks solid and uniform. Start by giving the piece a coat of white acrylic primer, slightly thinned with water. This dries quite fast (in about half an hour) with a slightly chalky texture which should be smoothed over lightly with abrasive paper. When the piece is dry you will almost certainly see bits you missed; it's best to go over these, if you can reach them, using a stiff-pointed fitch to get into the cracks. Turning the piece upside down at this stage will help you to get an even coverage.

For solid colour, simply repeat this process, using a good quality matt emulsion brushed well in. Again you may need two goes to arrive at an even finish, but don't overload the piece with paint or you will lose surface texture. When quite dry, give the piece at least one coat of well-stirred matt varnish, slightly thinned with the appropriate solvent and brushed on thinly but thoroughly.

If you prefer a distressed finish, which adds a subtle lift to the final colour, you can achieve this easily by applying primer as above, then brushing on colour and wiping it back randomly with a soft rag, so the white base shows through here and there. This looks softer than solid colour, and flatters the texture of the wicker. Varnish as above. A painted piece which is going to stand outside should have two coats of varnish.

PAINTING LLOYD LOOM

Off beat thirties' colours are worth considering here, such as pinks, almond green and cream. If you can stand the smell (wear a mask and work outside) and fancy a high-gloss finish, car spray paints are a possibility, but you will need more than you expect to give a solid colour – at least two cans to a chair. The advantage of these is that they cover finely, so the woven texture gets less clogged up. Alternatively use a standard oil-based undercoat, followed by an alkyd eggshell. Thin both slightly, brush on very thoroughly but not too thickly, forcing paint into the cracks and allowing coats to dry hard each time. One undercoat plus two thin top coats is about right. Eggshell does not really need varnishing when it's on furniture used occasionally, but if you want to make sure, follow with a coat of eggshell varnish.

Some people brush a coloured glaze over painted Lloyd Loom to enhance the weave, and this can look attractive used with discretion. Use the standard glaze recipe given on page 201, tinted with artists' colours. A couple of shades darker than the base colour gives a pretty effect. You will not need much glaze; 250 ml ($\frac{1}{2}$ pint) is about right for a chair. Brush on generously, leave for a few minutes while you carry on painting another part of the piece, then wipe back discreetly with a soft clean rag so the glaze settles more in the interstices. Leave to dry hard then varnish with eggshell varnish.

Finish off your chair with tailored seat cushions (see page 168).

CHAPTER 6

CHAIR COVERS AND CUSHIONS

One of the quickest ways to smarten up your living space is to re-vamp or re-cover your furniture with swathes of fresh and colourful fabric. If you are renting a flat, this is something you may want to do in a fairly *ad hoc* way – by flinging a large bedspread over an ugly sofa for instance. If the furniture is your own, then there are a number of economical ways of making more satisfactory covers. Which one you choose depends really on how good your furniture is and how much time you have to spare.

Close Covers

Re-covering chairs and sofas is quite a speedy way to improve their looks dramatically, and a great deal easier than re-upholstering from the frame out. It also takes less time and fabric than making a loose cover. The idea of renewing the outer skin of a piece of furniture may sound alarming, but if you are systematic and patient you can achieve excellent results. And if you prefer using a hammer to a needle, it is also more fun. A quite surprising number of upholsterers working today are women, which scotches the notion that this is a trade requiring immense physical strength. It is, however, rough on the hands. It is also messy, and best done in a garage, shed or spare room. However, there is no doubt that this area of DIY is a serious money-saver.

Tools and materials

Beginners can usually get by with a skeleton range of tools for this task. A tack lifter, tack hammer, plus a strong sharp screwdriver for forcing out recalcitrant tacks are essentials (see illustration page 13). So too are a curved upholstery needle, a double-ended needle for buttoning, upholstery twine and boxes of 12-mm ($\frac{1}{2}$-in.) upholstery tacks. Some upholsterers today make use of a power-driven staple gun rather than the old hammer and tacks routine, but there is not much point investing in one of these for a chair or two, and as often happens with high-tech gadgets, there is a downside to stapling. It takes less time to shoot them in, but much longer to prise them out again and a lot of loose covering needs tentative and light movement when slip-tacking the cover, until you have got it right, taut and shipshape. Besides, stapling is frowned upon in the best upholstery circles, being associated with other short cuts like foam padding and stretch webbing. On chairs with exposed or 'show wood' frames you will also need gimp, braid or grosgrain ribbon to cover the rows of tacks, plus gimp pins and a clear contact adhesive to fix this in place over the rows of tack heads.

In some cases – see below – you may also need unbleached calico, hessian or jute sacking, horsehair and wadding. A visit to an upholsterers' suppliers should fit you up with anything too specialized for your local shops (see Suppliers page 202). Horsehair or curled hair is hard to come by these days. It can be worth ripping an old, dilapidated piece apart to salvage the hair.

Preparation

Removing the old cover is the most tedious part of close covering. You should not just rip it off though, because the old cover pieces make useful templates for cutting new ones, saving a lot of time calculating and measuring. Remove the old tacks one by one. Do this by setting the screwdriver at an angle to one side of the tack and banging lightly with the hammer. This levers them up and you can then prise them up easily with the screwdriver or forked end of the hammer.

Remove the old cover in this order. Turn the chair upside down and take off the dust cover on the bottom. The outside arms and back come off next. Start by removing the tacks fastening these to the bottom rail and then work up round the side and top. Next deal with the inside arms and back, and lastly the seat cover.

Lay the cover pieces out flat, with the straight of goods (lengthways weave) all going the same way, to give you an idea how much fabric you need for the new cover. Allow 5 cm (2 in.) extra all round each piece because the old ones will have stretched in use. Most upholstery fabrics are 1.25-m (50-in.) wide, or more. Odd scraps can be used for covering piping cord if you are using it (see page 162 for piping know-how).

Fabric

Close covering looks best carried out in a close-woven, medium to heavy-weight fabric with a little stretch to it. Thick, tweedy fabrics are helpful to beginners, being firm and stretchy, and the texture disguises flaws in the workmanship. Most upholstery fabrics are expensive. You can save material by using cover stretchers – pieces of tough scrap material machined to the cover pieces where they will not show, which means from just below the cleft running round the seat to the point where they are tacked to the bottom rails. If your chair has a loose seat cushion, you can save a bit more by covering the underside of the cushion and the back part of the seat-cover proper with more scrap material. Denim, ticking or canvas are strong but cheap materials for upholstery. Handle these fabrics respectfully and smarten them up with fringe, braid or contrasting grosgrain ribbon, and they can look very distinguished. Their disadvantage, as with all smooth-textured fabrics, is that they show dirt more quickly. Keep on the look-out too for something special which could be used to re-cover a chair – a piece of old kilim rug (they often turn up at sales of household effects), second-hand curtains, often complete with lengths of fringe and braid which could be used to embellish the chair.

When choosing your fabric avoid large patterns with a pronounced repeat, unless you are fairly experienced at dealing with them, because they create a host of special problems in measuring and cutting in order to keep the pattern properly centred on back and seat, and symmetrical on inside arms.

Undercover work

To look really sleek and classy an upholstered piece should have a calico undercover, usually overlaid with a layer or two of wadding. The outside arms and back should be covered in with pieces of hessian too to prevent that caved-in look. If your piece was properly upholstered, it will already have these, and you can go straight ahead with re-covering. If not, you might well consider improving its looks by adding these underpinnings yourself. The materials are cheap, and fitting a calico undercover is good practice for installing the final one. You can build up meagrely stuffed arms, seat and back at the same time, which will make the whole chair more comfortable and twice as good looking. Use curled hair to build up the stuffing. This can be salvaged from an old chair or stool, or bought from upholstery suppliers; 1.5 kg of hair per sq. metre (5 oz per sq. ft) gives approximately 2.5-cm (1-in.) extra padding when compressed. Pick hair over to break up lumps, and then pack it on generously where it is needed – usually a thin layer over the inside back, a thicker one to correct hollows in the seat and a good puff over each arm. The calico undercover will keep it all in place.

Use the old cover pieces as a rough guide when cutting the undercover, adding on a few centimetres (inches) all round to accommodate the extra padding and allow for beginner's mistakes. Fit on and tack down as for the final cover (see below) but set the tacked edges (which should be double thickness or folded back, for strength) 12 mm ($\frac{1}{2}$ in.) within the tack holes of the old cover. Cut pieces of hessian or strong scrap material to cover in the outside arms and back and tack these down, folding the edges in, round the sides and top. Do not cover the bottom rail because the outer cover pieces will have to be pulled through here to be tacked down. Set the tacks 1-2.5 cm ($\frac{3}{4}$–1 in.) apart.

CUTTING AND FITTING THE COVER

Again, use old cover pieces as a pattern. Lay the new fabric out flat and arrange the old pieces – reconstituting their original shape carefully – on top, leaving 5 cm (2 in.) all round to allow for the old material having stretched. Allow more material where you have added padding. *Important*: All the old pieces must be laid out with the straight weave of the cloth corresponding to the straight weave of the new fabric. Squeezing odd bits out on the bias will booby trap your work, because bias stretches just where you need the cloth to be taut. Mark the outlines in chalk. Make sure you have not overlooked a vital piece (front arm panels) or forgotten to cut two of a particular piece. Then cut them out. Any joins should look considered – down the centre of a sofa back and seat for instance. Machine these up first, using a medium-sized stitch. The cover pieces are fitted (or 'installed' as upholsterers say) in the reverse order from the one in which you removed them – seat first, then inside arms and back, outside arms and back and any borders (the part from the seat to the bottom rail of an armchair) and arm scrolls, finishing up with a new dust cover and any gimp or braid trimming.

Stretch the seat-cover fabric smoothly over the seat, pushing the sides and back well down till the fabric hangs over the bottom rail. It takes some trial and error to get the cover pieces smooth and taut, without wrinkles, so do not hurry this part. Begin tacking with slip-tacks, or tacks driven only a little way in so they can be removed easily, while you are adjusting the piece. The object is to get a really tight fit, keeping the weave of the material running straight across and up and down the chair seat. Slip-tack first at the centre front and back, then in the middle of each side, straining the cover smooth and tight each time. Go on straining and slip-tacking round the seat, working outwards from your first tacks. When the whole piece is slip-tacked into position, give it a last critical smoothing over with your hands and correct any slackness by removing the relevant tacks, tightening and re-tacking. When you are satisfied you have got a perfect, tight fit, pull out the centre tacks, fold the cover edge under and re-tack, driving the tack home this time. Repeat around the seat. A double, folded edge stands up much longer to heavy wear than single thicknesses which are liable to tear. Make any further nicks needed to make the piece fit smoothly round the back posts and arm posts, folding the slashed edges in a little and tacking down firmly on each side of the post. The cover may need pleating to fit smoothly at the front corners (see illustration). You can leave the pleat as a pleat, or blind-stitch it (see illustration) with a curved needle and thread.

Do the inside back next. On a stuffed chair the back cover should be nicked to follow the curve of the arms. Push the raw edges well down into the fold here before tacking side pieces to the back posts and the bottom edge to the bottom rail. Turn all edges under again before tacking down.

The inside arms are often the trickiest part of a cover to fit well, as some pleating may be needed to fit the piece neatly round the arm front, and any bungling will show. The fewer and smaller pleats you can contrive, the better – this is done by working the fabric tightly round the curve, and keeping the whole piece with the grain or straight weave running vertically up the inside arm and over the curve. Begin by slip-tacking the centre of each side. Slip-tack right round except for the part to be pleated, making sure you get a smooth curve over the arms. Now make some experimental pleats, following the illustration and holding each one down with a slip-tack. When you are satisfied

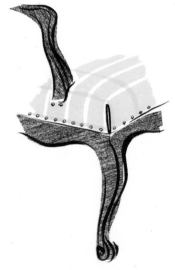

To make a chair seat cover perfectly smooth, you may need to pleat it at the corners

Right For a close fit on the arm front, make several small pleats (the fewer and smaller the better) and slip–tack them in place, before tacking down

Far right Leave the pleat as it is, or blind-stich it

that you have got it just right, tack it down permanently all round. Trim any extra fabric off round the pleated curve. Tear a strip of wadding to pad out the narrow panel, or scroll, down the centre of the arm front. The scroll cover piece is blind-stitched (see illustration) down over the top. If the scrolls are to be piped, tack the piping down first as shown (see illustration). Use hatpins to

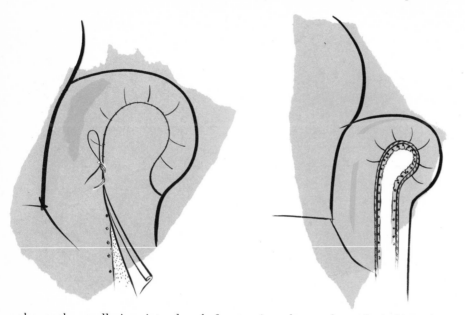

Far left Blind-stitch the scroll cover piece over the top

Left Piping the scroll makes a professional finish (see page 162 for details on covering piping cord)

skewer the scroll piece into place before turning edges under and stitching. An upholsterer's trick is to blind-stitch it from the top using two curved needles, one down either side simultaneously. This prevents it being pulled out of true.

The front border (part between seat front and bottom rail) of a sofa or chair should be tacked or stitched into place invisibly. Do this by laying the border piece, wrong side up, over the front of the seat so that the border edge meets up with the edge of the seat cover and then blind-tack or stitch. When the border is pulled down you cannot see tacks or stitching. A blind-tacked border, particularly when piped, looks tauter if you tack a thin strip of stiff cardboard down on top of the border and piping so as to wedge the border tightly against the piping. This prevents the border sagging a little between the tacks when pulled down tightly.

The border itself should be padded out generously with hair and felted cotton or wadding to give a smooth curve before the cover is pulled down and tacked into place under the bottom rail.

Before finally installing the outside arms and back, tack the lower edges of the hessian undercovering down. Set the outside arms in place first, making sure the upper edge follows the arm curve. This edge can be blind-tacked in position, or stitched, or tacked on from the outside, the tacks then being covered with glued-on gimp, or ribbon. This depends on the style of chair – gimp and trimmings look appropriate on Victorian furniture, but fussy on large stuffed chairs. A first-class upholsterer would neaten these edges with piping, but this is not necessary. The bottom edges of the outside arms and back should be brought right down under the bottom of the chair before being tacked down, unless the chair has an exposed wooden frame. Cover the outside back

A bedroom should be a retreat, one quiet place in a noisy household.
A touch of fantasy and escapism seems appropriate, and lace, flowers
and floating drapes give a boudoir-feeling with ridiculous ease.
Bathrooms are usually smaller spaces, but they also unleash all sorts
of exhibitionist or eccentric decorative schemes – who needs a sunken
jacuzzi or a mirror-panelled bath when you have bold colours,
flamboyant furnishings and whacky collections of memorabilia to
contemplate?

145

Right This detail shows how successfully paint can disguise tacky white melamine. The flimsy moulding allowed us to try two techniques, dragging on the surround, stippling on the panels, picking out mouldings with a further coat of glaze applied with a fine brush.

Below Verdigris stippling updates a curly black magazine rack, whilst a rose découpage hat-box cunningly picks up the floral themes throughout the room.

PROJECT 4: THE ROSE BEDROOM

This is the front first-floor room of a turn-of-the-century terrace house in a city suburb. Generous bay windows, good quality plank floor, and original lime-plastered walls are original to the house. The lime plaster emerged from under layers of wallpaper whilst ancient lino was peeled back to reveal the splendid floorboards, which only needed a good scrubbing. We went for a romantic look with pretty colours, florals, floating drapes on the bed. The home-mixed soft distemper on the walls, coloured aquamarine with universal stainers, turned out triumphantly on the lime plaster, drying to a velvety texture. The same stainers were used to tint a matching oil-glaze finish for a wall span of melamine-fronted cupboards, an inherited feature, useful but hideous. Universal stainers will tint both water- and oil-based paints. Doing a glaze number over the melamine transformed the room, losing the whole melamine expanse and pulling the room together visually. Rose-printed union curtains were secondhand finds, whilst the rose border was cut from a roll of cheap wallpaper, then pasted down. Laborious but effective. A charming 'deco' period dressing table was limed to lighten its colour, and a touch of silver leaf and paint picked up its detailing. A mosquito net hung from a cup hook provided instant feminine glamour to the bed.

Above Carl Larsson-type bows and swags make a decorative stencilled frieze round this low-ceilinged cottage bedroom. Anything heavier might have looked clumsy. But the eyecatcher here is the *trompe l'œil* treatment of fitted cupboards with sliding doors, painted up to resemble a colourful *armoire*, complete with iron hinges, dentil cornices and lurking cat.

Right The simplest unbleached calico drapes soften and screen a pretty bedstead, covered with a splendid patchwork of tiny solid blue and gingham squares. Books and china brighten up a cupboard which doubles as a radiator cover.

Above A tender and whimsical artist's bedroom, full of ingenuity and unexpected ideas. Bed posts are salvaged balusters with added finials. Shell decoration is painted free-hand. Mirror-backed candle sconces are a romantic alternative to bedside lights.

Left A bedroom can double as a quiet spot to work in – it would be delightful to write letters or novels at this sensible desk, with reference books to hand. A big picture removes any 'home office' associations and a cream Roman blind economically covers a large window.

PROJECT 5: THE STARRY BLUE BATHROOM

Another room in Jason and Kate's terrace house (see page 90). This was originally the back bedroom, complete with a tiny range and hob but, being a small space, it made far more sense as the bathroom. Inspiration for the deep blue paper sprinkled with pale stars came from a picture of a Swedish 'fatehbur', or display cupboard, in my book of Scandinavian interiors. The mahogany bath surround was another salvage-yard find, cut down to fit a shortish bath and French-polished for a rich lustre. The floorboards were treated with two bright coats of red oxide metal primer, which we varnished before adding a bright kelim rug. the spotted enamel kettle, antique mirror and colourful clothes basket are more treasures from the owners' bargain-hunting forays into junkyards and car-boot sales.

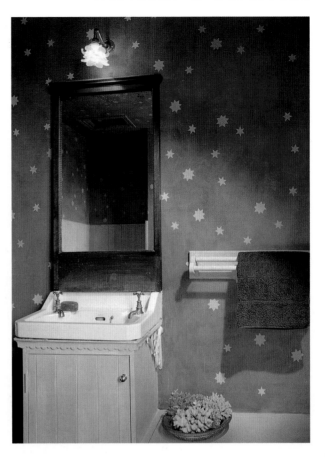

Right Jason wanted the starry-night sky effect on walls and ceiling. We used sea-blue colourwash, wiped over a mid-blue matt emulsion, to arrive at a deep but not dismal blue, with a painterly texture to it, thanks mainly to rough old plaster beneath. Stars were stencilled on randomly, using the same Driftwood paint used for woodwork throughout.

Above A small. ceramic basin, complete with brass taps, was given a fitted cupboard below for medicines and cosmetics. Plumbing is covered by a capacious box alongside, with a lift-up lid for storing cleaning materials. A simple white dowel rail holds towels. The mirror just happened to fit neatly above the basin. The pretty old wall light, complete with original frilly glass shade, gives just enough light to be useful. Cupboards were woodwashed again, but given extra coats of matt alkyd varnish as protection since they will get plenty of handling. The cupboard door is made of tongue-and-groove timber, cut to measure and battened behind.

Left If space allows, introducing more and unexpected furnishings can give a civilized, even luxurious air to a functional bathroom space. Walls here have been scraped clear of old paper and paint and retained in all their 'distressed' splendour of colour and texture. Note the splendid ceramic dishes displayed in the wall cabinet. An ideal place perhaps to display objects you like to contemplate but prefer to keep safely out of reach.

Above Several clever notions packed into a small compass. Panelling is salvaged, stripped and re-painted. The zig-zag edging to the bathroom shelf is a strong decorative accent easily cut from plywood using a jig- or fret-saw. Paint it a contrasting colour as here. Hand-painted flowerpots make amusing decorative holders for soap and sponges. The sun-in-glory medallion is a cheerful extra. Note the old-fashioned washbasin and ewer.

in the same way. Stitch the covers where outside back and arms meet, using the curved needle as shown for the seat cover corners. The stitches should be small horizontal ones, with the needle moving forward invisibly underneath.

Gimp and ribbon are glued in place using a colourless instant adhesive. Put plenty of glue on the wrong side, leave it to soak in for a moment, then stick it down, a small length at a time, over all visible tacks around the exposed wood frame. Ribbon is prettier than most gimp sold today, but a little tricky to stick round curves, where it needs to be pleated and tacked down with gimp pins. Use 12-mm ($\frac{1}{2}$-in.) grosgrain ribbon; anything else is too flimsy. Finally tack a new dust cover, which can be made of any scrap material, over the bottom of the chair.

GENERAL TIPS

When removing the old cover examine each piece carefully to see just how it was put on.

If you run stitching twine over a cake of beeswax (available from hardware shops) before using it, you will find the stitching goes more smoothly and the wax makes the twine stronger and prevents knots.

Clean upholstered surfaces by going over them frequently with a vacuum cleaner, banging the stuffing back into shape at the same time. Shampoo with suds only – an eggwhisk froths up a splendid amount of suds.

Loose Covers

Short of completely re-decorating, nothing so radically improves the look of a room as re-covering the main pieces of furniture. The shabbiest sofas and chairs take on sleek and prosperous airs when zipped into fitted covers in good plain colours or brilliant prints. Covering a chair is a bit like dressing a problem figure; there is lot one can do to disguise its bad points. Soft or neutral colours play down ugly shapes and lumpy contours. A corner-pleated valance or quilted band round the bottom hides bulbous feet and gives furniture a streamlined look. Understuffed chairs and sofas are greatly improved, both in comfort and looks, by a plump seat cushion (two in the case of a sofa) covered in the same fabric.

Anyone who can make clothes can make loose covers, and doing so will save a *lot* of money. I should explain, incidentally, that 'loose' in this context means removable; a loose cover can and should fit like a glove. Once you have grasped the principles of cutting and fitting, it is actually easier to make a well-fitted cover than a well-fitted dress. The chair does not move or scream when you stick pins in it, or mysteriously expand between fittings. Its contours are large and simple, and you can take as long as you like crawling round it adjusting seams. The sections of a cover are cut out in simple rectangles (measured of course), and then shaped, pinned and tacked *in situ*, and finally machined up in one operation. Piping is inserted at the pinning stage. Piping is invariably used by professionals because it looks neat and reduces wear on the seams, but it is a bit tricky to handle if you have never piped a seam before, and it does emphasize the shape of the chair, which might not be a good thing. Also it takes more material.

Before buying the material it is worth spending time measuring up the piece or pieces with some care. Any standard quantities that might be quoted to you by shop assistants or magazines invariably err on the generous side and you may be left with a piece of material too large to throw away and just too small to cover anything else with. If you have some idea of the particular fabric you want, so much the better, because furnishing fabrics come in varying widths. Standard British width is 1.36 m (54 in.) but some imported fabrics are 1.2 m (48 in.). Any of these widths will accommodate the average armchair without joins in any of the main pieces (I suggest you begin with an armchair for this reason) but the really wide fabrics also allow you to cut most of the smaller pieces from the off-cuts.

Avoid large patterns with repeats for the reasons given under 'Close covers'.

Measuring up

First consult the illustrations. There are ten sections to measure up for covering the chair shown, and these are designated alphabetical letters. A band or pleated valance round the bottom will require extra material, as would a seat cushion. Incidentally, this type of chair looks twice as luxurious with a cushion. The actual cushion need not cost much if you use the innards of old pillows and bolsters to stuff it with.

It helps get the plan clear in your mind if you draw a long rectangle on paper representing your length of fabric and draw out the pieces on it – not to scale, but just to ensure you have not left anything out. It is only the *length* of each section you have to worry about when working out the total fabric requirement.

Measure sections *a*, *b*, *c* and *d* lengthways, as shown by the lines, adding 13 cm (5 in.) to each measurement. This is for the tuck-in all round the seat, which anchors the cover to the chair. Then measure *e*, *f* and *g* – the back and

A shabby armchair can be given a new lease of life with fresh, well-fitting loose covers

Left Take measurements from the front for sections *a, b, c, d, h, i* and *j* (also *x* if you wish to make a valance)

Below Take measurements from the back for sections *e, f* and *g*

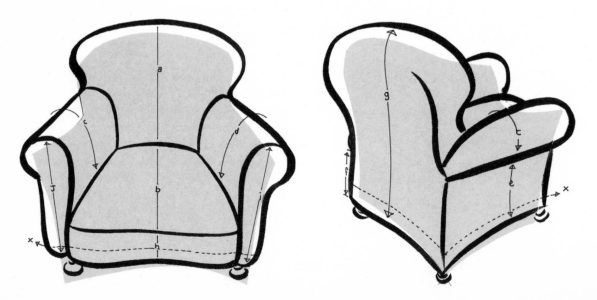

sides – from the seam in the original upholstered cover down to about 2.5 cm (1 in.) above where the legs begin if you are having a valance or quilted band (instructions for both come later), or down to the floor if you are finishing the cover with fringe or a plain hem, adding 5 cm (2 in.) for the hem in the last case. Finally measure h, hereafter called the 'border' for simplicity's sake, and i and j, known in professional jargon as the 'front arm quirks'.

Some types of chair have a corresponding flat piece (like ears close to the head) either side of the back, and these are called side quirks. If your fabric is a wide one, you should be able to cut quirks and border out of pieces left over from cutting the main sections. Add a 2.5-cm (1-in.) seam allowance to each length measurement. By totting up all your measurements you will arrive at a pretty exact idea of the quantity required. To measure up for a valance or band (the band takes the least material) measure right round the chair at the height where you want it to start. (Don't make it too narrow, a deep border of some kind improves the proportions of most chairs.) For a corner-pleated valance, which looks smarter than box pleats, or a gathered frill, add 60 cm (2 ft) to the all-round measurement. Now measure the drop down to the ground, adding 5 cm (2 in.) for hems and seams.

To measure up for a seat cushion, measure the length from back to front of the seat, add on 2.5 cm (1 in.) for seams and double the result. A seat cushion cover has an inset band running right round it (see illustration). Again you may be able to contrive this from odd pieces. If you are doubtful add 20 cm (8 in.) to your total length.

When measuring up for a sofa cover allow two widths across the back, inside back, seat, border and valance or frill. Also allow for two seat cushions instead of one. One point to remember when making up is that a two-seater sofa is generally covered in two widths with a seam plumb down the middle, whereas a wider sofa is covered with the width of fabric across the middle and seams at the sides. These practices may seem arbitrary, but actually they look better this way.

This may all sound like a lot of palaver just to work out your fabric requirements, but accuracy saves money at this stage. Once you have had a little practice you will be able to do most of the arithmetic in your head.

Cutting out

Marking out and cutting your cover sections follows much the same procedure as measuring up, except that this time you need width as well as length measurements and you chalk these on to the fabric itself. Measure every section from a to j across at the widest point, adding a 2.5-cm (1-in.) seam allowance. This measurement plus the length measurement you already have gives you a rectangle corresponding to each particular section. Measure and chalk out these rectangles on to the fabric, marking each one with its alphabetical letter so that you know where you are. Before cutting make sure (a) that you have not left out any pieces, (b) that your rectangles are laid squarely over the fabric so that the edges follow the grain (a T-square could help here), and (c) that you have not overlooked seam allowances here and there – allow 2.5 cm (1 in.) per seam. Cut out all sections except the seat cushion and valance or border.

Shaping and fitting

It helps to chalk lines down and across each section of material at the exact centre, and mark similar lines on the corresponding chair sections so you can pin each piece on squarely and make sure none of them gets pulled askew while fitting. *All pieces are pinned and fitted to the chair inside out.*

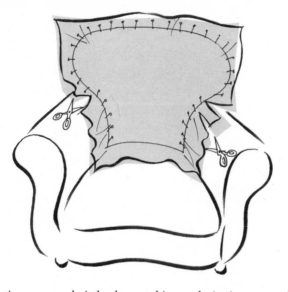

Pin section *a* to the chair back, using short diagonal nicks to let the fabric lie flat at the arm join

Place section *a* over chair back, matching and pinning centre lines. Tuck extra fabric in round seat, and into sides. Cut a short diagonal nick at both sides (see illustration) to let the fabric lie flat over the curve where the arm joins the chair. Repeat for *b*, *c* and *d*, tucking in extra fabric and pinning at centre marks. You may need to cut nicks in *c* and *d* as for *a* to make the fabric lie flat over the arms. Now pin *g* to the back, pinning *g* to *a* as these meet along the top seam line, following the curves either side. Smooth *g* to chair back and pin at sides. Now pin *e* and *f* to chair sides, pinning to *c* and *d* along the arms, and to *g* down the back. Finally pin *h* to chair front and then to *b*. I find it simplifies fitting to cut *i* and *j* (the quirks) to shape before pinning in place and attaching to the rest of the cover. To do this cut a newspaper pattern to the shape of the quirk on the upholstered cover and transfer this to your fabric pieces, allowing a 12-mm ($\frac{1}{2}$-in.) seam allowance all round when cutting. Now pin to chair quirks. You may need to shape *c* and *d* to curve smoothly over the arm fronts. This looks neatest done with two or three small darts. Pin these in place and then pin quirks to the cover sections all round – *j*, for instance, is pinned to *h*, then *c*, then *e*.

Now, having satisfied yourself that all your fabric sections are lying smoothly and squarely over corresponding chair sections, you can begin adjusting and tightening and trimming off extra material where necessary. Section *a* will need darting, for instance, to follow the bulges either side. If the seat overhangs a bit in front you may need to take a few tucks in *b* at each front corner if the border is to lie flat to the chair. If your chair has sides and back which slope sharply inward, giving it a top-heavy look like a butterfly-stroke champion (all shoulders and no legs) you can disguise this by letting the vertical seams at the back and sides drop instead of taking them in to lie close to the chair. When you think you have pinned your cover to perfection, tack all the main seams except for those round the quirks. Pull out the tuck-in round the seat and pin and tack this all round, making a diagonal seam where *a* meets *c* and *d* over the bulge of the arms. Tack all seams firmly, and not too loosely, as you want the edges to hang together while machining.

Unpin *i* and *j* (front quirks), machine any darts and machine up all seams except for one seam at the back, where you will put the placket and fastenings for the cover. Put the cover back on the chair inside out, smoothing out and tucking in, and now pin and tack *i* and *j* in place. Then machine.

The bottom of the cover should be finished off before you sew in the fastenings. I favour a machine quilted band because it uses the least material, is heavy enough to improve the hang of the cover, does not take long to do and looks solid and nice. It's best used on a fairly straight-sided chair or sofa. Shelving sides need a pleated valance.

An interlined band adds a finishing touch

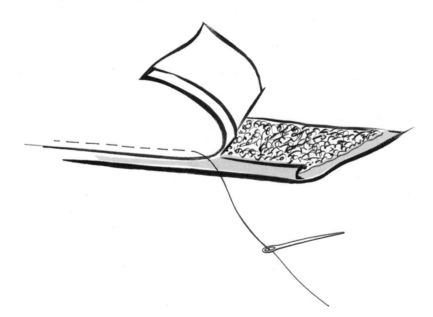

To make the band, cut the previously measured pieces and join into one continuous strip. Back it with something fluffy like a strip of old blanket or interlining, and a strip of plain scrap material so that you have a sandwich with fluffy filling. Turn a 2.5–4-cm (1–1½-in.) hem up over the filling along the bottom edge of the band and tack down loosely. Fold lining material under and tack over this (see illustration). Lay the band out flat and pin or tack all three thicknesses together here and there so they can be machined as one. Machine several rows all the way along your band in whatever grouping you like; a few rows wide apart, or one or two wide apart and several bunched together. It does not matter if your lines are not dead straight, and if the fabric puckers a little here and there as you quilt it.

To attach band to cover, draw a chalk line right round the cover on the *right side* at the correct height. Remove cover and pin band to chalk line, keeping right sides of band and cover together. Tack in place and machine.

To make the corner-pleated valance, cut your measured strip. Allow 15–20 cm (6–8 in.) at each corner for an inverted pleat. Chalk a line around the cover bottom where the valance is to start. Measure the width of each section separately along the line and mark it off on the strip, adding and marking off 15–20 cm (6–8 in.) for the pleats at corners. Fold pleats and tack down. Tack valance to chalk line, making sure pleat opening is exactly over chair corner and follows on the cover seam. Machine. Turn up hem round bottom and machine or hemstitch. The valance will look crisper if you line it, though this is more trouble. To line simply tack a piece of plain cotton the same size as the valance before pleating, and pleat, stitch and hem as one.

If you are edging the hem with fringe, or just leaving it plain, simply turn back the hem allowance and hemstitch or machine down. Fringe is stitched into place by hand. Cotton rug fringe is cheap and looks good on matt-textured fabrics. To give a plain hem a bit more definition, you could make a rouleau edging of the same fabric, by stitching a strip of the fabric over fairly thick cord, or even rope, if it is not too springy, as for piping (see illustration page 162). This is then machined or hand-stitched round the hem on the inside, leaving only the rouleau visible.

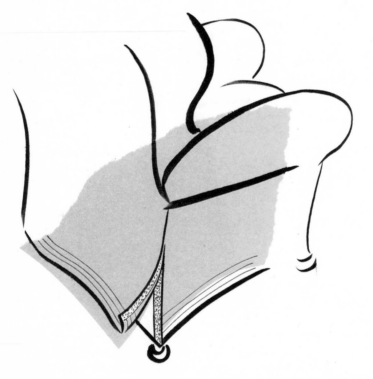

Velcro strips sewn to each side of the back opening are the easiest fastening

The easiest fastening for your loose covers is a strip of Velcro, machined each side of the back opening (see illustration). You will need to sew a strip of fabric to one side to give enough overlap for your Velcro to be hidden. There are other alternatives: a zip, inserted as for a garment, with the opening at the *bottom*; press-stud tape as sold in most needlework shops, machined on as for Velcro; or, cheapest of all, and perhaps the longest lasting, good old hooks and eyes, large size, firmly sewn to a neat placket.

Boxed seat cushions

First you need the cushion. As I said, any old pillows and bolsters can be cannibalized for the stuffing, the softer and downier the better. Buy strong feather-proof ticking for the cushion case itself because feathers work their way through any less closely woven fabric. The cushion cover will follow the shape of the case exactly, so cut the case to a pattern and use the same pattern for the cover. The cushion should fit tightly into the seat space since this looks more generous.

On chairs with set-back arms the seat and its cushion usually project; on other chairs it follows the line of the seat, coming well forward at the front edge. Lay a large sheet of newspaper over the seat and mark it round with a pencil, folding the paper to guide you. Make sure your pattern is symmetrical by folding down the middle.

Cut two pieces of ticking according to the pattern but add 5 cm (2 in.) all round to ensure that it fits the seat tightly when sat on. Measure round the edge of your ticking pieces and cut a strip 7.5–13-cm (3–5-in.) wide and long enough to go right round, with 2.5 cm (1 in.) for a seam at the ends. This strip determines the fatness of your cushion, which will depend on the depth of the chair seat, the ultimate height from the ground (you do not want to be perched too high) and the softness of the filling; 7.5–10 cm (3–4 in.) is right for most chairs. Really soft down filling is better stuffed into a very fat cushion as it squeezes down so far when sat on.

Tack the strip to both cushion pieces, wrong sides out, to make a bag (see illustration), making sure the pieces are squarely on top of each other by pinning first. Machine up, leaving ends of the strip open. Insert stuffing here in handfuls till the cushion is plump. Overstitch the gap in the string with small tight stitches. Make the cover in the same way, but sew up the ends of the strip and leave a section of the cushion cover seam open at the back so that you can get the cushion in. These openings are usually finished with a long zip, inserted as for a dress opening.

Your completed cover will be much stronger if you oversew the seams. This is worth the effort if you have bought a good, expensive fabric and want to get the most wear out of it. Use a machine for this.

Above
Boxed seat cushions look very smart in economical mattress ticking or sturdy canvas

Below
Tack the strip, wrong sided out, to both cushion pieces to make a bag

Right
A finished boxed seat cushion with its smart new cover

Piping

The illustration on page 162 shows a clever way of cutting material for piping that does not leave you with dozens of lengths to join separately. Piping cord should be boiled or put through a hot wash to pre-shrink it (if the cover is washable) before making up. Cut bias strips of material 4–5-cm ($1\frac{1}{2}$–2-in.) wide depending on the thickness of cord and material. Fold the strip over the cord, pin and machine, using a special piping foot, as close to the cord as possible. Covers are usually piped along all the outside seams. It is inserted, raw edges outwards, along all the seams after the sections have been shaped and fitted. Pin and then tack through cover edges (right sides together) and piping thicknesses all at once, tacking as near to the cord as possible. Don't pull the piping too taut, or the cover will pucker, but don't let it slacken either. Snip through the material, almost up to the cord, at the corners for a good fit. I think it is best to machine up the main seams with piping first, leaving the quirks to be fitted and seamed separately, because it may take a little adjusting before you get both quirks exactly symmetrical, with the piping evenly distributed round them. Machine up with piping foot, as before.

COTTON CHAIR 'PINAFORES'

There is a 'stalkiness' about chair legs *en masse* which can get a bit oppressive in a smallish room. A simple, elegant and cheap solution is to run up a set of pinafore type covers that conceal all these legs beneath valances that reach almost to the floor. In posh shops these will cost as much as the chair, but you can make them for peanuts if you use cotton duck (a type of close-weave canvas) and calico, like the set I made for the picture on page 59. I added blue piping, for smartness, but this is optional. The making takes about two hours per chair.

Materials

I allowed approximately 1.1 m ($3\frac{1}{2}$ ft) of cotton duck per chair, roughly half as much calico, as it is only used to line the valance, and 1.2 m (4 ft) of thick piping cord per chair plus approximately 1.1 m ($3\frac{1}{2}$ ft) of contrast coloured cotton to cover the piping. Make sure you have lots of pins, and also a piping foot for your sewing machine.

Method

Dining chairs vary considerably in their shape. The set of four I covered were junk shop finds, with high curving backs and cabriole legs: twentieth-century repro versions of a Queen Anne style, stained and varnished, with padded seats. The same covers would look just as good on squarer chairs, with straight legs, and be somewhat easier to make, since the heart-shaped top and the cabriole bulge of mine necessitated more fitting. I had to make a dart in the valance, for instance, to accommodate the outward curve of the front legs (see illustration).

Begin by putting your fabrics through a hot wash on your washing machine to pre-shrink them. Press the fabrics when damp if possible.

There are six pieces to cut out for these covers (see illustration). I started by measuring the back panel. Take the measurement of the chair back from top rail to floor, allowing for 4-cm (1½-in.) seams. Next take the inside of the chair back from top rail to seat, allowing for 2.5-cm (1-in.) seams. Measure the chair back at its widest point, allowing for 12–18-mm ($\frac{1}{2}$–$\frac{3}{4}$-in.) seams. Cut rectangles of the duck to fit roughly these measurements. If you are nervous of cutting into your cloth in this vague way (no pattern) allow a few centimetres (inches) in every direction for second thoughts. The beauty of using cheap fabric is that you can be a bit wasteful.

Next pin the two halves of the chair back cover as shown, inside out, on the chair. Trim as necessary. Covers like these do not have to be a glove-fit, but they should not be baggy either. Remove, fold in half to make sure that both sides are symmetrical, trimming where necessary, and making sure that both pieces are cut on the straight of the fabric. Lay the roughly measured and cut square of fabric over the seat, adjust, leaving seam allowances on all four sides.

Finally cut the valance. To do this take the seat to floor measurement plus a 2.5-cm (1-in.) seam allowance and the circumference of the chair seat, giving you a longish rectangle. Cut this in the duck and also the calico, which lines the valance.

If you are making several matching covers, now is the moment to cut the remaining covers, using your first set as a pattern. It is easy to get into a muddle with so many pieces of indistinguishable fabrics to cope with, so assemble the bits for each separate cover and keep them in separate plastic bags till you are ready to sew them together.

The Queen Anne chairs I covered required darts in the valance to fit over the outward curve of the legs

Below The six pieces needed to make a chair pinafore

Right Pin the two halves of the chair back cover, right sides together, on the chair

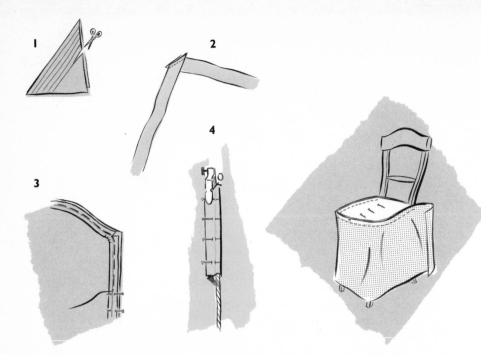

I A clever way of cutting bias strips for piping along a 45° fold

2 Join bias strips together to make a continuous strip

3 Baste the piping to one side of the back cover, before placing the other side of the cover over this, right sides together, and machining as close to the piping as possible. Make cuts in the piping material to accommodate corners neatly

4 To save time, you can machine across the shaft of pins

Left Pin the lined valance to the seat cover

Below The extra lengths of valance are hidden by the floating back panel

Piping should be made before assembling the covers. I piped the inside back and seat only, but the piping could continue down the back panel to the floor (see illustration). Measure the length of the piping fabric, along a 45° fold as shown. Each strip needs to be approximately 3-cm ($1\frac{1}{4}$-in.) wide. Machine all these together as shown (see illustration) to make one continuous strip. Next fold this round the piping cord and pin, then, using a piping foot on your sewing machine, machine the piping material as close to the cord as possible, stretching both a little as you go. You can machine across the shaft of pins (see illustration) to save time.

Machining across pins is a viable way to stitch the cover together too, if you are not too fussy, but you may find you have to re-do certain seams, thereby losing on the swings what you gain on the roundabouts. Fabrics have a way of stretching unequally, as you machine, leading to unwanted little folds and puckers. If using piping it definitely pays to go the slower way, which means pinning, then basting (tacking), then machining the piping round the seat and the back cover (see illustration).

Next machine the two halves of the back cover together, using pins only. You *must* use a piping foot if you are piping the cover because it allows you to stitch really close to the piping.

The valance and lining should be stitched together, inside out, round the bottom and side. Allow a good 12-mm ($\frac{1}{2}$-in.) seam all round. Turn the right way round and press flat to make a neat rectangle with one long raw edge, which goes round the seat cover. Baste this edge, smoothing the length flat on a long table.

Now lay the seat cover, piped or unpiped, upside down on the chair, fixing it in place if possible (I pinned it through the seat pad). Find the centre of the valance, and pin in place inside out on the seat (see illustration). Carry on

Below Line the floating back panel with calico

Right Continue piping right down the back panel to the floor

Above Pin the chair back cover to the seat and valance piece across the back of the chair seat

round the chair seat, pinning the valance so it clears the floor by about 12 mm ($\frac{1}{2}$ in.). Some people make inverted pleats on the front corners, but I like the simplicity of the shape shown. The two extra lengths of valance which meet at the chair back are hidden by the back flap (see illustration) so they can be attached by whatever seems the simplest means – two tapes, Velcro, even safety pins. Machine valance to chair seat cover, or baste first to try out, if in doubt.

Finally slip the chair back cover and the joined seat and valance piece back on to the chair, inside out, and pin the two together across the back of the chair seat (see illustration). This is a critical seam: too tight and the seam rides up off the chair back, too loose and the seat cover flops down off the front edge instead of delineating it trimly. So be prepared to fiddle about, pinning and re-pinning and perhaps tacking too, before the final '*coup de machine*' which unites both halves.

Note: Where two sections of piping cross, your machine may balk. Try sewing very slowly, turning the wheel by hand and easing the fabric through. Never force the machine as the needle will just snap. An alternative solution is to stitch these small bits of seam by hand, using stout thread, a thimble and sheer determination.

All that remains is to line the back floating panel (see illustration) using more calico. Do this with the assembled cover in place but inside out, pinning the calico lining on as shown. Machine, turn right side out and press flat and machine again right across to secure it, as shown.

Trim and notch all seams, especially on curves and corners, for a sleeker fit and oversew these by machine if you wish. Attach tapes or Velcro to the back panel corners as shown. Turn right side out, slide on to your chair and, hey presto, a neat tailored shape emerges. Classy stuff. If you hate repeating yourself as much as I do keep the first finished cover before you as an encouragement while you repeat the process again and again and again.

Re-caning Chairs

Sets of old dining chairs are increasingly hard to find. Attractive modern ones tend to be expensive, while sets of so-called antique chairs – usually Edwardian – command exorbitant prices. One cheap way round this difficulty is to hunt out old cane-seated chairs with the caning gone, and learn to replace it yourself. Chairs of this type, often with a piece of plywood tacked over the seat, turn up in junk shops and sale rooms for very modest prices by present-day standards.

There is less competition for these chairs, pretty though they may be, because most people cannot be bothered to find someone to re-cane them. Also, a professional re-caning job works out expensive. If you do it yourself the cost is minimal. Any tools needed can be improvised from what you have lying about – a length of wire to help thread the cane through, and something like an icepick to use as a bodkin in the last stages of caning.

Caning is not the mystery it looks. It is a straightforward, simple process: it is the perfect job to do sitting in the garden on a hot day. Any mending, strengthening or titivating of the chairs should be done before caning them. Old paint and varnish may need to be stripped off (following the method described on page 117). Most caned chairs were made of undistinguished wood and look better painted, stained a bright colour or 'distressed'. Any loose joints should be re-glued with wood adhesive and left to dry under pressure; a tight bandage of tape or string will usually do the trick. The rows of holes round the seat must be cleared of old pegs or bits of cane, or old paint if you have stripped them down. Banging a sharpish tool, like a bradawl or icepick, through the holes with a hammer will clear them but do not use so much force you split the wood.

MATERIALS

Seating cane is a split cane with a hard, glossy finish on one side. It comes in various widths, Nos. 2 to 6 being the ones most commonly used for chair seats. The standard pattern for cane seating has six strands of cane woven in and out of each other and passing through the holes, so you need a narrower cane for this, Nos. 2 or 3, or 2 for the first four stages and 3 for the next two to give a bit of variety. It is tempting to use the caning patterns which use only four strands, but these are not so strong and are really only suitable for bedroom chairs or chair backs. For beading – the cane which is laid flat around the seat – choose a thicker cane, No. 6. Split cane can be bought from most handicraft shops, or ordered by post.

METHOD

Soak the cane for a few minutes in cold water to make it pliable. Keep the extra cane in the bucket till needed (take it out at the end of each stint though,

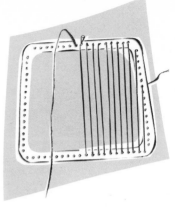

1 The last strands of cane on each side will have to go through holes along the sides

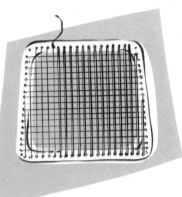

2 Thread the cane across the cane seat

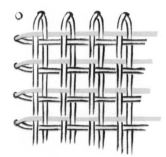

3 Repeat stage 1, taking the cane in and out through the same holes

or it will start some mysterious fermentation process). Keep a sponge handy to damp the cane as you work and keep it flexible.

Begin by counting the number of holes along the back and front of the chair. There will usually be more along the front as most chair seats are wider at the front. Find the centre holes. Start caning from the centre holes outwards because the last few strands of cane each side of the seat will have to be taken through side holes (see illustration) so as to keep them parallel with the others.

Take a strand of cane and make a pencil mark roughly half-way along it. Thread the cane up through the centre hole in the seat front to the half-way mark, stick in a peg (a small pencil will do) to hold the cane in place, then take the cane over the seat and down through the hole immediately opposite, making sure the glossy side of the cane is uppermost (throughout all stages). Now take the cane up through the adjacent hole, twisting it a little to keep it shiny side up, and pass it down through the opposite hole in the seat front. The illustration shows a frame half worked in this way. This may *sound* complicated but it is obvious once you come to do it. Continue threading the length of cane through front and back holes till you come to the corner holes at the seat front. Consult the illustration to see how to thread the cane into the side holes so as to keep the strands lying parallel. If the cane runs out before you have finished (one strand is usually enough to complete one stage of caning a seat but sometimes they break, or are shorter) run the end of the used-up cane over and over the nearest loop between two holes and pull it tight. Secure the end of the new length of cane in the same way.

Remove the peg holding down the other half of the cane and work the other half of the seat in the same way. Do not pull the cane too tight at this stage.

Stage two (see illustration) is worked in exactly the same way except that the cane is now threaded across the chair seat.

Stage three (see illustration) repeats stage one exactly, taking the cane in and out through the same holes, so that it lies over the previous strands.

Stage four (see illustration) is where the job gets slower because here the strand is woven under and over the previous ones. You are working across the seat as in stage two. The threading can be done with your fingers, but it speeds things up to improvise a threader. Use a 20-cm (8-in.) length of thick wire bent into a loop at one end to hold it by. Thread the wire in and out of the strands then slip the cane in alongside and remove the wire.

Stage five is where diagonal weaving starts. First check that all your woven strands of cane are neatly separated out into pairs as shown, as this makes the weaving easier to follow. In this stage of the caning the strand is threaded over a pair of horizontal canes, under a pair of vertical ones, and so on diagonally across the seat. Begin threading from the corner hole at the right of the seat front. Unless you make a mistake en route you should finish up at the left corner hole of the seat back. Work half the seat at a time. Note that two strands are passed through each of the corner holes to give the correct spacing.

Stage six, the final one, repeats the diagonal weaving process in the opposite direction (see illustration). Here the cane passes under the horizontal strands, over the vertical ones. The seat holes will be getting rather choked by canes by now, so you may have to use a pointed tool like an icepick to clear a space to slide the cane through.

4 Repeat stage 2, but threading the cane over and under the canes it crosses

5 Begin the diagonal weaving, threading the cane over a pair of horizontal canes, under a pair of vertical ones, and so on across to the opposite corner

6 Repeat the diagonal weaving in the opposite direction, going under the horizontal canes and over the vertical ones

BEADING

A wider beading cane worked round the seat sets the caning off handsomely and gives protection against wear and tear. Use No. 6 cane for the beading and No. 2 to bind it in place. Cut one end of the beading cane into a sharp point and push it well down into one of the corner holes. Then thread the No. 2 cane up through the next hole, pass it over the beading cane, keeping the shiny side up as usual, and down through the same hole. Continue along till you reach the next corner, where the beading cane should be cut to a point and pushed down into the corner hole. If the holes are so packed that it is difficult to get the No. 2 cane through, you can cheat a bit and work it through alternate holes, though this will not be so strong. Begin the next section of beading by cutting the cane to a point and driving it well down into the same corner, as before – this will help wedge both ends of beading securely. Carry on right round the seat. If any ends of beading threaten to work loose you can secure them by driving in a peg – a couple of matches cut to 2-cm ($\frac{3}{4}$-in.) lengths will do the trick. Check that all cane ends are neatly fastened off underneath, and trim off any excess.

Rush Seating

There is something altogether satisfactory about rush seats; the ribbed texture, the greeny-yellow colour of the rushes, the warmth and resilience that accommodates you. Make sure that you can recognize a piece that was intended for rushing; if some of the old seat remains, there is no problem, but you may light upon an old chair like the ladderback shown in our red kitchen (see page 91) completely devoid of seat and imagine that perhaps it was once upholstered. Usually a rush seated chair ends in raised knobs at the front corners, which keep the strands separate. The wooden seat frame will be roughly finished compared with the rest of the piece, and taper inwards, making it almost wedge shaped in section. All this helps your rushes grip as well as encouraging a comfortable lap of a seat in the final result.

Rushing is done with bundles of rushes, sold as 'bolts', which contain a mixture of thick and thin rushes. You also need a rushing needle, though the curved longish needles sold in upholstery packs can substitute; make sure the eye is large and generous, and the point not too sharp. A padding stick is helpful for pushing padding down into the seat, but people improvise with spoon handles, even paper knives. Use thin tough twine or string.

Rushes need to be damp to work with to make them stretchy and pliant; as the rushes dry the seat tightens up. It is better to start with too few rushes for the job than over estimate and be left with a surplus of damp rushes which need careful drying out again, laid flat. To damp them, run a shallow bath, lay the rushes in flat, under a weight, for two minutes. Try not to bend the rushes because this weakens them. Take them out, wrap tightly in a towel or plastic bag and leave overnight.

To start off a seat, pick out two rushes, one thick, one thin. Tug the tip of each rush (the thinnest end) to break off any weak bits, and wipe them gently from the tip downwards to the butt. Put the two rushes together, tip to butt, and

1 Tie the first two rushes, one thick, one thin, to the frame with string

2 Wrap the first rush 'rope' round the chair legs and frame in an anti-clockwise direction

3 Use a spoon handle to push the padding into the seat 'pockets'

4 The last strands of weaving will form a figure of eight

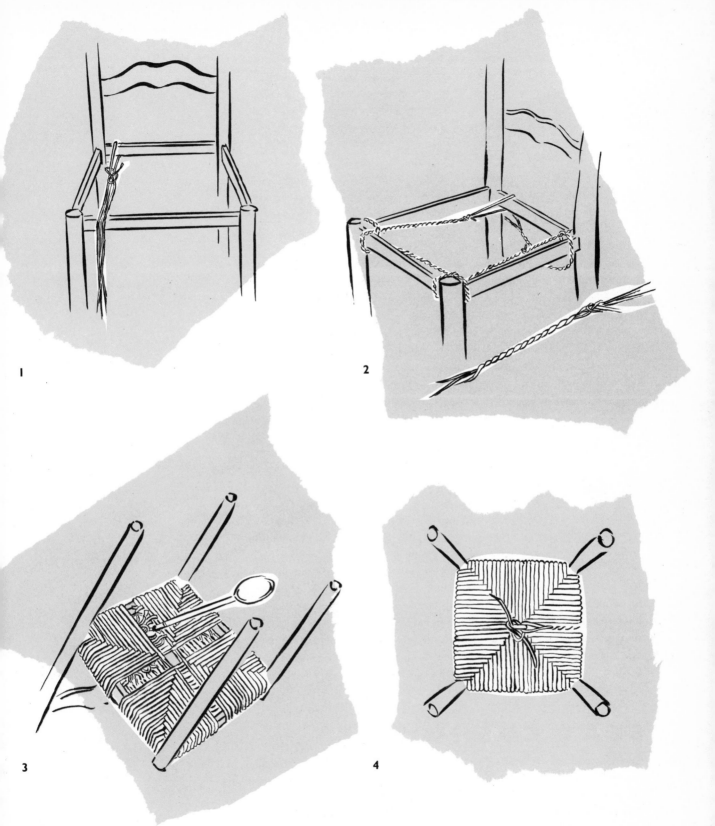

1

2

3

4

tie them to the frame (as shown) with string. Now twist the two lengths of rush together, to give an even, smooth 'rope', and begin wrapping it, working anti-clockwise, round the chair legs and frame, as shown. Twist the lengths of rush that show on the seat; the unseen part beneath does not need to be twisted.

As you reach the end of a rush, or both rushes, attach new rushes to each, following the thick/thin system, using a reef knot or half-hitch (see illustration), making sure that these joins occur in the unseen lengths, i.e. at corners or underneath.

As you weave away you will find that you are creating a double thickness of rushing, 'pockets' formed from a top and bottom layer of weaving. These need to be padded out with 'waste', in this case dry odds and ends of rushes (using damp rush for packing will cause mildew) which are pushed down into the pockets with your spoon handle, paper knife, or whatever, to create a taut, rounded surface (see illustration).

Carry on rushing till you have completed about 5–7.5 cm (2–3 in.) of seat all round, packed out suitably, then leave the seat to dry for 24 hours. Before starting to weave the rest, press the strands together as closely as possible to look dense and compact. Continue weaving as before. As you approach the centre it is harder to push in the padding; you may need to pad across the gap and weave over and under it, using the needle if necessary.

Unless the seat is a perfect square, the last strands of weaving will take a figure-of-eight form (see illustration) to fill in the central area. The final twist must be worked in place with the rush needle, and secured by tying the loose end to the opposite strand, underneath the seat. To finish up, tuck all knots and loose wisps of padding away into the seat so that the underside looks neat.

Cushions

Thrifty decorators are liable to go mad on cushions; not only do they help in livening up dull colour schemes, they're great as first aid for hard or lumpy seating. Floor cushions, covered with sound bits of old rugs and kilims beyond repair, make handsome low-level seats if you stuff them with something solid like bran or sawdust, and pile them up two or three at a go. Machine quilting for sofa cushions makes fine or cheap fabrics like calico and lawn look more interesting, and last longer. Quilting round stencilled patterns is another way of introducing colour and texture to basically cheap fabric covers. Whatever your taste runs to in covers, try to find the softest pads; a hard cushion (except on the floor) is a contradiction in terms. Down- and feather-filled cushions turn up in junk and jumble sales.

SEAT CUSHIONS

Cushions add comfort and colour to seat furniture. Depending on the shape and depth of the seat, a fat or lean squab-style cushion, piped and buttoned if you choose, does not take long to make. A skinny seat cushion can be padded out with layers of old blanket, piled up like sliced bread and then stitched through to make a pad cut to fit the exact size of the chair seat. Make a pattern from newspaper. Use the pad as a pattern for cutting two cover pieces adding a 2-cm ($\frac{3}{4}$-in.) seam allowance. Stitch piping (see page 162) round one of the pieces, then pin the other on top and machine together with the piping foot, leaving a section of the cushion cover seam open at the back so that the pad can go in. Finish this opening with a zip, inserted as for a dress opening. Insert the pad then add ties if the chair needs them. Don't button a thin cushion or it will be uncomfortable to sit on.

A fat cushion is made in much the same way, using a newspaper pattern to cut the seat cover pieces. But you will need to join the pieces with a third strip to make a boxed shape.

Buttons covered in the same material as the piping not only look decorative but help keep the filling evenly distributed. Use a double-ended upholstery needle and thin twine or linen thread to stab through the finished cushion in whatever grouping you fancy. Use flat buttons to anchor the stitching underneath.

STENCILLED AND QUILTED CUSHIONS

Quilting round a stencilled decoration gives the effect of appliqué and the stitched outline, which can be machined or handsewn, also gives the stencilled pattern more oomph. This is a cheap and cheerful way to make some bright

Cushions decorated with motifs, either handpainted or stencilled, which are then quilted round, are bright and cheerful

and lively cushions from a few metres (yards) of calico plus odds and ends of acrylic artists' colours. Or if you prefer, use special fabric paints (see Suppliers page 202).

This works best in a folksy idiom though I have seen versions on silk, usually featuring floral motifs. Bold designs with simple outlines are the most effective. Patchwork motifs are one source to raid for ideas: pineapples, flower baskets, a Log Cabin, the Texas star. Vegetables are fashionable at the moment and I can visualize bunches of carrots, red, green and yellow peppers, or cabbages all looking well. Then there are familiar and decorative household items such as patterned jugs, flowery cups and saucers, teapots (see illustration). If you prefer you can handpaint designs from a sketch directly on to the fabric, but converting a sketch into a stencil often results in a stronger image because the discipline of planning a stencil suppresses inessentials. And you never know, you might want to make many repeats, to give as presents, or even to sell, and this is where stencils – which allow a design to be repeated quickly – really score.

I suggest calico as basic fabric because it is so cheap and you can chuck out mistakes without feeling guilty, and because it is a natural cotton which improves with washing. But there are many other alternatives: silk, as I mentioned, checked cottons, velveteen. Use flameproof wadding to quilt on to, with a calico backing.

Stitch round the outline of your design on the cushion cover

Materials

You will need stencil card and a craft knife for cutting, a bushy brush and acrylic colours (or fabric paints) to fill in the design, plus a fine brush and an artist's flat-ended fitch to add borders or outlines. Masking tape can be useful too. A couple of metres (yards) of contrast fabric could make piping or a frill to set off your design.

The back of the cover can be simply quilted in checks or a trellis

Method

First work out your design and transfer this via carbon paper on to the stencil card. Make the design large enough to fill two-thirds of the space or more, if the cushion is generously sized (teeny shapes would be lost in the final effect). Cut the stencil using a sharp craft knife.

Pre-wash and iron the fabric, then stretch it taut on a table with a few drawing pins. Test colours and paint consistency on a spare piece first. An almost dry brush, charged with colour, is the ideal, with enough colour to register clearly but not so much water that you make a wet splodge. Practice will guide you. Use tabs of masking tape to hold the stencil card steady while you paint. Use bold colours and don't try to shade too realistically or you may end up with a muddy image. Use a fine watercolour brush with black to whisk in outlines, where appropriate, in the style of Omega Workshops or Raoul Dufy textile prints.

When dry, cut out the cushion cover shape allowing 2 cm ($\frac{3}{4}$ in.) for seams all round. Lay this on the wadding and backing and cut round. Baste the thicknesses together to keep the layers manageable as you sew, then machine round the design (see illustration). Use standard stitching, or a fine satin stitch if you have a swing needle, but keep the stitching outline simple. When

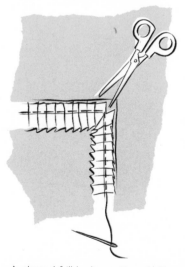

A pleated frill looks pretty; snip the corners before sewing to ensure a neat finish

completed, pull all loose threads through, knot and snip off. Press the cover with a damp cloth to ease out puckers and flatten it. The back half of the cover can be a single thickness of fabric, or very simply quilted in checks or a trellis (see illustration) to give it the same weight as the decorated front. If you use a painted border, piping will not be necessary, but contrast piping or a pleated frill look pretty. Tack these in place, snipping corners as shown, then lay both halves together, wrong side out, pin and machine together round three sides and a few centimetres (inches) of the fourth, leaving a gap to insert the cushion pad. Turn right side out and press again. Insert the cushion pad, then handstitch across the gap.

FLOOR CUSHIONS

These were often made in the past from the small rectangles of oriental carpet, flatweave or pile, originally destined for saddlebags. These pieces still turn up in likely places, but are not particularly cheap; their attraction is that the design is complete. Carving up clapped-out old rugs, too torn to mend (as on page 85), is less satisfactory, since you are stuck with bits rather than an entire design. However, attractive and lightly worn pieces of carpet, such as kilims, can still be sewn together with tough thread to make up into handsome and sturdy floor cushions. If you look around the shops, you will see that kilim cushions are horrendously expensive to buy.

The size of the usable bits of rug dictates the size of the cushion. Floor cushions are best rectangular; square pieces can be turned into sofa cushions instead. To look good the rectangle should measure something like 60×90 cm (24×36 in.). Use close-weave canvas to make the internal cushion cover, then stuff into this either sawdust or bran or even sand – all traditional fillings for floor cushions, which are solid rather than soft. They will be very heavy too, so double-stitch all the seams on the inner covers, to prevent them from bursting under pressure.

Cut the canvas cover 12 mm ($\frac{1}{2}$ in.) smaller on each edge than the salvaged piece of rug. With right sides together, machine both halves together on three sides, fill, then double stich the opening closed.

The cushion can be rug-covered on both sides or more thriftily covered only on one side with rug and with a strong, dark canvas or upholstery fabric used on the other. This makes the rug pieces go further and the cushion easier to sew up. Use a heavy-duty machine needle and extra strong thread to machine the cover pieces together. The best looking way to finish off these cushions is with a plain webbing in a toning colour (dye it to match) folded over and machined down all round as shown. Machine the rug piece to the canvas backing first to give a firm edge on to which the webbing can be applied. One end of the cover will have to be left open to insert the cushion and do remember that there is no 'give' in a cushion solidly filled like this.

There are various possible ways of closing up the open end. You could handstitch it shut using a strong needle, waxed thread and a thimble on your finger to drive the needle through. Or you could bind the edges with the same webbing and make webbing ties as shown. Don't get involved with zips; they are not strong enough to take the pressure and weight of a floor cushion.

Finish off a floor cushion with plain webbing folded over and machined down, mitring the corners (see page 98 for details)

Webbing ties make a satisfactory closing

PATCHWORK

Nearly everyone gets bitten by the patchwork bug at some time or other. The idea of making something beautiful and useful from all those bits and pieces of material one accumulates is extraordinarily appealing. Unfortunately, one usually runs out of steam rather early on and then large fragments of uncompleted patchwork go to swell the mountain of unfinished masterpieces in drawers and trunks. There was an awesome amount of patient stitching in those delectable quilts our ancestors made on long winter evenings. Women today are too impatient, or busy, or perhaps they have other ways of passing long winter evenings. So I thought it would be better to include a patchwork design that can be stitched up by machine. Log Cabin was an obvious choice, as all the pieces are straight-sided, and the piecing is straightforward. It is a popular Early American design, and one of my own favourites. The American Museum near Bath has a beautiful example made up in those demurely figured calicos, chintzes and percales which add to the charm of nineteenth-century quilts.

The correct thing was to use the same quality of material throughout in quilt-making, though mixtures of silk and velvet were admissible for the more sumptuous 'winter' quilt. There is good sense in this as an all-cotton quilt is washable, while a mixture of silk and wool might not have been.

Log Cabin was usually made up in half dark, half light patches, giving a stepped effect over a whole quilt. One block (one completed section of the pattern) on its own makes a very attractive cushion cover if you do not feel

I Log Cabin patchwork is an extremely pretty covering made of fabric remnants

2 Back with light cotton to make a cushion cover, or with strong cotton and an interlining to make a light cot cover

3 Link blocks together into lengths with narrow strips of contrasting or matching cotton

4 Join the lengths of blocks together in the same way to make your complete quilt

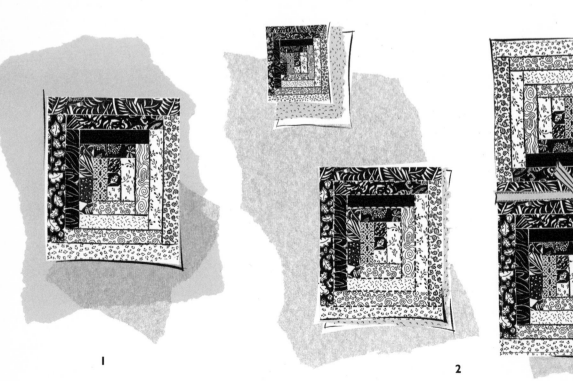

I

2

3

equal to making a whole quilt. A dozen blocks would make a child's cot quilt: three across, four down.

To make up, draw the pattern pieces on cardboard to use as templates. Cut out with a sharp craft knife. If you want to make the block bigger, add several more rectangles, increasing the length proportionately. When cutting the pieces allow a 6–12-mm ($\frac{1}{4}$–$\frac{1}{2}$-in.) seam allowance round each patch and make sure they are all cut exactly on the straight. You must make the *same* allowance on each patch, or you will get into a right old mess when sewing them together. Turn the seam allowance under and iron down to give you sharp creases as a guide for machining. Sew the first three small squares together by hand and then transfer to the machine.

To make up into a cushion cover, the pieced block only needs backing with light cotton before being made up in the usual way. If you want to make a light cot-cover (more decorative than warm) back the patchwork with strong cotton and perhaps an interlining of flannel (an old flannel sheet perhaps). Machine the blocks together along the outer seam allowances. Press them from the back over a damp cloth to flatten all the seams and smooth out any creases. Tack the backing and optional interlining in place to make sure the pieces stay properly aligned while finishing off. With an interlining it is advisable to machine-quilt the three thicknesses to make the coverlet more solid. Machine along the seams between the blocks, and round two or three squares in each block. Then, tack a wide coloured bias, or a bias strip of one of the patching materials, round the coverlet. Machine, and then turn back and hem.

For a warmer, more luxurious cover, interline with cotton batting or with one of the Terylene waddings which are easy to wash and quick-drying. Tack the three thicknesses of patchwork, wadding and backing together carefully as shown and then machine in an unobtrusive shade of cotton down the main seams and round as many of the smaller rectangles as you feel equal to. The more closely quilted a cover like this is, of course, the better it looks and feels. Then bind the edges with bias or matching fabric as above.

If you were contemplating making a full-size quilt, the easiest way to cope with such a weight of material would be to machine-quilt each block separately, leaving the outer edges of each block unstitched. Then use narrow 2.5-cm (1-in.) strips of contrasting or matching cotton, cut on the straight, to link the blocks together. Join lengthwise first, setting the blocks edge to edge, with the outer seam allowance ironed flat this time, and tack the strips in place over the joins as shown, folding in the edges of the strip of course. Machine down both sides of the strip. When you have completed enough lengths to make a quilt the size you want, start joining these together in the same fashion. By the time you are joining the third or fourth length of blocks, the quilt will be very bulky and difficult to manoeuvre, so set the machine on a large table to support the rest of the quilt as you work. This is a speeded-up way of making a quilt compared with the old way, where the whole quilt was made up first as with the cot-cover and then hand-quilted on a frame, but it has one snag – the backing will need further lining strips sewn into place to hide the raw edges. It is easiest to do this by hand. Use ordinary bias binding, hemmed down on either side, trimming off any pieces of surplus wadding or backing material as you go.

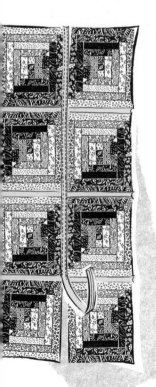

4

CHAPTER 7

FINISHING TOUCHES

Paper and Fabric Creativity

You've sorted out the basics, and your house now has decorated walls, floors, furniture and soft furnishings, of which you can justly be proud. Now comes the fun bit – all those finishing touches that make your home a reflection of your personality and which add charm and individuality to *your* castle: from re-vamped picture frames (and what to put in them), découpage, and the intriguing-sounding book doors, to covered or punched lampshades, and paint techniques like gilding and verdigris. You will add ideas of your own; these are a few suggestions to get you started.

DÉCOUPAGE

Taken from the French word for 'cutting out', découpage has understandably become something of a national pastime. It allows artistic butter-fingers to create decorative effects which look glossily professional and can be applied to almost any surface or artefact – screens to picture frames, tin trunks to tea trays. Découpage as a serious means of ornamenting furniture originated during the Renaissance, not so long after the new-fangled technique of printing made visual images accessible to a new public. Black and white printed borders of an elaborately ornamental sort were designed for use on painted furniture, picture frames, and the like, enabling craftsmen to arrive at complex efforts by simulating 'tarsia' or inlaid decoration, quickly, and without special skills. The 'commercial potential', as we would say today, of such charming deceits was not lost on either tradesmen, or their clientele.

The craze for oriental lacquer led to the production, chiefly in Venice, of much 'lacca contrafatta', or fake lacquer, relying on coloured cut-outs and many layers of shellac to give painted furniture something of the bizarre charm and glossy finish of the real thing. From cabinet-makers' workshops, the idea spread to affluent homes, where cut paper ornament, artfully tinted and 'Japanned', grew into a genteel pastime for late eighteenth-century ladies. They revelled in the production of pretty artefacts and knick knacks which this technique made so temptingly possible. Two centuries later, the idea is back in fashion, rendered more tempting still by the advent of photocopying, fast-drying, high-build varnishes and a wealth of suitable material for découpage which our ancestors would have found overwhelming in its variety.

Use a soft watercolour brush to tint the motif before cutting it out

To a picky eye, there is découpage and découpage; colour-printed cut-outs from wallpapers, or glossy magazines, stuck down and embedded in a deep layer of clear resin or acrylic varnish, lack the charm of hand-tinted cut-outs from photocopied black and white prints, finished in a subtler, less blanket fashion. However, the piquant possibilities of the genre – smothering wallpaper roses on old deed-boxes or adding a neo-classical foliage border to a picture frame – is open to anyone with a sharp pair of scissors and a few hours to spare. Finding suitable motifs for découpage is a challenge in itself. There are books of likely subjects – cherubs, flower sprays, cartouches, architectural borders – available (see Suppliers page 202). These ideas can be a bit samey, but on the other hand colouring them in yourself gives a whole new look. If you need many repeats of one motif, use a photocopier. Build up your own collection of old prints. These still turn up modestly priced if you keep your eyes open. Don't cut them up; again use a photocopier. Browse through art history books in a good library; most of them have a photocopying service. Search out likely wallpapers, black and white (Timney Fowler/Osborne and Little) as well as gloriously floral. American readers have access to some excellent wallpapers, like a china patterned one designed by Mary Gilliatt.

Materials

You need scissors and a craft knife, white polish (bleached shellac), tiny tubes of watercolour, two or three soft watercolour brushes, gum arabic (from artists' suppliers), a good quality decorating brush and a glider. For a 'crackled' and antiqued finish you also need a set of Le Franc Bourgeois varnishes – Vernis à Viellir, and Vernis à Craqueler (see Suppliers page 202) – and some burnt umber artists' oil colour.

Good subjects for découpage might be any of the following: trays, boxes and trunks, small round-topped tables, lampshades and lamp bases, metal waste bins, picture frames, nursery furniture, corner cupboards, desk sets, tole planters. Small découpaged boxes make charming presents, especially if you plan the decoration as a surround to the recipient's initials. Use Letraset transfer letters for these, or a calligraphy stencil. Or practise till you can do a handsome set of initials yourself with Indian ink and a fine brush.

Method

The subject for découpage should be carefully painted and rubbed down for a smooth finish. Dark green and black were traditional background colours. Cream, ochre yellow, soft red and mulberry are also effective. Bear in mind that Le Franc Bourgeois varnishes will yellow and darken all the colours you use (both the background and the painted motifs). Tint the motifs with soft brushes before you cut them out, using the watercolours sparingly (see illustration). Subdued colours usually look best, especially with formal, architectural ornament. Coat the motifs when dry with shellac – this toughens the paper as well as sealing your painting, making it easier to cut.

Use scissors and/or a craft knife to cut out the designs. It is not necessary to cut into very complicated motifs where there is a risk of tearing fine bits. You can fill in some areas after the design is stuck down using the background colour of the piece.

A homely tea tray customized with a découpage marigold design

To stick the cut-outs, coat their backs with gum arabic. This has the advantage over modern adhesives that it allows you much more time to experiment and juggle your pieces round for the best effect. When you like the effect, press down in place, coating with more gum if necessary and leave to dry. (A hairdryer will speed this up.) Coat the entire piece with shellac and leave to dry. If you are not using the craquelure finish, your work needs only a light antiquing with a little burnt umber, wiped on with a soft rag and rubbed back for a tinge of age. When dry (leave overnight) cover the whole piece with a tougher varnish preferably matt or semi-sheen.

If you want the craquelure finish – and it does help tie the decoration in with the paintwork – paint it over thinly but thoroughly with ageing varnish, or Vernis à Viellir. Try not to miss anything out, holding it to the light to check. Leave for around 50 minutes, till tacky but not wet, and re-coat with the second Vernis à Craqueler. Again make sure you don't miss bits out. Within 15 minutes or so the surface will begin to crack up. It is only the transparent varnishes which are cracking, so the effect is not yet dramatic. If you can leave the piece overnight to dry and crack naturally, so much the better.

The next step is to wipe burnt-umber oil colour over the whole surface with a soft rag, rubbing it in and rubbing it off again, so the cracks show up dark. This process adds hundreds of years in a moment. Finally coat the whole piece first with shellac, then, when dry, with a varnish as above.

Note: The best antique découpage was varnished repeatedly (up to 40 times), with careful rubbing down in between, till the varnish was deep enough to make the cut-out edges almost undetectable to the finger tips.

UPGRADING CHEAP LAMPSHADES

I have been debating whether or not to include recycled text from my original book on making lampshades from silk materials, such as pleated cotton. The snag is, the wire frames on which these shades were stretched and stitched have simply vanished from the department stores where they once featured, next to Haberdashery and Paddings. A wire frame cost next to nothing, whereas a custom-made fabric shade (nothing gives a softer or kindlier light) costs considerably more. So why don't craft shops, and other public-spirited small

Use newspaper to make a pattern for covering a lampshade

With more and more people working from home, some form of
workspace, ideally secluded and private, more often squeezed into a
corner, alcove or recess in an already restricted living space, is
becoming a necessary part of home planning. Studies and halls may
seem to have little in common either decoratively or functionally,
except that often you find them rolled into one — a tiny office squeezed
into the below-stairs recess, which used to be a broom cupboard.
Planning decisions are imperative when space is so limited.

PROJECT 6: THE BROWN PAPER STUDY

A small box-room, featuring a quaint Arts and Crafts triangular window but little else, seemed cut out for conversion into a quiet study or office in this terraced house. As found, the walls were papered but tattered, the floor covered with a grim carpet. Extravagance here was the sisal matting and old desk, which I cleaned up using methylated spirits and wire wool and then re-stained. The chair, however, cost next to nothing from an office supply shop. We chose ordinary brown wrapping paper for the walls, liking its neutral but warm colour and its sheer thriftiness. Taking the paper up to the ceiling would have made the room top heavy, so we stopped at the picture-rail level and added a simple stencilled border.

Above Shelving is crucial in any home study, yet it need not be expensive. Here, we customized a simple set of shelves from a chain DIY store with matt blackboard paint, which has excellent covering power. A final coat of varnish protects and seals.

Below Postcard-sized Greek vase prints from an old catalogue look twice as impressive when generously mounted. Frames were cut from unpainted beaded moulding, painted black and dull red and finished with glass and backing.

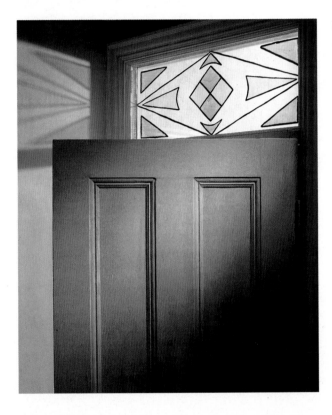

Above Once plainly glossed, the study door is transformed beyond recognition with a 'grainy' layer of oil glaze. We achieved this by 'flogging' tinted oil glaze in light golden brown over an eggshell base, using a long-bristled 'flogger' brush. This gave an easy but effective imitation of blond wood 'graining' – a treatment which we extended to the radiator and the surrounding woodwork. The half-light cunningly mimics stained glass when special glass paint is applied with a steady hand.

Dramatic backdrop to a designer's workplace: a whole wall has been papered with favourite images, photocopied and stuck down to create a contemporary print-room effect. One extra long wooden table gives plenty of elbow room, whilst twin lights are positioned to be both practical and stylish focal points.

Desk-top travel via layers of old maps pinned to cover walls and cupboard doors in this attractive and eccentric workspace. For an idea like this to work, it *needs* to be over the top. Two maps, neatly framed, would not be the same thing at all.

Left An eye-catching mural, inspired by a Greek vase painting, is the first thing everyone notices in my own front hall. Stencils, also taken from classical ornament, pick up the theme and add colour and definition to an apricot-yellow distemper, which was chosen to import warmth into a rather dark space. The stairs are stained a mahogany/walnut mix and varnished. I added light stencilling to soften the effect. One corner of a large oak bookcase shows on the right. This was originally a dark varnished piece, which I limed to make it look less bulky. The hall floor is paved with York stone slabs taken from my cellar, while the passage beyond is floored with second-hand bricks laid flat onto a concrete screed.

Top right Charleston, the Sussex farmhouse where Vanessa Bell and Duncan Grant entertained the luminaries of the Bloomsbury Group, is one of the most atmospheric and idiosyncratic houses to visit. Note the extraordinarily subtle colouring and wall decoration. Vanessa and Duncan decorated everything themselves, using mainly home-made distemper, which they mixed and tinted with powder colour. Charleston is a must to visit for anyone sensitive to painterly decoration.

Right Dark green panelling, an old ladderback chair and low table are set off by a splendidly vivid floor painted in green and yellow checks. A small hall needs little more in the way of furnishings, except coathooks perhaps. A bold use of colour defines and expands a limited space.

If in doubt, go overboard for colour. Powdery blue tinged with violet, as here, offset by terracotta floor tiles and a curly iron balustrade makes an immediate impact. The big mirror is contrived from an antique picture frame and is positioned to double the light cast by the gilded lantern overhead. Mirrors are potent elements in putting spaces together. Try them in different positions before making up your mind.

enterprises, stock wire frames so that people like me can enjoy the masochistic satisfactions of puncturing themselves copiously on the road to the perfect lampshade?

An abridged version of how I cover cheap card shades follows as do a few simple ideas for making card and fabric shades more interesting. These look more appealing and cast a gentler glow.

Covering shades

There are so many attractive, interesting hand-made papers, and pretty fabrics around; using one of these to cover a boring cheap shade doesn't take long and makes a big difference to the light cast through it, as well as its looks.

Choose a plain white shade in card or fabric-covered card, in your preferred shape. Make a pattern in newspaper of its shape, by pinning and trimming the paper till it is an exact fitting cover (see illustration). This is easy with cylinders, but less straightforward with cones. Use this to cut a cover in fabric or paper, allowing a 12 mm ($\frac{1}{2}$ in.) hem all round for glueing. You may decide to fold fabric or paper in and stick it down top and bottom, in which case you will need this extra allowance. Nick it as shown. If you prefer to use a coloured binding, the extra allowance can be trimmed away to the shade edges, but the overlap down the shade seam will be needed to glue the piece together. Position the side seam of the cover over the shade seam so as not to have too many dark shadows. Use clear paper adhesive to glue paper, PVA for fabric, and stretch the cover material tight and taut before glueing. Don't dab glue all over the shade and cover because this may show up as dark spots in the finished shade. Alternatively, with a fabric cover, you may prefer to machine the main seam, pressing it flat.

A bias-binding in a contrast colour makes a neat binding or edging for these covered frames. Glue the wrong side of the bias (better than ribbon because it bends to fit curves) and the outer and inner edges of the shade, leave for the stated time, then press the bias over the edges, stretching it as you go.

If you want to fold in the top and bottom of the fabric or paper, cut out nicks for a neat finish

Painting shades

Use transparent, watery colours (acrylic plus acrylic medium) to paint blurry stripes, checks or stencil shapes around a shade. Stencilling a small repeat motif doesn't take long but will give any shade considerable charm.

Puncturing shades

A development of punched tin, this can work very effectively on a dark card shade. Use a sharp upholstery needle, or compass point, to pierce holes in a pattern. Constellations is an obvious choice, but pretty nonetheless. Another variant which is more subtle but more laborious is to trace off a pattern – stencilled ivy trails, bunches of grapes – on to the card shade, then cut round these – not fully but half way through – with a sharp craft blade. What you are doing is using light as a modelling agent, so be prepared to experiment. What should happen when you lift the cut edges slightly is that the light gleams out through the cuts to create a chiaroscuro version of your original design. This technique is a traditional one used in the USA.

Painted Finishes

VERDIGRIS: THE PAINTED VERSION

Verdigris (literally, greeny-grey) is the name given to the natural patination that develops on copper and bronze exposed to oxidization via wind, sun, rain and fresh air. Some anonymous clever-clogs discovered a few years ago that this subtle, distinguished green-blue-grey surface could be readily imitated by stippling on suitable paint shades in a determined sequence. Anyone who keeps their eyes open will have met the finish on anything from wicker garden furniture to photo frames. In my studio classes we have shown people how to verdigris entire roomfuls of terracotta flower pots; it may be a familiar look, but achieving it never fails to please. Whilst I like it on flower pots (which look like posh cache-pots) I think its full potential as refurbishment is best seen on twirly black metal objects and decorative knick-knackery dating back to the late thirties. At this time the Californian hacienda style became desirable everywhere in the wake of movies starring such imperishables as Bogart and James Cagney, socking it to each other in whitewashed patios and raftered interiors all awriggle with scrolled black metalwork. This, for your information, is the background to this exotic and un-British metal craftwork, which surfaces in the form of wall-lamp brackets, standard lamps, decorative plaques and firescreens and interesting oddities like the magazine rack (page 147).

In their found state (black and twirly) they give me the creeps. I cannot see them sitting comfortably in the interiors of the low-key nineties: but with verdigris finish, it's another story. Softened and 'antiqued' by the verdigris paintwork, this faked up metalwork borrows the dignity of the noble materials such as copper and bronze on which old patination is natural and beautiful.

The process is lovably simple – anyone can do it. You need two colours that make up the verdigris blue-green: a turquoise blue plus a lime green. These can be standard emulsion colours in sample pots. You don't need much – a cosmetic jar-full, for example, will do a metal chair. In my classes, we stipple these, one after the other, over a sludge-coloured base coat (we have our own verdigris kit, see Suppliers page 202), and a water-based emulsion, using a rounded but fat stippling brush (see page 53).

You can send for our kit or put together your own shades. If the metalwork (wicker, terracotta, resin, plaster) is in reasonable shape it may only need a good clean and a light rub down with wire wool to give a key for the water-based sludgy base. On metalwork, I give the whole thing a priming coat of red-oxide metal primer, for bonding and to prevent rust. When dry, brush this over with a coat of sludgy base paint, covering everything and leave to dry. Spread some newspaper under your piece as waste paper to work off excess paint. Subtle verdigris stippling involves 'pouncing' or lightly jabbing the smallest trace of colour – first turquoise then green – with the bristle tips, on to the whole sludge base, not to obliterate it but to just 'mist' with colour. The trick is to pick colour up on the brush, then work it up into the bristles while blotting off moisture, by pouncing on to the newspaper.

When the paint seems almost too dry for the brush to make a mark then this is the moment to start stippling. Mist or powder the turquoise evenly over the surface: it will dry on contact. Repeat, but more sparingly, with the lime green. If there are any relief mouldings or other features then use colour to emphasize these with a heavier build-up. Outdoor pieces should be protected, when dry, with a coat of near-invisible, matt, non-yellowing varnish (see Suppliers page 202). Indoor pieces need nothing more than the paint, though some people like to add a subdued gleam with a gilt wax cream rubbed on here and there with a fingertip (see Suppliers page 202).

GILDING

Simple gilding

Water-gilding with real gold leaf on red bole and gesso is beautiful, but to do it yourself requires some setting up in the way of tools and materials, and much practice. In its straight-from-the-gilder state it is a bit dazzling for most tastes. But it is possible to achieve a very acceptable effect of worn, antique gilding, using a minimum of equipment and Dutch Metal transfer leaf (actually thin leaves of brass) which is much easier to apply than the loose sheets used in water-gilding. Dutch Metal is definitely brassier than true gold, but the whole skill in this technique is to distress it by one means or another to suppress the gleam and give the surface a mysterious patina. This is done partly by rubbing the transfer leaf back to a red underlay, partly by 'dirtying' the leaf with thin glazes. I know professional gilders who make increasing use of this sort of finish, not just because it saves time and works out cheaper, but because their customers like it better. It is particularly effective on carved and moulded frames.

Materials

You need interior-grade filler, Milleput (a putty-like material) for minor patching, real gesso (see Recipes page 200) or acrylic gesso (more expensive, but comes ready to use and dries fast) for re-surfacing rough textured wood for gilding. You also need red-oxide metal primer, one or two books of Dutch Metal transfer leaf, Wundasize, cotton wool, fine-grade wire wool, a standard decorator's brush and assorted artists' oil colours – burnt sienna, burnt umber, black – for glazing.

Method

A previously gilded frame may show bald white patches where moulding or ornament has been chipped off. Small cracks and chips can be mended with interior-grade filler, larger missing portions can be built up with Milleput, following the maker's instructions. Sand any repairs smooth when dry. Shellac the repairs to seal, then paint the frame – or the replacement part – with red-oxide primer.

After repairing your frame, if necessary, coat it with size, then begin laying on the gold transfer leaf

If you are gilding a plain wooden frame, it will need several coats of gesso to build up a fine smooth surface for the leaf. Apply two to three coats, letting each one dry in between. Sand these lightly to give a fine smooth texture, then seal the gesso with a coat of shellac. When this is dry, paint with red oxide to give an overall opaque colour. Rub down lightly with wire wool, and brush down. The frame – or replacement part – is now ready for gilding.

Wundasize has the advantage over standard Japan Gold Size of considerable flexibility; the leaf can be laid after half an hour or less, and the size remains workable for up to 24 hours. All of this gives a beginner more latitude. Coat the frame evenly with the size, using a soft clean brush. After half an hour begin laying on the transfer leaf (see illustration). Each sheet of leaf is attached to a backing of waxed paper which makes it easy to position, leaf-side down. After positioning, press firmly from the back, using fingertips or a pad of cotton wool. You can see the leaf becoming detached from the backing as the size grips it. Peel the backing away to leave a golden strip. Position the next leaf slightly overlapping the first, and repeat over the entire surface. You will find difficulty at first persuading the leaf into grooves and around moulding, and your gilding may show 'skips' where the leaf didn't take. When this happens you can usually cover the 'skip' with a tiny corner of leaf left on a sheet. If this doesn't stick, dab on more size, wait 30 minutes and try again.

Experts cut the transfer sheets into sections using sharp scissors to fit the surfaces of the frame more closely. This makes it easier to get a good 'fit' and is less wasteful of the Dutch Metal. The 'skewings', or tiny scraps of leaf, can be saved in a plastic bag and used for various fancy finishes.

When the frame is completely 'golden', leave for a few hours or overnight to settle, and for the size to harden. Then run a smooth cloth, or cotton-wool pad, over the surface to flatten it out and remove any loose leaf. The gold will look very shiny so the next stage is to distress it. Begin by gently rubbing the surface with fine-grade wire wool, going in one direction on flat bits, round and round on bumpy ones. The idea is to raise the red underlay here and there by gradual attrition of the leaf. More red should 'ghost' through on raised areas to simulate normal wear. Start cautiously and see how you like the effect, then work through to the red more vigorously where it looks appropriate and attractive. Take care not to rub through the red paint.

By now the frame should be acquiring a warmer red-gold colour and more texture. When you think you have gone far enough, start applying 'dirtying' glazes. Use artists' oil colour thinned to fluidity with white spirit. Brush the glaze on or swab it on with a rag. Leave a few minutes, then wipe off again, leaving more colour in the grooves and carvings for contrast. Try any or all the colours mentioned above. Stipple colour into undercut or heavily moulded bits. Don't forget to antique the sides as well as the front. When the frame looks convincingly old, leave it to dry off for a day or two. Some people finish frames with shellac as protection but I think this is unnecessary. For further ideas on frames see pages 191–193.

Polychrome on gilding

This could be a further development of the type of gilding I have described. Here, instead of dirty colours, brush on rich hues – crimson, green, blue – either in layers, rubbed through, or in great overlapping splodges, which are also rubbed through to blend them together and to raise muted gleams of gold. This sounds odd, but if you look closely at frames on early Italian paintings, you will find effects like these, which are rich but muted and subtle all at once. Use Plaka colours for this.

ANTIQUED PLAIN COLOUR

Suppose you have a wooden frame you don't want to gild, but which looks too dark for your picture. Here a subtle lightening can be achieved by using a technique similar to the distressing effects described above. This effect is based on a coat of light coloured paint – off-white, grey, raw sienna – with shading and ageing colours rubbed on and rubbed off. Some texture in the wood is helpful here, so you can dispense with gesso and even primer. Standard oil-based undercoat tinted with oil colours makes a good base-coat. When this is dry, brush, rub or stipple on thin washes of darker shades – grey-greens, sepia and so on. This 'modelling' with colour is a sensitive process which cannot be reduced to a formula. Looking hard at frames you like and trying to copy them is the best training.

CHEQUERS, PAINTED DECORATION, ETC.

I have a frame around a modern watercolour, quite flat, which an artist friend decorated for me, simply, but entirely successfully, with dark green chequers on a brown-paper coloured ground. Both tones pick up colours in the painting. Imaginative treatments like this are not hard to copy, but too rarely seen. This effect is excellent for a modern work, but there are more traditional subjects, like Greek-vase prints, which could be treated to a suitably classical band of ornament. Any of the borders seen on Greek vases could be painted in white or gold (or both) on to a dark picture frame, and then distressed and dirtied to 'knock it back' again.

MAKING NEW PLASTER-CASTS LOOK LIKE ALABASTER

Making plaster reproductions of attractive subjects – cherubs, medallions, Wedgwood plaques – is something of a minor industry today. The results are cheap and appealing, but in their pristine state are as startlingly white as cheap dentures. It is easy to give them the look of alabaster, and the effect is highly convincing.

Materials

You will need a soft brush, orange or bleached shellac (white polish), liming wax, and rottenstone, which is a dust-coloured powder much used in antiquing processes and obtainable from specialist shops (see Suppliers page 202).

Method

Brush cold water over the entire piece. When it has soaked in follow with a coat of shellac. Orange shellac will give a warmer tone than white polish. Leave to dry, then stipple liming wax all over the piece. Leave for a while, then gently rub it back, leaving some whitish deposit, especially on a 3-D piece. If you want to dramatize the piece, stipple rottenstone powder into crevices or features. With a soft rag or brush gently polish up the surface, leaving some lime white and rottenstone five o'clock shadow, for contrast.

   Note: Plaster-casts are brittle. Some have inherent weak spots – air bubbles perhaps. So handle them carefully at all times and work on them on a flat surface, moving them as little as possible till dry. Bits that break off can be stuck back again with a good adhesive, such as thixotropic glue.

Filling the Gaps

Sooner or later one has enough of posters and the urge hits you to put something more personal on your walls. It used to be possible to find old prints, unmounted, quite cheaply but nowadays the market for these is so brisk, you will need to cast your net widely (that is if you like prints). I found a whole set of small reproductions of Greek vase paintings, which we framed up for the brown paper study, for a snip. They were smaller than postcards, but with a generous mount and matching frames they look good hanging as a group. I think of modest stuff like these little pictures (probably taken from a nineteenth-century catalogue) as space fillers: background material for larger and more impressive subjects. If you can paint yourself then relieving the blankness of your walls will not present a problem. But what can the inartistic do in this situation?

   Well, obviously, there are reproductions, and their quality improves all the time. Good museums will offer plenty of choice in this line. But however good the colour reproduction, an oil painting inevitably loses in being transferred on

An inexpensive classical print looks stunning when framed and mounted properly

to paper. Drawings reproduce far better, as one might expect. No one would despise a reproduction of one of Matisse's blue nude cut-outs. Attractively framed, these will add colour and life to your rooms. Screen prints and lithographs are also good choices. If you haunt galleries you may find an original you can afford, making the nucleus of your *own* collection.

Photographs are becoming increasingly popular and exhibitions are held regularly of work by famous and less famous photographers. A collection of black and white photographs, simply mounted and black-framed, looks dramatic in the right place. Architectural drawings have something of the same crispness, and are now eagerly collected. If you find a drawing reproduced in a book that you particularly like, have it photocopied, and maybe a little enlarged on to an off-white paper. Mounted and framed, it will look just fine. You could try your hand at colouring in photocopied botanical prints, using watercolours or gouache, as people did in the eighteenth century with attractive and now collectable results. Old sepia photographs have become something of a cliché, but originals can be of historical interest as well as looking good.

If you yearn for colour and texture, old fabrics are an area to explore. Old embroideries, even swatches of old cotton prints, can look rich and interesting properly displayed, and you will have the added satisfaction of knowing that you have helped to conserve a special piece of work from the rough and tumble of use and wear. Chinese embroideries on silk, pieces of fine old lace, ethnic embroidery and batik can all look distinguished and colourful but you will need to spend some thought on their display. A box type frame, with some depth to it, generally looks best, so the fabric has space around it instead of being squashed up against the glass. Odd shaped pieces will need mounting on to fabric, using transparent thread and preferably keeping the mount stretched on a frame as you work. This can then be fixed to a backing and framed. The right fabric makes a difference. Plain blue looks good backing lace; silk embroidery needs a fine but neutral backing – nothing shiny to compete; ethnic pieces may work well on natural hessian or calico dipped in strong coffee or tea to soften the colour.

Children's pictures and drawings are so lively and endearing one is tempted to keep all of them. This leads to trunkfuls over the years. I think one should frame some of them, from time to time, for their charm and as a record of the budding individual in question. Little objects, of no great intrinsic value, can look handsome in attractive frames. I have been gradually collecting tiny plaster impressions taken from carved seals and rings, mostly of antique subjects, and exquisitely finely detailed. Some of these displayed against marbled paper or red felt, in a mahogany grained box frame, make interesting wall decorations. So do collections of unusual shells, and of course butterflies. But take pains over their setting; the things are so beautiful intrinsically, it upsets one to see them housed in a tacky mass-produced frame.

FRAMES

As you see, there is no shortage of things worth framing; the problem is often the frame itself. Fine old frames have become so sought after there are auctions of frames alone. This does not surprise me because I have always been a frame fancier, and not a little of the time I spend in galleries and museums is actually devoted to peering at the detail and workmanship of especially interesting frames. Framing is both a craft and an art and, in its higher reaches, a peculiarly selfless art in that its aim is to be at once perfect and invisible: it focuses your attention on the painting or drawing, not on itself.

Once in a while, if you are lucky, you may come across a hand-carved pearwood frame, much battered, its burnished gilt in tatters. Mostly we have to make do, either with junk frames, mended, restored and perhaps given a new paint finish, or with new frames – better than they used to be in some respects but too glitzy to do much for their contents.

Junk frames, if you collect enough of them, and can find suitable material to fill them make an impression if you have them in quantity – too many to take in individually, so your eyes simply register a fascinatingly busy wall. Nothing is more atmospheric, but such a collection is the reward of many hours of pottering through antique markets, junk yards, thrift shops and all the other places where such trophies come to light. The frames are picked up for their own sake, the prints mostly separately, and the fun is arranging a perfect marriage.

Re-finishing and restoring old frames

This is the place to start, because though it is quite possible to make one's own frames up from standard mouldings, and a great deal cheaper, most people will cut their teeth on a junk or second-hand frame which just needs tinkering with in the way of minor repair, new glass, or a radically improved finish. The pleasure of working on frames is that the area is slight but the effect great.

Examine the frame carefully, back and front. Is it ebonized (smooth and black), or varnished oak, or gesso moulding on a wooden frame? Since any or all of these may reach you coated in pink gloss, white emulsion or cheap gold paint, it may take some detective work to ascertain what you are dealing with.

Experience has taught me that most frames overpainted in cheap gold paint were once properly gilded, often very finely. If the moulding looks bold and handsome (not gingerbread) this may well be the case. The odds are that you can remove the overpainting and rescue the original water-gilt, because gold leaf is not affected by paint removers if you work carefully and gently enough. You simply brush on the proprietary stripper, leave till the paint bubbles up, then gently wipe it away with soft wire-wool pads and rags.

Do this a section at a time. It will not happen in a minute, but to strike gold in this context is deeply satisfying. The gold leaf will not be perfect, or it would not have been overpainted, but it is now fashionably threadbare, with patches of red bole underlay showing through. Once cleaned – and this may require all sorts of *ad hoc* tools if the moulding is undercut or complex (nail-files, pen-knives, knitting needles) – let it rest overnight. Pick off any last shreds of cheap paint, then polish with a soft rag.

If there are chunks of moulding missing you have another problem. Artists' suppliers (see Suppliers page 202) supply rubber solutions for making moulds, which are used to cast replacements in fine plaster, but this is for the serious would-be restorer. Most people are better off simply camouflaging the wounds and mutilations. A substance called Milleput, a putty-like material, can be

Picture frames can be stencilled, potato-printed or painted freehand

Embellishing a mount with strips of
marbellized paper

used to build up a rough approximation of the missing chunks. These can then
be painted red (iron-oxide red) to simulate red bole and given a canny lick of
gilt cream to tone them in with the rest of the frame. If narrow strip mouldings
have dropped off leaving white gaps, just paint these a dirty colour to 'lose'
them. Dirtying repair work makes it inconspicuous – the best disguise.

Oak frames, very popular in the late nineteenth century, look good cleaned
of old paint or varnish and waxed. You may need to wire-brush any oak which
has been overpainted, in order to clean out the grain. In this case a limed
finish (see page 118) pale, interesting and good housing modern work, might be
in order. Many oak frames came with a gilt slip inside the glass. This will
usually be in good repair, but if not, rub gilt cream on to it subtly, to give a
threadbare rather than bright gold effect.

Glass can of course be readily replaced. Make sure it is picture-glass weight.
A framer will insert all this for you reasonably, but if you think you may be
reconstituting many frames you might consider investing in a staple-gun type
gadget which shoots framing 'points' into the frame to hold your picture, mount
and backing in place. This can save hours spent fiddling about with tiny pins
and a tack hammer.

A decent mount makes a big difference to lesser art works and will bridge
the gap between a small picture and a large-ish frame. The best mounts are
still cut by a professional hand, but there are inexpensive gadgets which will
cut a clean 45° bevel round your mount 'window', with a little practice. The
bevel can be gilt and coloured lines can be inked round the 'window'. Use a
pen and real inks for this. Fill in the broader gaps with a pale watercolour
wash. Today there is much use of narrow marbled paper strips, narrow gilt
strips, and other embellishments to dramatize the presentation of minor art.
Looking around at what is on display in smart shops will familiarize you with
the alternatives.

I came across a wonderful mount treatment in an antique fair. It was
surrounding Pompeiian prints, and made of gesso, layered on over cardboard
till it was thick enough to crack when slightly bent with one's hands. With
practice it is possible to create radial regular looking cracks, redolent of age,
which, with a shellac finish and a gilt bevel, could pass for ancient ivory.

SILHOUETTES

If you can't draw for toffee but the idea of making some sort of personal record of your family and friends appeals to you, why not try silhouettes? These little black-on-white profiles can capture an excellent likeness – a silhouette cut by Mrs Leigh Hunt of Lord Byron was acclaimed by all his friends as the 'best likeness of his Lordship ever made'. They are entertaining to do and, nicely framed, make charming things to hang on your walls or give away as presents. I have never known anyone who wasn't secretly gratified at having their features recorded. If you can obtain a good profile snap to work from, it can all come as a big surprise. One reason modern silhouettes make a poor showing compared with eighteenth- and nineteenth-century examples, is that our clothes and hairstyles are dull and shapeless compared with the fantastical wigs, beribboned caps and shepherdess hats ladies wore then, not to mention the ruffled fronts and queues and high collars in which the gentlemen caparisoned themselves. I don't see why one shouldn't introduce a touch of fantasy into silhouettes by showing your contemporary Miss as an eighteenth-century belle, or a portly male relation handsomely got up *à la* Prince Regent.

If you just want to play at making profiles to while away a rainy day, all you will need is a quantity of squared paper, some tracing paper and carbon, Indian ink and a candle. That is, if you propose to get your silhouettes the old way by interposing your sitter between a candle flame and a piece of paper pinned to the wall where you trace round the shadow with a black biro. It takes a little experiment to get this right; people *will* move their heads and candles will flicker. One of those lantern torches which throw a strong, concentrated beam might be better. Simpler still, use a clear profile snapshot. If you are using the shadow-on-the-wall method, trace your profile off on to paper, then reduce the size via a photocopier. When you have got it right go over the outline with Indian ink and a mapping pen, or fine nib. Paint the profile in carefully inside the outline with ink till quite black and, when dry, cut it out and mount on white card. If you are working from a snap, trace if off carefully. If it needs to be made smaller, photocopy and reduce.

The old profile artists used many different ways of getting their silhouettes some of which you might like to try. As well as simply inking a profile straight on to card, or sticking a cut-out on to card, they sometimes used the reverse procedure, in which the white card from which a profile had been carefully excised was stuck over black paper. This was known as 'hollow cut'. A hollow-cut profile, thought to be of Jane Austen, turned up pasted into an old edition of *Mansfield Park*. A great find this because only one other likeness of her, by sister Cassandra, survives. Another method was to paint the silhouette on to the back of a piece of plain, or domed glass. This cast a light shadow on to the white backing, adding to the interest of the picture. Or the silhouette might be set slightly above the white card, to cast a more pronounced shadow. Shades were often embellished with fine white shading about the hat, hair and clothes, though the face was always left plain black. The shading can either be added afterwards with white ink and a fine pen or sable pencil or, better still, because more delicate, by shading in the two-tone areas very carefully and cautiously with diluted ink, leaving the highlights white.

Silhouettes of your family and friends, nicely framed, make charming things to hang on your walls or to give away as presents. A touch of fantasy with the addition of a period wig or helmet will also amuse

BOOK DOORS

Until recently, I had never heard of a 'book door', but then in the way these things happen, 'book doors' seem to come up in the conversation twice a week, and looking into the idea I began to see that this was a decorating trick with interesting possibilities. There is one snag to 'book doors': to make one involves mutilating a lot of old books. However, we are *not* talking about leatherbound, gold-tooled volumes, or about the sort of classics any sensible person likes to have around. As a tireless consumer of second-hand books, I know from experience that it is possible to collect a sack-load of old books with decent cloth bindings but of no literary merit, quite speedily and cheaply, and this is your raw material.

Book doors — either painted in *trompe l'oeil* or made from the spines of real books — are always conversation pieces

Let me explain the 'book door' concept a little. It originates, like so many decorating gambits, in grand houses of the eighteenth century. Libraries were mandatory in the homes of anyone with cultural pretensions, magnificently fitted out with mahogany or oak bookcases, filled with books bound in half-calf (maybe not much read but they looked good) and topped by a row of busts of famous writers and philosophers. These handsome rooms would have been entered through the usual handsome doorway. However, it was often necessary to provide a second inconspicuous doorway, to the lavatory or a smoking room or simply to escape tedious visitors. Rather than break up the symmetry of the book-lined walls, the architects, or their clients, hit upon the solution of a 'book door'. This could have been as elaborate as a hinged bookcase, swinging open at a push, or as light-hearted as a flat 'jib' door, inserted among the bookcases and covered with rows of false books, sometimes real spines glued down, sometimes painted in *trompe l'oeil*.

If the thought of cutting up old books, however abysmal as literature, upsets you, the *trompe l'oeil* painting is a viable option. Books on shelves are a favourite subject with *trompe l'oeil* painters, not only because they are easy to paint and look attractive, but also because they offer the possibility for family jokes, witty allusions, puns and *double entendres*.

In a contemporary home, a 'book door' takes on a rather different role: mainly or entirely decorative. Books are friendly looking things – lots of them lined up together create a civilized atmosphere. I know of a lift in an elegant West Country hotel the walls of which are done out with books (cut off and stuck down), so that it feels like a book-lined 'snug' rather than a standard elevator. I can think of all sorts of contexts for a spot of bookishness: giving substance to alcoves too shallow for real shelving; disguising those boring flush doors that people went for when Modernism was the thing; giving visual interest and charm to flat MDF doors on cupboards; filling in alcoves either side of a chimney breast; disguising a door that breaks up the visual unity of a room; or simply making a joke, or a secret, of an uninspiring door to, say, the downstairs loo.

How architecturally convincing you want to make it is up to you, and the given materials. Shelves may simply be painted in, or counterfeited with strips of nailed-on batten. Architraves can be real, or painted, the book spines likewise. But cannibalizing cheap second-hand books is undoubtedly easier, and probably more fun.

Architraves, mouldings and shelving should match what is present in the room, whether real or painted. The background to your books, whether glued on or *trompe l'oeil*, is best done in a dirty, dark colour, burnt and raw umber mixed to a sludgy brown, with darker shadows. On to this, and your rows of simulated shelves, you simply stick or paint rows of books, adjusting the colours nicely for contrast, and not being too regimental about positioning, relative heights and so forth. Use a sharp scalpel or craft knife to slice book backs off cleanly, and a strong adhesive to stick them down, with a couple of strips of masking tape to hold them in place till the adhesive dries. Painted books are best worked in acrylic colours. The fun of *trompe l'oeil* of this sort, aside from the laughs you can have thinking up titles, is the opportunity it offers to bung in realistic detail – propped up postcards, photos, invitations, personal clutter of every kind. You can use felt-tip or metallic pens for writing in titles. Use a spray fixative to secure your work, if painted in different media, before varnishing with an invisible colourless matt varnish.

Household hints

I used to find something romantically pleasing in dust and cobwebs: a gentle patina of neglect misting over mirrors and bookshelves. I still find ghostly old houses in overgrown gardens poetic and moving, but reluctantly, I am more and more coming round to the view that what looks poignant in decaying mansions, or noble ruins, looks plain squalid in modest homes where life is being actively lived by people, children and animals perhaps among possessions of no great value or distinction. There is nothing poetic about dog hairs on chairs, and I refuse to let my children persuade me that our long kitchen table looks more appealing with its deal planks spotted with grease and splashed with wine stains. They argue the futility of scrubbing the table daily to an unblemished pallor, when, by the next morning, the job will have to be done all over again. I maintain that a household which doesn't keep to certain minimum standards of cleanliness and order is on the slide towards despondency, and beyond a certain point, dirt in whatever form simply looks – to me – dispiriting. Whereas the moment, albeit brief, when equilibrium is restored, surfaces clean and planks immaculate, is both soothing to my spirit and deeply satisfying because – like the Japanese tea ceremony – it gives dignity and meaning to the trivial, repetitious, but nourishing rituals of daily life.

All of which is a long preamble to a list of what used to be called 'Household hints'. Whole books of these were published in the inter-war years, probably with the intention of educating a new generation of servantless, middle-class women in the skills and domestic routines that they formerly relegated to their maids, cooks and handy-men. They usually covered a swathe of topics from straight cleaning tips, to recipes for whitewash *or* 'face wash', to a first-aid drill. I used to read these tomes with absorbed attention as a child, marvelling at the brisk solution apparently always to hand for anything from chapped hands to an infestation of bedbugs. On re-reading, some of the advice borders on superstition, and old wives' tales (such as the interminable hints for bleaching freckles), but there is also much common sense, practical knowledge and resourcefulness born of thrifty housekeeping in a period when aerosols and even washing machines were unknown.

I think some of these nuggets of womanly wisdom are worth recalling today; usually the materials are cheap, relatively 'green' and effective. With the general revulsion against devastating rain forests and blasting a hole in the ozone layer, plus a simple wish to trim needless expenditure, there may be something we can learn from traditional, thrifty practice.

CLEANING

Cleaning glass

Rub first with a rag or cheesecloth wrung out in cold tea, then polish dry with handfuls of newspaper. Unlike the squeegee method this doesn't leave streaks, and recycling newspaper and left-over tea seems a good idea.

Newspaper is excellent for polishing glass

To soften water for washing-up or floor mopping add a splash of household ammonia or washing soda to the water in the sink or pail. This cuts grease and softens the water. A splash of vinegar in hot water brings glasses to a clear sparkle.

Cleaning copper and brass

The old chef's formula of a half lemon dipped in fine salt and flour, worked round and round on copper and brass, is a good way to clean and polish these without leaving the black residue of metal polishes. The flour softens the scratching action of the salt. Kitchen-ware thus cleaned will not glitter but has a mellow glow and is visibly clean.

Badly tarnished brass can be cleaned off quite quickly by steeping in vinegar. Any cheap vinegar will do. Swab it on, or immerse the item if small, and watch the tarnish melt away. It will need polishing with metal polish if you want a bright shine, but the worst is over.

Cleaning brick or stone floors

To clean these deeply add a spoonful of caustic soda to the cleaning water. Go cautiously – it will froth up and fume. This is a powerful de-greasing agent, for occasional use only. It should be rinsed off with clean water, and a string mop (not squeegee type) well rinsed out.

Touching up scuffed black leather

Indian ink, brushed on with a small brush, is a handy way to hide the scars and scuffs which keep appearing on black leather shoes and bags. It can also be used on black velvet which has developed bald patches. Leather should be polished with shoe polish as usual after 'inking'.

Home-made furniture polish/cleaner

A little ordinary vinegar and/or artists' turpentine shaken up with boiled linseed oil and applied with a clean rag helps to clean and bring up the colour and grain of polished wood furniture, without leaving a layer of gunk behind as so many instant spray polishes do. The secret is elbow grease; much rubbing is the mystery ingredient, of more value than a host of chemicals.

Getting whites clean

The old way to get white linen shirts and the like spotless and snowy was first to soak, then to boil them, slowly. I still use this for smaller things like pillow cases. I add a sprinkle of powdered stain remover to the boiling water, and cook the lot up very slowly in a huge metal pan on the Aga slow plate. I then put it through the washing machine, or handwash, depending on how much there is and how strong I feel. This method does give cleaner collars and dishtowels than any other. Hanging whites outside in the sun, or on a frosty night, helps bleach fibres naturally.

Rugs in the snow

A Swedish friend reminded me of this wheeze, which dates from the days before carpet shampoo or vacuum cleaners and is of course convenient in a snow-bound country like Sweden. Come a good snowfall, any old rugs are

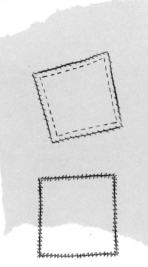

Patching sheets seems to be a thing of the past, but it can double the life of bedlinen

spread outside on the snow and brushed with stiff brooms and handfuls of snow on both sides. This cleans the fibres, and gets rid of a lot of loose dirt, without wetting the rugs too much. A good shake and they are replaced indoors.

The best way to clean rugs otherwise is to beat them, pegged on a line, and using a cane carpet beater. This dislodges dust and dog hairs without beating down the fibres, as a Hoover does when, that is, it isn't sucking them up. Damp tea leaves, scattered, then brushed or hoovered up, are also brilliant dust and hair attracters.

Moth proofing

I have given much thought to this infestation, which has cost me more than I care to add up in terms of designer goodies chewed to a cobweb, or more dispiriting, because more subtle, clandestinely nibbled-at key spots – armpits, crotch, elbows – which only reveal themselves in use, embarrassingly. Moths like human secretions; they also notoriously like woollies, and wool and silk mixtures. I have tried every commercial deterrent, with little effect other than smelling like an old clothes' shop myself. I have also tried herbal nostrums like lads' love and lavender. My final thought on this is that an ounce of prevention is worth a pound of cure. I buy cheap plastic clothes' bags from Ikea, with hangers inside, and store all my moth-attracting garments therein. A bore, but it works.

Dry cleaning v. washing

Most natural fabrics can be washed successfully, despite what the labels say (they are over-reactive) if you go carefully. I wash any cotton, linen or silk fabrics in the washing machine on a delicates setting, or by hand if the colours look likely to run. I obviously don't wash tailored jackets with all sorts of interlinings and linings which may behave differently. I wash wool blankets on a wool setting. I also wash old-going-on-antique curtains in linen or cotton (if they have that greasy, grimy texture) either in the machine on 'delicates' or by hand, steeping them in a lukewarm bath. The critical part is to ascertain whether any of the dyes will run. I have also washed a sturdy patchwork cotton quilt in the washing machine, but I don't recommend this for anything with fragile components. If in doubt, don't, but more often than you might think, consider the washing machine: cleaning bills can be horrific.

Patching

I sometimes wonder if anyone under the age of forty knows how to patch a torn pillowcase or sheet (jeans maybe, but that is another ball-game). Patching torn or worn areas can double the life of bed linen. My grandmother, raised on the Argentine pampas, was the queen of such making-do. I like a patched fabric myself; what it loses in newness it gains in long-service badge of honourable intent.

Recipes

Traditional gesso

Gesso was traditionally used as a base for water gilding, to provide a super-fine surface for decorative furniture-painting, and to prime canvases. Traditional gesso is cheaper than acrylic gesso, and gives a finer finish which is porcelain smooth when rubbed back with abrasive papers. It can also be tinted with powder colour to make a high build paint, which can then be burnished. Venetian furniture makers wrapped low-grade pieces of wood furniture in linen, then gessoed them before painting, to disguise rough wood and the tell-tale signs of a hurried assembly such as cracks and patches.

Ingredients
For approximately $\frac{1}{2}$ l (1 pt) of gesso
$\frac{1}{2}$ l (1 pt) water
1–1$\frac{1}{2}$ tablespoons rabbit skin glue granules
3–4 tablespoons whiting

Method
Use a small pan which will fit inside a larger one to make a *bain-marie*. Leave granules in water overnight to 'fatten', then heat gently in the larger pan with a couple of inches of water in it until they are melted. Sift whiting in gradually, stirring to break up lumps. The consistency should be just thicker than single cream. Test by dabbing a little on one palm and pressing your hands together; as you separate them there should be a slight resistance or stickiness.

Brush gesso on evenly, let each coat dry *completely* before applying the next, brushing at right angles to the previous coat. Sand the gesso to smoothness with medium, then fine abrasive paper.

Distemper

This is a home-made paint with which to experiment, which yields exquisite colours in the pastel range, with a dry, ridgy texture that is soft and delicious. The prettiest distemper – 'soft distemper' – is the most fragile, i.e. it rubs off. It is made from glue size, whiting and dry colour and water only. A superior size, like rabbit skin glue, makes it less powdery and more tenacious. This is the mixture we used for the Rose Bedroom (see page 147) and it is one I recommend for interiors which do not suffer and wear. Oil-bound distempers are tough enough for exterior use, but the texture is less appealing, though it erodes away pleasingly on outside walls. I would buy an oil-bound distemper rather than make it (see suppliers page 202).

Ingredients for soft distemper
For a small-to-average room
5 kg (11 lb) whiting
2–3 l (3$\frac{1}{2}$–5$\frac{1}{4}$ pt) water
1 kg (2$\frac{1}{4}$ lb) rabbit skin granules
dry colour

Method
This is a bulky paint, needing much forceful stirring in large containers. It is made to this method in Scandinavia today, where distemper is still commonly made and used in remoter areas. It is a rule of thumb approach (like many bread-making recipes) perfected only by experiment and experience.

Put water into a large plastic bucket. Pour in whiting through a sieve until it peaks a few inches above the water. Leave overnight to fatten. Do likewise with the granules of size, adding enough water to cover, in a separate container. The next day, ladle off the first few inches of the clear water on the whiting bucket, and stir hard to mix. In Scandinavia they use a propeller-type attachment on an electric drill, but a tough power-driven whisk or cake mixer would suffice, but make sure that your gadgets are in good working order, properly earthed, and go cautiously. If this sounds too stressful, just use your arms and a stout wooden spoon.

Gently heat the glue size until it is fluid. Dissolve the powder colour in water, *thoroughly* – a dash of methylated spirit may help some pigments to dissolve thoroughly. The ratio of glue size to distemper base is around 5–10 per cent of the total volume. Add the fluid, warm size gradually, stirring vigorously, and test the mixture by brushing on to a board. It should be of brushable consistency, but thicker than emulsion, and should dry with a rigid texture but not be so friable that a light rub leaves your hands floury. Add dissolved powder colour, stirring hard to disperse evenly. Go cautiously; you can always put more in, but you can't take it out. Remember that wet distemper is many shades darker than dry, so test the colour on card, using a hairdryer to speed drying, before deciding.

Apply distemper with large brushes. One coat should cover. Standard emulsion makes a fine base for distemper; bare plaster may need a preliminary 'sizing' to seal the pores. But do not try to put an emulsion coat over an existing distemper; only distemper goes over distemper. *New* plaster should not be sized, in this case apply distemper directly to the plaster.
Note: A small proportion of emulsion glaze added to this distemper recipe will strengthen it, but in my experience the less you adulterate the primitive formula the more appealing the result. In old societies, where this was the standard house paint, people just brushed a new coat over the old one when it started looking shabby.

Limewash

Ingredients
1 kg (2.2 lb) lime putty
water to cover
earth or mineral pigments

Method
Put the lime putty (broken up into lumps) in a large sturdy bucket, cover with water, and leave to steep. Dissolving can be helped along by pounding it with a rolling pin. Avoid splashing it on your face and eyes, and wear plastic gloves.

When the putty is completely dissolved, add more water to bring it to a fluid, milky consistency. Dissolve powder pigment in some of this limewash, then add this concentrated colour to the bucket gradually, stirring well each time and testing the colour on paper or a board.

Masonry to be limewashed should first be wetted thoroughly, to help the mixture to bond and penetrate the surface. Brush the limewash onto the surface. The paint becomes more opaque as it dries, but at least three coats will be needed to build up a strong colour with covering power. The bonus is that every time you re-paint the limewash colour grows richer, and the surface tougher. Wherever limewash is still used as an exterior finish it is easy to pick out buildings treated this way; their colour sings out with a rare intensity, even when the paint is old, weathered and flaky. No more satisfactory exterior paint has ever been invented.

Home-made oil-based paint

This recipe will give a lean, fine-textured paint finish with a vivacity of colour and texture quite different from any commercial oil-based paint. If you are into restoring antique painted furniture this might be a paint to consider because it will look closer to the original finish than anything you can buy and use straight from a can. This recipe is one used by Scandinavian conservationists.

Ingredients

0.7 kg (1½ lb) boiled linseed oil
0.2 kg (½ lb) titanium white pigment
1 kg (2¼ lb) zinc white pigment

Method

Mix the ingredients together. Terebine dryers are added to the mixture in a ratio of 2–5 per cent of the total weight. To tint this basic mixture use powder colours as follows. Pale colours are made by mixing dry colour with linseed oil before adding to the basic paste. To make dark colours tint the linseed oil, then add white pigments gradually. For a mid-sheen finish the basic paste should be diluted with a mixture of two-thirds oil to one-third white spirit, mixed together and added gradually to make a brushable consistency. For a shiny finish, thin only with linseed oil.

Acrylic scumble

Various proprietary brands of acrylic scumble are coming onto the market, and their advantages – drying speed, non-yellowing properties – make them highly interesting to decorative painters today. Since acrylic systems look like overtaking oil-based ones it makes sense to familiarize yourself with these state-of-the-art products.

Mixing a 'scumble', or glaze, with an acrylic product is straightforward enough but sufficiently different from making up an oil glaze to be worth describing in detail.

First of all, acrylic scumble is water-based, which means that tinting must be done with water-soluble pigments, such as artists' acrylics, gouache colours, dry pigment or Universal Stainers. Of these I prefer gouache, because the colour dissolves readily, is powerful as a tint, and comes in a wide range of pure colours. But the others are cheaper, and satisfactory.

The next point to bear in mind is that the scumble looks milky white in its container, with a consistency like mayonnaise. It becomes transparent only as it dries, like PVA-based adhesives, for instance. This means that the colour you mix in the mixing vessel looks fairly unlike the colour which will result when the scumble is brushed out over the surface to be decorated. This means you will need to keep checking your scumble mixture on white paper to monitor the final shade. As it dries fast this is not a big problem. But expect the mixture in your bowl or paint kettle to look peculiar, porridgy, not at all like the clear transparent colour you will finally achieve.

Drying time for acrylic scumble varies from ten minutes to one hour, depending on how warm the weather is.

As far as 'malleability' goes, or the capacity to take decorative patterning, whether dragging, ragging, rag-rolling or stippling, acrylic scumble strikes me as a very satisfactory alternative to its traditional oil-based equivalent. Dragging, especially, seems to flow extra smoothly with this mixture; ragging looks crisp and rag-rolling dramatic. The appropriate base for acrylic scumble finishes is a vinyl silk, or water-based eggshell. The chief reservation I have about this formula is that the end result is more shiny than matt, mid-sheen is probably the best description. If you prefer a matt finish, the solution would be to cover the finish with one coat of matt acrylic varnish, which will subdue the shine.

Metallic paint

Use bronze powders mixed into fast-drying shellac. Bronze powders come in a wide range of metallic shades, which can be intermixed, or layered for excitement. Pour a little shellac into a saucer then gradually mix in powder to make a fluid, or pasty mixture, depending on what you are painting. Use orange shellac for richer shades, bleached shellac (white polish) for pale or silvery tones. Clean brushes immediately after use in methylated spirit, or the shellac will harden irretrievably. This paint can be used on most surfaces, including fabric, though it will not be flexible enough for dress fabric.

Stencil paint

Acrylic artists' tube colours are ideal for most stencilling, as they dry fast, reducing the risk of smudging, and are not so pasty that they clog the stencil. They can be extended and made transparent by mixing in a little acrylic medium, or they can be lightened by the addition of a little white emulsion. Alternatively, use ready-mixed colours.

Oil glazes

When oil glazes first entered the DIY repertoire a decade ago, most people rushed out and bought a can of 'transparent oil glaze' or scumble, tinted it with artists' oil colour, and slapped this on their walls. The result looked sticky, like jam. Since then the pros have worked on distancing themselves from such crude efforts, using less and less transparent oil glaze, more and more standard oil undercoat, tinted as required. This is not strictly a 'glaze', being cloudy, matt and chalky, but it gives effects more in line with clients' tastes. It is also much more difficult to handle, drying faster, and yielding less crisp 'effects', whether ragged, dragged or whatever. Undoubtedly, to eyes attuned to the reticent, matt charm of fresco, this is more attractive and easier to live with. The best advice I can give to beginners, is to mix up one of each recipe given, in small quantities, and try them out on painted boards, to familiarize yourself with the behaviour and consistency of each. Let them dry before you decide, too.

The next problem is to re-mix on a room scale – say one litre – the colour you liked on your board. Make rough notes of colours used, and in their relative proportions. Be prepared to fiddle about for several hours; this is normal, even for professionals.

Beginner's glaze recipe

1 part commercial oil glaze
1 part white spirit
tinting colour
1 tablespoon of white oil-based paint, like undercoat or eggshell, can be added per ½ litre to soften the hard-edged effect

Standard glaze recipe

1 part commercial oil glaze
3 parts white spirit
tinting colour
1 tablespoon undercoat or eggshell white paint per ½ litre

All-purpose glaze recipe

1 part raw linseed oil (slow drying but makes a harder finish when dry)
1 part white spirit
1 part clear matt varnish
tinting colour
For a softer effect, add up to 1 part white undercoat

Suppliers

TEXTILES

New

Z. Butt
24 Brick Lane
London E1 6RF
Tel: 071 247 7776
Undyed calico, muslin, etc.
Cheap.

Java Cotton Co.
52 Lonsdale Road
London W11 2DE
Tel: 071 229 3022
Hand-blocked cotton batik;
sarongs.

J. D. McDougall Ltd
4 McGrath Road
London E15 4JP
Tel: 081 534 2921
Undyed canvas, hessian, etc.
plus wool fabrics.
Contact for appointment.

Russell and Chapple Ltd
23 Monmouth Street
Covent Garden
London WC1 9DD
Tel: 071 836 7521
Canvas, hessian, etc. Good
range.

Sheraton Textiles
60 Wentworth Street
London E1 7TF
Tel: 071 247 3822
Exotic prints (including 'wax'
prints) in extraordinary
colours.

Whaleys
Harris Court
Great Horton
Bradford BD7 4EQ
Tel: 0274 576718
Undyed silk, linen. Cheap.

Old and Second-Hand

Alyson Burden
4 Anley Road
London W14
Tel: 071 602 1973
Freelance seller of old
costumes, trimmings, etc.
Contact for appointment or
for antique fair dates.

Penny Philip
5 London Road
Bath BA1
Tel: 0225 469564
European (esp. French)
country-style fabrics, quilts,
curtains, plus furniture and
ceramics.

Spread Eagle Antiques
22 Nelson Street/8 Nevada
Street
Greenwich
London SE10
Tel: 071 858 9713
Old/antique textiles, clothes,
inc. theatrical and ethnic.

Susannah
142–144 Walcot Street
Bath BA1 5BL
Tel: 0225 445069
1920s and 1930s fabric,
quilts, trimmings, curtains.

CURTAINS

Curtain Call
The White House
Sutton Scotney
Near Winchester
Hants
SO21 3JW
Tel: 0962 760254
Second-hand curtains and
service to remake old
curtains.

The Curtain Exchange
Branches throughout the
country
133 Stephenson Road
Fulham
London SW6 2PG
Tel: 071 731 8316
Wide range of good-quality
second-hand curtains.

Judy Greenwood
67 Fulham Road
London SW6 5PY
Tel: 071 736 6037
Antique and grand second-
hand curtains.

McKinney Kidston
1 Wandon Road
London
SW6 2JS
Tel: 071 384 1377
Antique curtains and old
textiles.

Sarah Meysey-Thompson
10 Church Street
Woodbridge
Suffolk
IP12 1DH
Tel: 0394 382144
Large range of antique and
recycled curtains.

PAINTS, TOOLS & MATERIALS

Specialist

J. W. Bollom
121 South Liberty Lane
Ashton Vale
Bristol
Tel: 0272 665151
Glazes, varnishes, tinting
colours.

C. Brewer and Son
(branches nationwide)
Paints, paper, brushes,
glazes, wood stains, shellac.

Brodie and Middleton
68 Drury Lane
London WC2B 5SP
Tel: 071 836 3289
Stage painters' suppliers

Canopy International
Unit 25
Parmiter Industrial Estate
Parmiter Street
London E2
Tel: 081 993 1172
Sheet metal work, punched
tin.

Cornelissen and Son
105 Great Russell Street
London WC1B 3LX
Tel: 071 636 1045
Pure colour in dry pigment;
tube paints, gesso, whiting,
bronze powders, rabbit skin
glue.

Fiddes and Sons
Florence Works
Bridley Road
Cardiff
Tel: 0222 340323
Wood finishing materials –
shellac, stains, varnishes.

Foxell and James
57 Farringdon Road
London EC1M 3JB
Tel: 071 405 0152
Acrylic lacquers, varnishes,
stains, rottenstone, etc. plus
good range of paints.

Green and Stone
259 Kings Road
London SW3
Tel: 071 352 0837
Glazes, brushes, craquelure,
gesso, rabbit skin glue.

W. Habberley Meacows
5 Saxon Way
Chelmsley Wood
Birmingham B37 2DB
Tel: 021 770 2905
Gilding materials, bronze
powders, brushes, shellac.

A. S. Handover
Angel Yard
Highgate High Street
London N6 5JU
Tel: 081 340 0665
Specialist brushes, shellac,
gilding materials, craquelure.
Catalogue.

John T. Keeps and Sons
15 Theobalds Road
London WC1X 8SL
Tel: 071 242 7578
Scumbles, varnishes,
brushes, flat oil, eggshells.

E. Milner
Glanville Road
Cowley
Oxford OX4 2DB
Tel: 0865 718171
Specialist brushes, glazes,
varnishes, etc.

John Mylands
80 Norwood High Street
London SE27 9NW
Tel: 081 670 9161
Dec. paints, shellac,
varnishes.

Nutshell Natural Paints
10 High Street
Totnes
Devon TQ9 5RY
Tel: 0803 867770
Earth and mineral pigments,
casein paints, varnishes,
waxes.

John Oliver Paints
33 Pembridge Road
London W11
Tel: 071 221 6466
Own range of paint colours
plus historic shades; papers,
borders.

Paint Magic
(main branch)
116 Sheen Road
Richmond
Surrey TW9 1UR
Tel: 081 940 5503
Paint Magic paints
(Colourwash, Woodwash,
Verdigris, etc.) plus range of
historic colours in emulsion
and distemper. 48-hour
colour matching service.
Mail order.

Paper and Paints
4 Park Walk
London SW10 0AD
Tel: 071 352 8626
Historic paints, matched
glazes, stencils

E. Ploton
273 Archway Road
London N6
Tel: 081 348 0315
Brushes, gilding materials,
rabbit skin glue, craquelure.
Low prices.
Mail order.

Putnam's Collections Ltd
55 Regents Park Road
London NW1 8XD
Tel: 071 431 2935
Paints in vibrant colours and
chalky textures imported from
Mediterranean.

J. H. Radcliffe and Co.
135a Linaker Street
Southport PR8 5DF
Tel: 0704 537999
Comprehensive range inc.
own scumble glaze,
varnishes, etc. Catalogue;
mail order.

Rowney and Daler
12 Percy Street
London W1A 2BP
Tel: 071 636 8241
Artists' paints, glazes,
brushes, gilding materials.

Stuart Stevenson
68 Clerkenwell Road
London EC1

Tel: 071 253 1693
Fine art and dec. products,
tools, materials, inc.
craquelure, whiting, rabbit
skin glue, blackboard black.

Alex Tiranti Ltd
27 Warren Street
London W1P 5DG
Tel: 071 253 1693
Gilding and patinating
materials, acrylic gesso,
bronze powders, cast-making
materials, pigments,
varnishes.

Lewis Ward and Co.
128 Fortune Green Road
London NW6 1DN
Tel: 071 794 3130
High-quality specialist
brushes, custom made if
required.

Conservationist

Colourman Paints
Cotton Clansford
Staffs.
Tel: 0785 282799
Historic colours.

Hirst Conservation Materials
Ltd
Laughton
Sleaford
Lincs. NG34 0HE
Tel: 0529 7517
Historic mortars, plasters,
coatings, pigments, as raw
materials or readymade.
Colour matching service.

National Trust Paints
Farrow and Ball
Uddens Trading Estate
Wimbourne
Dorset BH21 7NL
Tel: 0202 876141
Historic colours; distempers,
flat oil, eggshell, emulsions.
Mail order.

Potmolen Paint
27 Woodcock Industrial Estate
Warminster

Wiltshire BA12 9DY
Tel: 0985 213960
Traditional paints.

Society for the Protection of
Ancient Buildings (SPAB)
37 Spital Square
London E1 6DY
Tel: 071 377 1644
Information and leaflets on
making and using limewash
and distemper.

*

Paint Magic
Franchise selling Paint Magic
range of paints, tools,
materials.

The Stulb Company
PO Box 597
Allentown PA 18105
USA
Tel: 215 433 4273
Old Village paint colours –
authentic and good quality.
Catalogue; mail oirder.

*

Paint Magic
Angie Gill
Emu Creek
Waucha 2354
NSW
Australia
Tel: 067 779119
Agent for Paint Magic range
of paints, tools and materials.

Porters Original Limewash
11 Albion Ways
Surry Hills 2010
NSW
Australia
Tel: 022 111620
Historic paints (limewash,
distemper, etc.) Excellent
colour range. Catalogue.

Stencils

Elrose Products
PO Box 30
Rickmansworth

Herts. WD3 5LG
Tel: 0293 285577
Stencils, paints, brushes.
Catalogue; mail order.

Paint Magic
116 Sheen Road
Richmond
Surrey TW9 1UR
Tel: 081 940 5503
Paintability Stencils,
Furniture Painting Patterns,
paints, brushes; courses.

Pavilion Stencils
1a Howe Street
Edinburgh EH3 6TD
Tel: 031 225 3590
Own range of stencils;
brushes, paints, cards.
Catalogue; mail order.

The Stencil Store
91 Lower Sloane Street
London SW1 8DA
Tel: 071 370 0728
Stencils, paints, brushes,
cards, craft knives; courses.
Mail order.

Découpage

ARC Prints
26 North Street
Clapham Old Town
London SW4 0HB
Tel: 071 720 1268
High-quality repro. of 16th-
19th c. engravings.
Catalogue.

Dover Book Shop
Earlham Street
London WC2 8PJ
Tel: 071 836 2111
Books for découpage.

Paint Magic
116 Sheen Road
Richmond
Surrey TW9 1UR
Tel: 081 940 5503
Books, motifs, materials.

CANE & RUSH

Chairpersons of Marshfield
40 High Street
Marshfield
Chippenham
Wilts. SN14 8LP
Tel: 0225 891431
Cane, rush, seagrass.
Mail order (send s.a.e.).

Eaton Shell Shop
30 Neal Street
London WC2H 9PS
Tel: 071 379 6254
Cane and seagrass.
Mail order (send s.a.e.).

PICTURE FRAMES

Brian Campbell
5 Peary Place
London E2
Tel: 081 938 1109
Bespoke frames.

J. Fisher and Sons
21 Bevenden Street
London N1 6BH
Tel: 071 253 8655
Non-finished wood mouldings
(soft and hard woods).
Mail order.

Framing Workshop
78 Walcot Street
Bath BA1 5BG
Tel: 0225 482748
Basic framing equipment and
materials; will also cut and
joint mouldings or make up
frames.

D. and J. Simons
130 Hackney Road
London E2 7QS
Tel: 071 739 3744
Frame mouldings, mount
board, tools and sundries.
Mail order.

BARGAIN HUNTING

Antique/Junk Shops

Ian Crispin, 95 Lisson Grove,
London NW3. Tel: 071 402
6845
McGovern's, 221 Belsize Park
Road, London NW6. Tel: 071
624 3322
This and That, 50–51 Chalk
Farm Road, London NW1.
Tel: 071 267 5433
Camden Passage Antique
Centre, London N1
Hobnob's, 29 Fonthill Street,
London N4. Tel: 071 263
4720
Wichmore Antiques, 14 The
Green, London N21. Tel: 081
882 4800
The Secondhand Shop
(various branches)
Anything Goes (various
branches)
Toots, 1 Colworth Road,
London E11. Tel: 081 518
7997
Cobbler's, 49 West Ham Lane,
Stratford, London E15. Tel:
081 519 8237
Nelson's, 709 Romford Road,
Manor Park, London E12.
Tel: 081 478 2587
Easton Express, 259 London
Road, Romford. Tel: 0708
745651
Tower Furniture, 63–65 Old
Kent Road, London SE1. Tel:
071 231 1278
Humphreys, 16 Dartmouth
Road, Forest Hill, London
SE23. Tel: 081 291 3023
Austin's, 11–23 Peckham Rye,
London SE15. Tel: 071 639
2725
Spread Eagle Antiques
(various branches)
Greenwich Antiques, 15
Greenwich Church Street,
London SE10. Tel: 081 858
4060

The Trading Post, 47
Charlton Church Lane,
London SE7. Tel: 081 853
5662
John Tolley, 93 Catford Hill,
London SE6. Tel: 081 690
4650
The Silver Sixpence, 14
Catford Hill, London SE6.
Tel: 081 690 0046
Oddiquities, 61 Waldram
Park Road, London SE23.
Tel: 081 699 9574
Hillyer's, 301 Sydenham
Road, London SE26. Tel: 081
778 6361
Aladdin's Cave, 146 Maple
Road, London SE20. Tel: 081
778 4873
The Griffin, 911 Garratt Lane,
Tooting Broadway, London
SW17. Tel: 081 767 6579
Tony Davis, 23 Battersea
Rise, London SW11. Tel: 071
228 1370

Auctions

Hornsey Auctions, 54–56
High Street, London N8. Tel:
081 340 5334
Belmont Auctions, 152 High
Road, London N15. Tel: 081
880 1562
Abridge Auction Rooms,
Market Place, Abridge,
London N15. Tel: 0992
812107
Jarvis Auctions, 263 Arch,
Railway Approach, London
E10. Tel: 081 539 1941
Mayfair Auctions, 7 Dartford
Street, London SE17. Tel: 071
703 1984
Rosens Auction Rooms,
144–150 London Road,
Croydon. Tel: 081 688 1123
Chancellors Auctions, 74
London, Kingston-upon-
Thames. Tel: 081 541 4139
Thomas Moore's Auction
Rooms, 217–219 Greenwich
High Road, London SE10.
Tel: 081 858 7848
Roseberry's Old Railway
Booking Hall, Crystal Palace

Station Road, London SE19.
Tel: 081 778 4024

Markets

Bath: Flea Market, Tram
Shed, Walcot Street, Sat.
Market, Guinea Lane, Wed.
6.30a.m.–2.30p.m.
Brighton: Market, car park
behind railway station, Sun,
5a.m.–noon
Bristol: Antique Market, Corn
Street, Fri. 9a.m.–3p.m.
Glasgow: Flea Market, by

Mercat Cross, Sun.
London: Bermondsey Antique
Market, corner of Long Lane
and Bermondsey Street, SE1,
Fri. from 5a.m.
Brick Lane, Chiswell Street
and surrounds, E1, Sun. a.m.
Picketts Lock Antiques and
Collectors Fair, Picketts Lock
Lane, N9, first Sun. of month
Newcastle-under-Lyme: The
Stones Antique Market, Tues.
9a.m.–4p.m.
Norwich: Cloisters Antiques
Fair, Wed.

9.30a.m.–3.30p.m.
Richmond: Duke's Yard

Antique Galleries and Salvage Yards

Bermondsey Antique
Warehouse, Bermondsey
Street, London SE1. Tel: 071
407 2040
LASSCo, St Michael's Church,
Mark Street, London EC2.
Tel: 071 739 0448

MacNeill's Art and Antique
Warehouse, Bermondsey
Street, London SE1. Tel: 071
403 0022
Robert Whitfield Antique
Warehouse, Bermondsey
Street, London SE1. Tel: 071
407 5960
Tower Bridge Antiques
Warehouse, Tower Bridge
Road, London SE1. Tel: 071
403 3660

Acknowledgements

Publishers' acknowledgements

28 above IPC Magazines Ltd/ Robert Harding Syndication; 28 below Stylograph/Casa de Marie Claire/Planells; 28–29 Tim Beddow; 30 above Marie Claire Maison/C. Dugied/J. Postic; 30 below Ianthe Ruthven (Nicola Wingate, Saul Print Rooms, 43 Moreton Street, London, SW1. 071 8211577); 31 Graham Henderson/Elizabeth Whiting & Associates (Designer: Sasha Waddel); 32 Scoop/Elle Decoration © J. Dirand; 57 Marie Claire Maison/P. Hussenot/R. Roy/ A. Comte; 60–61 Nadia Mackenzie; 61 Jeff McNamara; 62 above Marie Claire Maison/G. Chabaneix/ C. Ardouin, 62 below William Stites; 63 IPC Magazines Ltd/Robert Harding Syndication; 64 Marie Claire Maison/G.

Bouchet/J. Postic; 89 Vogue Living/Quentin Bacon; 92 Bent Rej; 93 above Daniel & Emmanuelle Minassian; 93 below Marie Claire Maison/R. Beaufre/C. Puech; 94–95 Tim Beddow; 95 above IPC Magazines Ltd/Robert Harding Syndication; 95 below Dennis Krukowski; 96 Stylograph/Maison Francaise/ Godeaut; 148 above Simon McBride; 148 below Ianthe Ruthven; 149 above Nadia Mackenzie; 149 below Marie Claire Maison/P. Verger/A. Comte; 152 left Tim Beddow; 152 right Simon McBride; 180 Agence Top/Pascal Hinous; 181 World of Interiors/Tim Beddow; 182 June Buck/Elizabeth Whiting & Associates (Designer: Jocasta Innes); 183 above Ianthe Ruthven; 183 below Camera Press; 184 Jean-Pierre Godeaut (Designer: Florence Lopez).

The following photographs were specially taken for Conran Octopus by Nadia Mackenzie:
25–27, 58–59, 90–91, 145–147, 150–151, 178–179.

Author's acknowledgements

'Hands on' books, like this one, involve even more people, in even more taxing ways, than most. I need to thank particularly all the people who generously lent us their own real rooms to do a number on: Helenka and Nigel, Ruth and Jeff, Jason and Kate. This involved extraordinary trust and patience, as whole sections of 'home' became no-go areas, littered with ladders, paint cans, brushes, and dust sheets. Sarah, Angie and Dave helped me make the rooms happen; their good humour and sheer muscle were a terrific boost. On the production side I have a whole team to thank: Louise, particularly, for imperturbably 'minding' the most complex operations; Anne and Alison for supporting and inspiring from the wings; Paul for imposing a visual elegance on the beast; Nadia for taking endless pains over photography; Lynne Robinson for brilliantly translating my rough scrawls into clear and lively illustrations. And there are a host of good and helpful people, dealers, restorers, paint experts – too numerous to mention individually, but without whose lively comment and insights this book would have been less fun to write and less useful to read.

Index

Page numbers in *italic* refer to illustrations and captions; where illustrations, captions and text co-exist on the same page, text reference only is given.